PELICAN BOOKS
A531

CHILDHOOD AND ADOLESCENCE

J. A. Hadfield was born in the South Sea Islands of English parents. He was educated at Eltham College and then proceeded to Oxford University where, after taking a degree in Arts, he read theology for three years. At Oxford he fell under the influence of William McDougall, the psychologist, under whom he did some research work on the relation of anthropology to psychology. The deeper interest in abnormal psychology thus gained led him to take his degrees in Medicine at Edinburgh University with a view to the treatment of nervous disorders, then in its infancy. During the First World War he served as Surgeon-Lieut. R.N. until, towards the end of the war, he was transferred to the Army, where he worked once more with McDougall as Neurologist in the War Hospital at Oxford. Between the wars he practised in Harley Street in psychological medicine, was appointed Lecturer in Psychopathology and Mental Hygiene in London University, and was one of the founder members of the Tavistock Clinic, later becoming its first 'Director of Studies' for the training of doctors in psychological medicine. In the Second World War he was Officer in Charge of Division and Director of Studies at the 41st General (Neuropathic) Hospital. More recently he has been the British President of the International Society for Clinical and Experimental Hypnosis, and of the Society for Medical and Dental Hypnosis.

Among his numerous writings are *Dreams and Nightmares* (a Pelican Book), *Psychology and Morals*, *Psychology and Mental Health*, and *Mental Health and the Psychoneuroses*.

D0988502

CHILDHOOD
AND ADOLESCENCE

J. A. HADFIELD

PENGUIN BOOKS

Penguin Books Ltd, Harmondsworth, Middlesex, England
Penguin Books Inc., 3300 Clipper Mill Road, Baltimore, Md 21211, U.S.A.
Penguin Books Australia Ltd, Ringwood, Victoria, Australia

—

First published 1962
Reprinted 1962, 1963, 1964, 1965, 1966, 1967

—

Copyright © J. A. Hadfield, 1962

—

Made and printed in Great Britain
by Hazell Watson & Viney Ltd,
Aylesbury, Bucks
Set in Intertype Baskerville

To my three sons
Ian, Douglas, and Gordon
victims of the principles herein described
this book is affectionately
dedicated

CONTENTS

EDITORIAL FOREWORD

IT well may be that the social historian of the future will pick out as one of the outstanding changes in the twentieth century that in the pattern of family life, and more especially in the relations between parents and their children. At the beginning of the century Edwardian youth was sitting in judgement on Victorian parents, and the judgement was apt to be harsh. Since then it has been more widely agreed that there were some good Victorian parents and some happy Victorian homes. More important than the change in judgement is the change in behaviour in the home life of young married couples, the grandchildren of the parents of the nineteenth century. Children may still often feel that they are not understood, but they cannot always in fairness say that their parents *do not try* to understand them.

The most striking change is in the role of the father in the home. Many young fathers today behave like mothers. Unlike even their Edwardian parents they feel no embarrassment at pushing a pram. They change the baby's nappies, they bath the baby and put it to bed. They enjoy doing these things. In short, they give to their children everything a mother can offer except a breast to feed from. The significant change in the pattern of family life is at present limited by the facts of social class and educational opportunity. We must impatiently await the evidence of sociologists and criminologists, regarding the delinquency rate of the children of today's more enlightened young parents, and evidence regarding delinquency rates generally, as opportunities for educating for parenthood are extended to the less privileged classes which at present produce so many of the young thieves and thugs.

The changed pattern of family life in the educationally

privileged classes is due to many and complex causes. Among these, one, but not perhaps the most important, is the impact of the teaching of Freud and other 'depth' psychologists, who have traced the effects on later life of emotional difficulties in the early years. Not less important for the diffusion of enlightenment and understanding has been the work of those, such as the author of this book, who have been able to select with critical discrimination what in the new psychology is sufficiently established and can be applied to the school and the home. Dr Hadfield is perhaps best known to the Pelican reader as the author of *Dreams and Nightmares*. He is known to others for his writings on mental health, and to very many teachers and parents, who as students attended his lectures in the University of London, first at King's College and later at Birkbeck College and the Institute of Education. This book makes available the content of some of those distinguished lectures to yet another generation of teachers and parents.

C. A. MACE

PREFACE

THE material for this book has been derived from four sources :

The first source was the Leytonstone Homes of about three hundred children, where I was Consultant Psychologist. These Homes were under the care of Miss Muriel Payne, whose experiences there were embodied in a book with the engaging title of *Oliver Untwisted*.

To these Homes I took students from King's College to investigate the stages of development in childhood. The students were known as 'Uncles' and 'Aunts' and played with the children. At the same time they investigated the children's activities and interests under the very free conditions which prevailed in the Homes. The full statistical records of these researches were unfortunately destroyed in the blitz in London. The general findings, however, had already been incorporated in my lectures. It is from these lecture notes that I have drawn the descriptions of child development contained in this book.

The second source of material was that obtained from the analysis of patients suffering from behaviour and psycho-neurotic disorders, which has been my main work for the last forty years. These disorders are usually found to relate back to experiences in the early years of life; and in reviving these early experiences we are, of course, all the time studying the reactions of childhood, and discovering how and why the disorders occur.

A third source of information was the diaries I kept of my three sons in their early years of life (not later) as well as a cursory observation of nine grandchildren, merely to put to the test conclusions I had already reached. Such observations of one's kith and kin are, however, liable to be prejudiced, and conclusions from this source require to be judged in the light of other evidence.

The fourth source of information was the publications of others. I have drawn upon the work of Gesell, upon material contained in the *Handbook of Child Psychology* (1931), edited by Murchison, and the *Manual of Child Psychology* (1946), edited by Carmichael. I have also found valuable the writings of Susan Isaacs. In common with all students of psychopathology and mental hygiene today, my work has been greatly influenced by Freud, especially in his mental mechanisms (conflict, repression, symptom formation); but not in his psychopathology! My method, however, has always been to make my own observations first and then to read books to modify, correct, or confirm my findings. It is hoped that this book will illustrate the advantage of combining the two methods of direct observation and analysis.

One pitfall of direct observation is that we are too apt to read our own interpretation into the child's behaviour. That is to commit the 'psychologist's fallacy', which means that we ascribe to a child our own interpretation of its behaviour. We commit the psychologist's fallacy when, seeing a dog slink away when found stealing a joint of meat, we say, 'You see! He knows he is doing wrong!' We are here ascribing to the dog our own interpretation of its behaviour, and what *we* should feel if we were caught in similar circumstances. To say that 'he knows that he is doing wrong' is to endow the dog with a moral sense. The explanation is much simpler, namely that last time he stole meat he got a beating, and the chain of reflexes is now reproduced and his fear revived.

This fallacy of reading into a child's mind our own interpretation of its behaviour is a very common one and one not easy to avoid. It is more common amongst child psychiatrists than child psychologists.*

* A particularly pernicious form of this fallacy is that of assuming a special theory, Freudian or otherwise, and interpreting the child's behaviour in terms of child theory. Still more is this the case when

Analysis has certain advantages over direct observation of the child. If a child is behaving in an abnormal way, whether in bed-wetting, sullenness, obstinacy, depression, or refusing to take his food, we may have theories as to why he is behaving in this manner, but there is no guarantee that our view of the case is correct, and the child is too young to tell us, even if he knows. But if we take an adult patient and by free association revive his early experiences, he can now tell us precisely why he bed-wetted or refused his food. We may, for instance, think that a child bed-wetted because his urine was too strong or because he was not disciplined enough, whereas, reviving the experiences as an adult, he can tell us that it was because he was too *much* 'disciplined' and this was his way of getting his own back, by being a 'nuisance'. So we may discover why one child developed a phobia, another became a sex pervert, another a hysteric. Analysis is therefore a most valuable corrective to direct observation; and indeed is the most accurate way of discovering the cause of abnormal behaviour.

Again, we may have our theories as to how to bring up a child – perhaps by strict obedience, perhaps by letting him do what he likes – but we have no means of knowing what the results of such treatment will be till years later, when it is too late, or when we have lost all interest.

In analysis we can discover what precisely was the result of a mother treating a child in this or that way. By this means we can study what methods of treatment produce

the child's behaviour is interpreted symbolically to fit in with our theory. You can prove anything that way! If a child playing with trains bumps them together, this may be interpreted as a child's interest in coitus between the parents. May be! But it could be given other interpretations. As well may we interpret it to the child as representing the sun bumping into the sea at sundown, and then, when the child continues to play in those terms, to assume that this confirms the Sun Myth theory! By the same argument one could prove that all the neuroses were due to morbid curiosity, sex being only a form of curiosity. Indeed Adler maintained that all sex was part of the urge to power!

good behaviour on the one hand, or delinquency or a neurotic condition on the other. Guesswork as to why a child
probably becomes a rebel or develops a phobia is not good
enough in these days; analysis tells us definitely how these
conditions are developed in a way that direct observation
cannot do.

So by discovering the causes of abnormal behaviour and
observing scientifically the effects of different types of treatment, we may not only discover what *not* to do with our
children, but more positively draw up at least tentative
principles of *how* to bring up children to health and happiness.

All the same, you cannot base child psychology on the
study of abnormal cases, as the analyst is prone to do. That is
why direct observation is necessary to test the findings we
have come to in analysis. By experiment we can see whether,
when a child is treated in this or that way, he responds
in the way we should expect from our analysis of such
cases.

Therefore, when we have developed our theories from
analysis as to how best to bring up a child, we still need to
make a direct study of the child to confirm or correct what
we have discovered. Thus direct observation of a child's behaviour, analysis into the causes of his misbehaviour, and
experiment are all necessary if we are to get an all-round
true picture of childhood. It was in order to make a direct
study of childhood that I, though primarily an analyst,
took over the job of Consultant Psychologist to the Leytonstone Homes.

Direct observation of the child is also made in clinics,
where children are allowed to play freely, especially in play-
therapy; in schools; and in the laboratory, where the child's
reactions are studied under prescribed conditions – for instance, we may study how a two-year-old reacts to a strange
animal like a lizard, both when he is left to himself with this
animal and when another person is present. This last method
has been developed by Arnold Gesell.

These observations are all of value and make their contribution to child study.

But as Susan Isaacs (my predecessor at the Institute of Education) emphasized, we cannot get a true picture of the child except in his *spontaneous* activities. That is why at her day school in Cambridge she allowed children to do as they liked. So at the Leytonstone Homes we studied the children mainly in their play-times, where, under Miss Payne, they were allowed a much larger degree of freedom than in most residential homes, although not as much as in Susan Isaacs's day school.

The study of children in a residential home has, however, one great advantage over that in day schools or clinics. No child psychologist can get a true overall picture of the child, except by a *twenty-four hour study* of him. We need to know him when he has his bath and goes to bed no less than when he is playing with his toys; to know him when he is sick and when he is romping with others.

Many child psychologists lack this experience, which led a woman, who had consulted an unmarried woman doctor, to remark : ' 'Er ! To advise *me*, wot's buried me five !' The one had knowledge, the other had experience !

THE PROBLEM

THE PARENTS' DILEMMA

PARENTS in these days are in a state of bewilderment as to how to bring up their children. This is not surprising considering the conflicting views, even amongst experts, on the question.

In the Victorian period it was a simple matter. There were certain rules and standards of behaviour to which the child had to conform. He had to be obedient, docile, well-behaved, seen and not heard, and made to fit in with social requirements and moral standards. The sooner we started drilling him into this conformity the better. To make a child of good behaviour was the height of the Victorian mother's ambition, and to lick him into shape, the prerogative of the father when he came home from work.

Curiously enough, this worked out not too badly in many cases, notwithstanding the derogatory remarks that are apt to be made about the Victorian era. For after all, it was a period which produced many men and women of great initiative, enterprise, and inventiveness, comparing not at all unfavourably with men and women of the present day. It made the Victorian age one of the outstanding periods in English history.

The cynic might ascribe these good results to the survival of the fittest in a rigid climate which only the more robust children could stand ! But that is not the whole story.

The truth seems to be that strictness matters little as long as there is love and a sense of security in the home, together with outlets given for activity in other directions. These conditions flourished in many families, and children brought up under them were none the worse for their strict upbringing.

But if that period produced some very fine characters, it

also produced some very fine neurotics, for where there was strictness without affection, there was insecurity; and insecurity is the basis of neurotic disorders.

There were, it is true, some sons who broke away and made good in the Colonies. There were also some daughters, of a more robust breed, who broke all convention – and their parents hearts – by launching into careers and becoming really useful. But too often unmarried daughters were condemned to live at home, to do little else than arrange the cushions for their aged mothers of thirty-eight. And too many sons, unable to get outlet for their energies, rebelled against restraints and became wastrels and delinquents.

In those times many respectable homes had to mourn their 'wandering boys'; and many a sorrowful mother complained, 'What have I done to deserve this?' But that was only a rhetorical question, for she rarely stopped to inquire what she *had* done. Indeed, her very question implied that she had done nothing at all to deserve this! For in past generations few parents would ever admit that unfortunate results were in any way their own fault, or due to the wrong method in which they brought up their children.

In a way it was not, since they knew no better. It was the fault of the system, for parents had themselves been taught by educationalists and moralists that strict obedience to moral rules was the only way to bring up children in the straight path. They did what they thought was right and what the teaching of the time and the experts told them to do.

All this has now changed. Nowadays we hear very little about strict discipline; the emphasis is on freedom.

This change has come about to some extent because the children of Victorian parents, resenting their *own* strict upbringing, have determined that their children should not have to suffer the same torment, and so have given them greater freedom. Sometimes, to make sure that they avoid such disasters, they have gone to the opposite extreme with equally unfortunate results.

No doubt this change has also come about as a result of the two world wars, when parents were absent from their homes or were too preoccupied to exercise discipline. In any case, wars tend to release primitive impulses, especially aggressiveness and sex, and so result in greater freedom, not to say licence — for licence is freedom without aim.

But perhaps the greatest influence in bringing about this changed attitude from discipline to freedom has been the teaching of the psychologists and especially the psychoanalysts. Freud taught that neurotic disorders originate in the repression of natural instinctual tendencies like sex and aggressiveness, which, being repressed, come out in the perverted form of neurotic disorders.

If this was true, it was natural that many amongst the public (and also amongst the educationalists, who should have known better) translated Freud's teaching to mean that we should never frustrate or discipline the child, but on the contrary should let him do exactly as he liked; otherwise we may be laying in store all kinds of neurotic disorders for his later life. It sounded so logical; if repression produces neuroses, then don't repress the child if you wish him to grow up without a neurosis. Child Guidance Clinics therefore provided rooms where children could fling water about and be as dirty as they liked. Enterprising enthusiasts opened up 'Free Schools' on these same principles. Discipline was not only at a discount it was to be discouraged. These experts sometimes forgot that what may be of value for neurotic children are not necessarily sound principles for bringing up the ordinary child. Ira Wile, the American child psychologist, tells an amusing story illustrative of these 'progressive' methods. A mother who came to one of these schools with a view to entering her son was being interviewed by the headmistress in a lobby when the dinner bell rang and out rushed all the children. One bumped into her on this side and one on that, but no apology was made until at last one boy bumping against her said, 'I beg pardon!' —

whereupon the headmistress remarked to the mother, 'You must excuse him, he is just a new boy !'

This 'do as you like' policy was, of course, a misrepresentation of Freud's teaching and of his use of the word 'repression'. He used the word in the purely technical sense of an unconscious process. Repression, as we shall see (p. 139), is entirely different from restraint and self-control, which are conscious processes and concerned with desires and impulses of which we are fully aware. Freud, it is true, has taught us the evils of repression. But to conclude that, unless a child is allowed to do what he likes, he is storing up for himself some dreadful neurosis is a travesty of his teaching. To take another example, it is true that smacking on the behind often arouses a child's sex feelings, and so may be the first steps to developing a masochism (the sex desire to have pain inflicted on one). Indeed, I have had for treatment an adolescent girl who used to commit delinquencies for no other object than to get beaten and experience the sex pleasure that beating gave her. Corporal punishment is therefore as undesirable as it is unnecessary, and we should find better ways of discipline. But to think that corporal punishment will almost certainly lead to sex perversions is a distortion of the facts. It fortunately takes far more than that to produce a sex perversion, and many of us are witnesses to the fact that a thrashing may leave no more marks upon the mind than it does upon the body.

These conflicting theories of the 'experts' have naturally bewildered parents. But their confusion and bewilderment have had at least one good result, namely in making the more intelligent parents face up to the issue and *think* ! This has resulted in a new interest in the child as such, and in a complete change of attitude on the part of the parents.

For whilst parents of a former generation were very unwilling to admit that bad behaviour or a neurosis of the child could in any way be due to their treatment, the mother of today is all too ready to admit about her difficult child, 'I think it must be something in the way I have treated him

that makes him behave like that. I wish I knew what it was!'
She is only too willing for these causes to be investigated,
and to take advice. For it is not only the bad parents who
get unfortunate results with the child, but very often it is
the well-meaning parents who are only too anxious to do all
they can to bring him up well, but lack the necessary guiding
principles.

It is for such parents, confused as they are by the clash of
modern teaching with old-fashioned ideas, that this book is
written, in the hope that it may be of some help in making
the principles of parenthood clearer. The purpose is not to
advise; it is rather to put the parent in possession of the facts
from which the right conclusions may be drawn. That is
why it is addressed to the *intelligent* parent.

In brief, we are coming to realize that we are not restricted
to a choice between neurosis and libertinism; nor, as we
shall see (p. 114), is there any incompatibility between discipline and freedom.

RULES AND PRINCIPLES

Unfortunately, we cannot prescribe rules for bringing up
children. How much easier for the parents if they could be
provided with a set of concrete answers for such questions as,
'What do I do when my boy is jealous of his sister?' 'tells
lies?', 'won't go to bed?', 'plays about with his food instead
of eating it?' Or, 'What do I do with my girl who is always
day-dreaming?', 'is spiteful?', 'tries to boss everybody?'

There are no potted rules for these conditions. What the
parent can do depends on many things – the circumstances
of the case, the cause of the condition, the temperament of
the child himself (each child reacts very differently to the
same treatment), and on the *way* the problem is handled. In
any case, it may not be what the parents do with the child
that is of importance, but what they do with themselves. It
is just as likely to be something in the parents' own attitude
of mind that makes the child naughty, as something in the

child himself. For instance, the parents' preference for another child (although, of course, they 'never show it') is
quickly sensed, and note is intuitively made that the
mother takes a little longer in kissing the favoured child
good night. Owing to these varying circumstances rules cannot be made, for rules, admirable as they are, cannot take in
all the circumstances of a particular case.

To take a commonplace illustration : A mother asks,
'What am I to do when my boy bites his younger sister? Do
I bite him back, as his father suggests; or do I punish him,
as his Granny suggests; or do I follow what the psychologists
tell me, and not frustrate him?'

I have known parents bite a child back, not by way of
punishment or from vindictiveness, but simply to show him
how much it does really hurt, and such treatment has done
the trick. But, let us admit, it is very hard for the mother,
when her baby is hurt, to bite back her older child *without*
any vindictiveness, although she may think she is doing so.
This is where we need to examine ourselves and our own
attitude, as well as the child.

In any case, the child is most likely to *interpret* this biting
as being vindictive, even if it is not. That is where we need
to study *him*. If the action is felt to be vindictive, he may
stop biting his sister for fear of retaliation, but he will hate
her all the more – which is hardly the end we desire. In
every case, we should find out *why* he bit his older sister –
perhaps she deserved it ! – and to punish him would be an
injustice. Where is your 'rule'?

Indeed, unexpected results may follow. Since a small child
learns more by imitation than by teaching, it is quite likely
that this boy will follow his mother's example and carry on
the good work, biting when she is not looking. She has, in
fact, taught him to bite back when he gets the chance ! On
the other hand, the mother's biting him 'to show him how
much it hurts' may be so successful that it convinces him
what an effective weapon biting is, with the result that he
keeps it up his sleeve, as it were, for future use ! Some

parents, of course, are frankly vindictive. 'I don't want any of this nonsense!' says the father. 'He deserves it and must be taught a lesson!' One cannot say offhand that such treatment is altogether unsuccessful, because very often a child knows he is doing wrong, and accepts the punishment as deserved. In any case, it is better to give him a good smack and have done with it than for the mother to be 'grieved' with him for the rest of the day. The latter method may teach him the effectiveness of 'being grieved' so that, realizing the devastation it produced in his own mind, he quite automatically, when he later marries, uses this same weapon with his wife, and gets into sulks if he does not get his own way. All this requires intelligence as well as intuition on the mother's part. Even then she must expect to make mistakes. What the fate of a child whose mother never made a mistake would be, I shudder to think!

Take another illustration from ordinary life. I have known parents stick to the rule that the child must be made to eat up all he has on his plate – and that's that. This insistence is usually backed up by the statement that 'Some poor children would be only too glad to have it!' – to which the child's natural reaction is 'Then let them have it!' (He does not say so, however, for fear of getting a smack.) But if it is his health we have as our aim (and, after all, food is intended for that purpose and not for the teaching of morals), it is wrong to make him eat what he does not want or need.

By all means teach him not to be wasteful. But this can better be done by the mother not piling up his plate with more food than he needs, on the grounds that it is 'good for you'! Whether or not he eats 'what is put on his plate' surely depends entirely on what *is* put on his plate. If the truth were told, in most cases it is because the mother can't bear to think that he does not want the food she has taken so much trouble to prepare.

To apply this rule indiscriminately is detrimental to the child's health. To force him to eat more food than he has appetite for means that he cannot digest it and will become ill-tempered – and then be blamed for that! To force an 'acidosis' child to eat fats (because such a child is often thin), when he cannot digest fats, is to make him sick or get migraine. Nor must he be expected to eat them when he is in an emotional state – as when he is angry at being taken from his games – for any emotion checks the flow of gastric juices, with the result that he *cannot* digest his food and often sicks it up. Then the mother says, 'I don't know what to do with that child!' – which at least is true. She then retires to her bedroom with a psychoneurotic headache, nursed in self-pity, while the child still suffers a psychosomatic indigestion, nursed in anger.

A placid mother is the best aid to a child's digestion.

But while we cannot lay down rules, because so much depends on the circumstances of the case, we can be guided by *principles*.

Rules are concerned mainly with behaviour, whereas principles depend on *aims or ends* in bringing up the child. If we are guided on principles, we ask ourselves why we do these things, what will be the result of this or that treatment, and vary our treatment in accordance with those ends.

OUR AIM

When a mother asks 'How am I to bring up my child?' the obvious reply is, 'What do you want him to be?' We must have some idea of our aim before we can devise the means to secure that end.

So we ask, in return, 'Do you want him to be a success in life, or to be rich? Or do you want him to be clever and win honours? Or do you want him to be happy, whether rich or poor, successful or not? Or is it your idea that he should be good and moral, of service to his fellows and to the community?' What we should *do* with the child depends entirely on our *aim*.

I suppose most of us if asked these questions would be somewhat vague, and if we are frank would answer 'A bit of all sorts !' That is not too bad an answer, for in fact they are not altogether incompatible, and each has its points. But no one of them, taken by itself, is entirely satisfactory.

Success is good : but many very successful people suffer from nervous breakdowns. Indeed their very success is because they are driven on by anxiety which catches up on them in the end.

Again many a mother, particularly the religious mother, wants her child to be 'good and well-behaved'. This is a very good aim, but not entirely satisfactory, for there are many children who are compelled to be good and conform to social demands to such an extent that their own individuality is crushed. They grow up to be very good but very sapless. This is particularly the case if they have been made to conform by fear and strict discipline.

High moral standards of behaviour are desirable, but they alone are by no means the gateway to a healthy and happy life. Many men with high moral standards, including some clergy, are victims of sex perversions, as many medical psychologists will tell you. There is obviously something wrong !

What then shall be our end and aim? The answer is not so difficult. The standard and aim we shall adopt is that of mental health. What then do we mean by mental health? *By mental health we mean the full development of the child's whole personality.*

Mental hygiene consists in the maintenance of mental health and the prevention of mental and emotional disorders.

This definition conforms with what we mean by physical health. By physical health we mean that all the functions and organs of the body – heart, lungs, liver, skin, and brain – are working fully and completely.

So it is with the personality as a whole. Nature has provided the child with a large number of potentialities, capacities, instincts, and patterns of behaviour and intelligence to enable him to cope with the problems and difficulties of life and to maintain existence. All these are necessary to life, and our aim as parents should be to give the fullest opportunity for the development and use of all these capacities.

But that is not all. As in the body, these functions and capacities need to be coordinated and harmonized if they are to be used most effectively.

How is this brought about? It is brought about by their being directed towards a common end or aim. *Ends, aims, and ideals are necessary to mental health and the coordination of the personality.* How these aims and ideals are provided we shall see later (pp. 134, 141).

In establishing this completeness and fulfilment of the child's personality as our aim, we are following nature. Every living organism is working towards its own fulfilment. Every tree and plant, every insect and animal is working towards its own completeness. Prune a tree and it will grow more branches. Make a wound in your flesh and all the resources of the body set to work to heal that wound until the body is whole again. The so-called *vis naturae medicatrix*, or natural healing force of the body, without which no medical or surgical skill would be of any avail, is always working towards this completeness. In the body we call it health; in the personality, wholeness; in religion, holiness. The root idea in all these ends is the same, namely completeness and fulfilment.

This idea of 'fulfilment' is not incompatible with those already mentioned like success or goodness; indeed it includes them all.

The child who is mentally healthy, that is, all of whose functions and capacities are fully developed, will obviously be both efficient and successful, for all his energies are employed to their full capacity. For the same reason he will have a strong will and character, for the will is the activity or function of the personality as a whole. He will also be intelligent, so far as he is constitutionally capable of being so, for curiosity and a desire for knowledge are natural in every child, and if they are encouraged by the parent and an opportunity is given for the exercise of his intelligence, he will be able to cope with the problems of life.

The mentally healthy child will also be moral. For man is by nature a social animal who likes to be with others and hates isolation. The child enjoys playing with other children, belonging to a gang of children, and later to a community. So he learns to cooperate and conform to the social pattern. This theme we have developed in Chapter 6. If the child enjoys privileges by belonging to a community, he soon learns that he must be prepared to conform to the customs of the community and obey its laws. That does not mean that the child conforms to a single pattern and lacks individuality. For every child is born different from every other child, not only physically but in personality; and the early experience of every child is different from every other. So each child as it grows up also develops an individuality different from every other, and so can make his distinctive contribution to the community to which he belongs.

WHAT THE PSYCHOLOGIST TELLS US

A great change from the static to the dynamic has taken place during this last half century in our conception of the child.

In Victorian times, following the teaching of the philosopher Locke, the child was regarded as passive, like a piece of wax on which impressions had to be made. In psychology, we heard a great deal about sensations, impressions, perceptions, conceptions, and so forth. In education, the successful boy (or girl) at school was one who listened intently, absorbed what was taught him, retained it in his memory, and trotted it out most accurately in examinations, so that he won scholarships to college and ultimately became a teacher or professor.

Nowadays all this has changed : we hear less about sensations and perceptions and far more about instincts, potentialities, drives, and dynamic urges, in the child. The new-born child is no longer regarded as a piece of wax upon which impressions are to be made; every child is born a going concern. Far from being a gramophone record whose function is simply to record and to reproduce what is recorded, the child is an internal combustion engine, capable of spontaneous activity.

This change in our concept of the child has affected the way we educate our children. Education and the bringing up of a child no longer consist merely in strict obedience, good behaviour, conformity to social custom, and cramming with knowledge. They consist in giving expression to these native potentialities, including the child's natural desire to learn, and directing them to right ends.

But it must not be thought that this dynamic point of view went unchallenged. On the whole, it is the generally accepted theory in Britain. But no sooner had this theory of innate potentialities got well under way than a very different theory was being advanced in America, *behaviourism*. This theory emphasized the importance of environment in shaping the character and destiny of the child, reducing the influence of hereditary factors, like the instincts, to a minimum.

This also had a profound influence on education, for the outcome was that, provided you brought up the child in the right environment, you could do anything you liked with him and make anything you wanted out of him. Watson, the originator of behaviourism, went so far as to say, 'Give me a dozen healthy infants, and my own specific world to bring them up in, and I will guarantee to train any one of them to become any type of specialist I might select, doctor, lawyer, artist, or even beggarman, regardless of talents, abilities, or ancestry.' It was an entire swing away from the dynamic point of view. Environment was almost everything : heredity and innate factors were at a discount.

But behaviourism was also riding for a fall, for no sooner was it well in the saddle than another aspect of child psychology came to the fore. This was the principle of *maturation*.

Detailed study established beyond doubt that children not only inherit what we call the primary instincts, but they develop certain *patterns of behaviour*, which are not and could not be due to the environment. Moreover these patterns of behaviour emerge at certain ages. Thus, very simply, children crawl at a certain age, walk a little later, and begin to talk at a still later phase. These capacities emerge *irrespective of environmental influences*, and therefore must be innate.

The theory of maturation differed somewhat from the theory of the instincts as proclaimed by William McDougall, for, while McDougall's instincts were dynamic urges, the theory of maturation was more specifically concerned with particular patterns of behaviour. Both theories, however, emphasized innate factors and thus differed from the behaviourists who ascribed almost everything to the environment.

Which of these different theories we adopt must profoundly affect our attitude towards the child's training. If we adopt the Victorian attitude we arm ourselves with a stock of moral maxims which we must at all costs hammer into the reluctant child, making a deep impression that will last him through life. If we adopt the behaviouristic view we set to work to develop as many serviceable conditioned reflexes in the child as we have time for, and make of him a little automaton, as described in Huxley's *Brave New World*. If, on the other hand, we follow the dynamic psychology we make use of the child's potential forces and encourage him to use and direct them. If, however, we accept the theory of maturation then we shall study the various phases of development as they emerge so as to give to each of these potential forces full opportunity for development; then each may make its maximum contribution to the whole personality.

The truth is, of course, that all the theories are true

except in so far as they are exclusive and deny truth to the others. Innate and environmental factors work together. A child has the innate capacity to crawl. But he cannot crawl without a floor to crawl on. On the other hand no amount of training will enable him to crawl unless he has the capacity to do so. The urge or capacity comes from within ourselves; the environment provides the opportunity for its expression and development.

WHAT THE MEDICAL PSYCHOLOGIST TELLS US

At this point the medical psychologist picks up the story. Those of us who treat nervous disorders, such as nervous breakdowns, anxiety states, hysterical paralyses, sex perversions, and behaviour disorders, such as bad temper, jealousy, lying, and self pity, find (a) that they are distortions of the dynamic impulses we have described, (b) that these distortions are due to repression, and (c) that the roots of the repression almost invariably go back to environmental experiences in the early years of life. (This does not apply to mental deficiency and insanity, which by contrast are mainly innate or constitutional conditions.)

It is true that there may be later causes, such as shocks, illness, war-strain, accidents, worry, and love affairs, which *precipitate* the appearance of the disorder itself and are therefore often regarded as the sole cause of the trouble. But in the majority of cases these more recent events would not have produced the breakdown were there not predisposing factors, going back to experiences of early childhood.

There are reasons why this should be so; for it is during the first three or four years of life, as we shall see later (pp. 72 f.), that the child's personality is organized. If his personality is well organized in these early years, he is capable of going out to meet all the ordinary difficulties of life with confidence and assurance. On the other hand, if his personality is badly organized in these early years he will be incapable of coping with life and must resort to subterfuges like neuroses in order to escape. His house is built upon sand, and when the winds of adversity blow, he fails to adapt himself to the conditions of life and falls victim to its storms.

If then it is true that psychoneurotic conditions and behaviour disorders originate in experiences in early childhood, *it should be possible by avoiding these conditions to prevent these disorders happening.* The *cure* of neurotic disorders is the function of the medical psychologist. *The prevention of neurotic and behaviour disorders depends on right parenthood.*

Such prevention is a matter of great urgency for several reasons.

First, because of the *widespread nature* of these disorders. Some general practitioners report that as many as one third of all patients attending their surgeries exhibit some form or another of neurotic symptoms. These patients are commonly told that there is 'nothing wrong with them', by which the doctor means nothing organically wrong with them. This led one hypochondriac to have carved on his tombstone the words, 'I *told* them I was ill!'

Secondly, prevention is a matter of great urgency because of the *severity* of these illnesses. A patient who is harassed by a chronic anxiety which no doctor can relieve, a hysterical pain which no medicine can cure, or who is the victim of a sense of guilt which no priest can alleviate, is doomed to life-long misery and despair. Morbid self-consciousness, blushing, or stammering may seem trifling or even humorous to others, but they make social life unbearable to the victim; such people have been known to take their lives to escape such misery.

A further reason for urgency lies in the fact that once these disorders have become established they are *very difficult to cure.* It may take months, if not years, to cure a patient radically of a neurotic fear or obsession which would have required perhaps only three or four treatments in childhood to put things right for good. It is not simply that prevention is better than cure; it is the only practical way of solving the problem of the neuroses. They are difficult to cure because their causes are unconscious, very often going back to fears in the first year or two of life, and long since forgotten.

Analytic treatment is a long, arduous, and expensive process, well worth while for those who are cured thereby, for they are transformed from fear-ridden, nervous wrecks into healthy and happy human beings; but quite inapplicable to the thousands who require treatment.

Obviously, unless our methods of treatment are radically and miraculously improved, *the only hope of dealing with the problem of these neuroses and abnormal forms of behaviour is by prevention.*

Fortunately, the vast majority of these disorders can be prevented. We can state this categorically, for when by analytic treatment we discover the causes of any particular neuroses in a patient we almost invariably find them to lie in conditions which could have been avoided had the parent dealt with the child with greater understanding. Indeed, the greatest service that analysis has rendered is not in the cure of the few who are fortunate enough to have treatment, but in the light it has thrown upon the causes in childhood of neurotic disorders, enabling us to devise means of preventing them.

THE CHILD'S NATURAL EQUIPMENT

Nature has supplied every child with certain items of equipment with which to start the journey of life. All these, from reflex actions, instincts, and emotions of intelligence, reasoning, and purpose, are rightly regarded as biological means of adaptation to life and should be studied as such.

I have written fully of these potentialities in *Psychology and Mental Health* (Chapter 3) under the title 'The Sources of Behaviour'. A brief note however is called for here, for they are the raw materials with which the parent has to deal and out of which the child's personality is developed.

Some of them are very primitive, like the infant's clinging

to the mother, as the starfish clings to the rock, and the need to be close to her. This gives the infant a sense of protection and security. Denied it, the infant suffers from 'separation anxiety' which may later take a neurotic form of a fear of leaving home; or agoraphobia, which is defined as a fear of open space, but which in reality is a fear of loss of contact. This kind of behaviour we call a 'tropism', defined as the tendency of an organism to move in a particular direction. The migration of birds and fishes and the turning to the sun of the leaves of a plant are further illustrations.

But these tropisms, valuable as they are, may lead to harm. The migration of birds to a warmer climate is desirable, but this strong urge may lead to disaster in a cross-channel storm. Something more is required.

Reflex action. An infant in the first year of life is almost entirely a reflex animal. Its characteristics of behaviour, such as swallowing, breathing, crying, the beating of the heart, the movement of the bowels, the retraction of the foot when hurt, getting sick when eating poisonous berries, blinking to protect the eyes, are all devices in the service of self-preservation.

But reflex actions are not enough. They lead the moth to burn itself in the candle and the child in the fire. In any case, the number of reflexes which nature can supply is limited; and nature has not managed to develop a reflex for every conceivable situation in life. So she must think again – if I may be dreadfully anthropomorphic !

Conditioned reflexes. This she does in the first place by enabling the child automatically to form new reflexes. Conditioned reflexes are *acquired* reflexes, which have been formed or conditioned as the result of environmental experience. A moth has its wings singed but goes on flying into the candle. Not so the child : the child once burnt avoids the fire, and, frightened by a dog or stranger, learns to avoid them.

All 'habit-training' is based on the formation of conditioned reflexes. A meal eaten by an infant starts the peristalsis of the bowels which results in evacuation, by reflex action. If with a meal you put the child on a pot, it still evacuates. But in doing so it acquires a new reflex. For after that, the mere feel of the pot is enough to start the bowels moving. Thus you train a child in regular habits of evacuation. It is automatic.

So the infant can be trained to be hungry only at certain times, some three times a day, some four, or five. Later it can be taught to wait its turn at table instead of grabbing.

Habits are thus formed which are in conformity with social convenience. There is no repression whatsoever; and in any case children are spontaneously producing these acquired reflexes with every experience of the day. So why not make use of this capacity so conveniently provided by nature?

A gun dog is trained, in the same way, to wait, even when the pheasant rises, to dash for the bird at a signal, to bring it back with a soft mouth instead of devouring it, and to lay it at its master's feet, instead of taking it to its lair. The dog enjoys it all : there is no repression.

The formation of such habits is based on primitive tendencies (you could not get a cow to retrieve a bird !). They are modifications and developments of native instincts. Would that a parent had as much patience as a dog-breeder in developing such reflexes !

Unfortunately, even conditioned or acquired reflexes may lead to harmful results. A child is not naturally afraid of the dark but is of a loud noise. But if there is a terrifying thunderstorm which awakens a child in the night, the child may thereafter be afraid of the dark with which the noise was associated.

Many phobias of later life, we find in analysis, originate with this type of experience – a fear of water in a child that slips in the bath, or a fear of cats in a child who in the pram had its face sat on by a cat in search of a warm place.

A child who feels left out and neglected because a newborn baby has arrived goes off his food. His mother gets worried over this and fusses over him, and so he gets attention. Thereafter he will automatically refuse his food in order to get it. What was previously the result of the need for attention now becomes the means of getting it. At school, on the other hand, he eats like a horse.

A child's behaviour is thus *automatically* modified by the *results* of its own actions. This process goes under the name of 'feedback'. An illustration in physics is the thermostatic control of central heating, and in physiology, the maintenance of an even body temperature in winter and summer. Thus an effect can become a cause. So *a child learns from the effects of its action*, apart from any training or teaching.

Pleasure and pain are of great biological value in adaptation to life. It may take numerous experiments to produce a conditioned reflex, as every child knows who has to train a dog, and as every mother knows who trains a child to pass motions at regular times. But only one experience of the pain of burning himself may be enough to stop a child touching a fire ever after; *once* bitten twice shy. Similarly one severe smacking of a child who messes itself may be enough to make the child stop passing its motions and thereafter suffer from constipation !

Pleasure encourages, pain inhibits a child's actions. On the whole pleasurable experiences like eating and running about are health-producing, whereas painful experiences like suffocation or injuring a foot are hurtful. But there are exceptions; for some pleasurable things, like the child's attraction to red berries or sexual attractions in adolescence, may be harmful.

Rewards, including praise, which give pleasure, encourage a child, and should be used freely by parents. Punishments, like slapping the hand of the child who always grabs, inhibit the child (though here again, there is no hard and fast rule), for the slap may make the child more rebellious so that it does it the more.

Pleasure and pain are therefore shortcut methods for the modification of behaviour.

Emotions, like fear, anger, sex, and maternal love, are an advance on conditioned reflexes, which are very mechanical and release only a limited amount of energy.

Biologically speaking, the most characteristic feature of the primary instinctive emotions is that they are *powerful drives* (as the word e-motion implies). *Emotions are the accumulation of energy before discharge*, with the result that when this energy is discharged, like a head of water at a dam, all resistance is swept away and all obstructions to the attainment of an object removed. Incredible deeds are performed under the emotions of fear and rage. Emotions endow us with superhuman strength. They are far more effective than reflexes, and more valuable to the organism in coping with life.

But valuable as they are, the emotions themselves, left to themselves, cause a great deal of trouble. Blind rage is not always the best way of achieving our ends; and the man whose sex instincts are so strong that when frustrated he murders the girl who is the object of his desire gets nowhere – except perhaps to the gallows.

Furthermore, the emotions, left to themselves, conflict with one another, sex with anger, fear with sex. This not only leads to disorders in the personality, but often the emotions in conflict are each repressed and neurosis results.

Thus the very strength of the primary emotions makes them difficult to control, and adds to both the child's and the parents' problems, for much of a parent's energy is necessarily engaged in checking a child's natural impulses, like cruelty and self-will, and directing them to more useful ends.

Intelligence. Something more is required if the organism is to adapt itself adequately to life. So Nature, like a kindly mother says, 'I can't give you reflexes for every conceivable situation; even the conditioned reflexes take time to develop and you may be destroyed in the process; and the emotions, while they give you added power often fight amongst themselves and lead to trouble. So I give you *intelligence* to enable you to get on with the job yourself.' Intelligence enables us to make the best use of our emotions *in accordance with our ends and aims*; and that often means restraining our emotions and using them to better purpose.

Let us see how intelligence works. (I use the word intelligence in its popular rather than its academic sense.)

If a boy finds himself in a field with a dangerous animal, his natural impulse is to escape by dashing away for all he is worth in response to the emotion of fear. So far so good. If the dangerous animal is a mad bull, merely to run away is not intelligent, for the bull can run faster than he can. Better to escape up the nearest tree. All right! But suppose the dangerous animal is a snake : to climb a tree could be the worst mode of escape, for the snake can climb a tree and has got him cornered completely. That is why he needs to use his intelligence, which regulates his behaviour according to the circumstances of the case.

To take a more commonplace illustration than bulls and snakes. If a child is told to turn on the bath water, and does so, but leaves the tap on till the water overflows, he may excuse himself by saying, 'You only told me to turn it on!' The mother replies, 'Use your intelligence, child!', for obviously the object of turning on the water is to fill the bath only enough for a bath. Intelligence must always take into consideration the end in view.

Intelligence is an *innate* quality. We either have it or don't have it; we have it in lesser measure like the mentally deficient or in greater measure like the boy capable of a university course. Being an innate quality, it is constant throughout life – and no one can turn a moron into a professor.

But a great deal will depend on what use we make of our intelligence, and that depends largely on training. In the war mental deficients were better at making roads than ordinary soldiers.

Knowledge. Intelligence is quite different from knowledge. Intelligence is the innate *capacity* to grasp a situation or devise means to ends. Knowledge is *what* we learn.

But the two interact; for the more knowledge we have the more effective will be our intelligence; and the more intelligent we are the more use we can make of the knowledge we acquire.

In the case of the boy in the field, it was only if the boy *knew* that bulls moved fast and that snakes could climb trees that he could use his intelligence most effectively. But you can conceive of a dull-witted country yokel who *knew* these facts but had not the intelligence to apply them. A familiar phrase 'All men are born equal, but some are more equal than others' has some sense in it. It is a mistake to give all children the same education; each child should have the education which is *fitted to his capacity*.

Intelligence is shown in two ways : a child may show his intelligence in the way he is able to *grasp* a situation – you do not need to tell him twice, as the saying goes – another with practical intelligence may be better able to *devise means* to achieve an end. The two qualities may be separate in different boys – one boy may be able to grasp a situation but not be able to do anything about it; another can do anything perfectly well if you tell him what is required. But they often go together, as in the case of the boy or girl who quickly grasps *how* to mend a fuse and proceeds to do so, how to drive a car, how to mend a bicycle puncture, how best to retrieve a football from a stream, and how to sail a boat against a wind.

Purpose. All true intelligence as we have said, is determined by the end or aim in view. *Purpose is the conscious pursuit of ends*. Most of the important decisions of our lives are determined by our aims–whether it be getting a job, satisfying our scientific curiosity, or bringing up our children well.

Children should be taught at an early age to motivate their actions according to ends and aims, by pointing out to them that if they spend their pocket money on sweets they will not be able to get the doll's dress they wanted; that if they don't share their toys with others the others will not share their toys with them.

The pursuit of ends is the most effective means of self-control. The boy who wants to buy a bicycle will deny himself the cinema he wanted to go to. The pursuit of ends is thus the most effective form of self-discipline, which is the only discipline worth while. The man who has aims and ends in life does not need to submit himself to fictitious self-discipline.

Intellect is something different from intelligence. The intellectual child is what is usually called the 'brainy' child. He is not always the one who knows best how to get a car out of a ditch, although he may know all the books have to say about leverages. Intellect is, again, an inborn quality. Intelligence in the ordinary sense is a more practical quality enabling us to cope with the problems of life. *Intellect I would define as the innate capacity to organize our knowledge.* It enables us to do most extraordinary things in engineering, electronics, and science. Don't worry if your child is not intellectual. He may have a great deal of practical intelligence, which is just as valuable.

Reason. The child of three or four is capable of reasoning. That is why he asks 'Why should I do that?' – for he wants a reason; and his own acts are determined by his reason. 'I want to get a bicycle because I can then go to the sea and bathe when I like.'

In earlier childhood the child's 'reasoning', if you can call it that, is based on the contiguity of experiences. A child, mentioned by Stott, held his hand under the tap for a long time and the water turned hot : the child assumed that it was *because* he held his hand there for a long time that the water turned hot. Logicians are fond of pointing out the 'fallacy' of *post hoc ergo propter hoc*. Very often it *is* a fallacy to maintain that because one thing follows another it was caused by it; but that is how a child does in fact argue. Nor is it surprising that a child argues in this way, for very commonly his own experience suggests that he is right. In conditioned reflexes there is no inherent connexion between a bell and the flow of saliva, between the feel of a pot and a child's passing a motion; but just because one is made to *precede* the other, it does in fact become the *cause* of the other.

This often leads to disastrous results. Because a patient of mine, as a child, disobediently went into her sick mother's bedroom and the mother died, she assumed it was *because* she went into the bedroom that the mother died; and the patient suffered from a sense of guilt for years. A boy has irritation of the penis and therefore handles it. A circumcision follows which terrifies him; and he concludes that it was *because* he played with himself that he was punished by the operation. This may mean the repression and arresting of sex, which later produces a perversion.

Intuition, like reasoning, is a means of drawing conclusions; but whereas in reasoning you are aware of the data from which you draw your conclusions, and the logical process which leads you to come to that conclusion, in intuition you come to the conclusion *but are unaware as to how or why you do so. Intuition is subconscious inference,* whereas reasoning is conscious inference from known facts.

But that does not mean that intuition is 'out of the blue'. It is in fact based on observation and past experiences, although at the time we are not consciously aware of this.

Children are very intuitive even when they cannot reason. A child, for example, takes a dislike to a man visitor. The mother says, 'Oh, but he is so nice; he bought you a present. Why don't you like him?' It makes no difference, the child just repeats, 'I don't like him,' without knowing the reason. But the 'reason' may be that the child has observed, without knowing it, that the visitor smiles with the lips but not with the eyes. His lips are friendly but his eyes say, 'I hate the brat. I wish she was out of the way!' The child also observes that the man always comes when the father is out and that the mother is particularly excited when he comes. The child instinctively senses that the man is up to no good, and has come to that conclusion without knowing why, but nevertheless from observed facts. It comes to a correct judgement, but from subconscious data. Likewise, a child easily senses that the mother loves another child more, however careful the mother may be 'to treat both exactly alike'.

These are a few items of the equipment which Nature supplies for the child. As they are developed in the course of evolution – the lowest forms of organism being motivated only by tropisms and reflexes and the highest by reason, intelligence, and purpose – so they appear in more or less the same order in the child. For the child recapitulates the history of the race.

A parent should have a good knowledge of them and of the complications to which they sometimes give rise. For a child is motivated at one time by its instincts, another time by reason; at one time by conditioned reflexes and another time by intelligence; at one time by intuition, at another by the pursuit of ends – and sometimes by several at once. It is not surprising that the parent is somewhat bewildered. But if the parent supplies the right environment of steady love and affection and provides the child with the opportunity to express itself in freedom, then, like a plant given good soil and sunlight, the child will flourish.

*

The discerning reader will come to realize that there are two themes running through this book.

The first is that all these potentialities which nature provides, the higher as well as the lower, intelligence as well as instincts, are *biological* functions designed by nature to enable the child to adapt himself to life. Even some psychologists have not appreciated this fact and will study such functions as memory or intelligence as though they were simply entities in themselves. But we cannot fully understand these potentialities unless we take into consideration what they are *for* any more than we can understand the structure of the eye – the lens, the pupil, the retina – without understanding what they are for, what purpose they serve in enabling us to see. Apart from their purpose they are meaningless structures. So with the various potentialities we find innate in every child. Memory, for instance, enables us to make use of past experiences; imagination to foresee the results of our actions.

The second theme, which follows from the first, is that the function of the parents is not to 'build up' the child by training and moral maxims, but to *make use of* the potentialities which nature has provided as a starting point, and direct these potentialities to the health and happiness of the child. This theme will be discussed further.

2

MATURATION

GROWTH AND DEVELOPMENT

WE not only grow, we also develop. Growth is increase in size; development is change in form.

The distinction is observed throughout nature. The grub not only grows, it develops into the chrysalis and then into the butterfly, an entirely different creature. The frog not merely grows, but develops from a tadpole; from a water-breathing animal to an air-breathing animal. At each stage the animal is a different entity, a different being, as a result of such development. So miraculous is this change that the grub is unrecognizable as the butterfly.

So it is with the child. He not only grows from infancy through adolescence to adulthood; he also develops. If we only grew we should all be big fat babies. There are indeed some people who conform to that pattern, like the Fat Boy of Peckham in Dickens's story, who spent his time eating and sleeping (a condition medically recognized as Fröhlich's syndrome, characterized by, amongst other things, a lack of sexual development).

Normally, growth and development proceed together, and that is presumably why Gesell * does not make a distinction between the two. It is true that we cannot separate them, but we can distinguish them, and indeed it is necessary that we should do so if we are to understand the child.

For sometimes a child, like a mental deficient, grows without developing. At other times he develops without growing correspondingly. The type of boy we call the 'lout' is one who is big in body but deficient in intellectual development.

* *Infancy and Human Growth*, p. 3. No effort, he says, 'will be made to maintain a distinction between *growth* (dimensional augmentation) and *development* (differentiation)'.

Small people are by no means the least intelligent. Thus a dwarf may be more intelligent than a giant, who has an excess of certain hormones. A David can outwit a Goliath, and Ulysses can defy the one-eyed monster Polyphemus. I stress this distinction because it is of practical importance.

Physical growth and size in a child may determine his place in the world. Every boy wants to be a 'big man' and every girl 'grown-up'; understanding thereby that they will have greater power than they have now, and be able to withstand the superior strength of the adults, who, as seen through a child's eyes, have all the advantages and can whisk him off to bed at the most inappropriate moments, however violently protesting! This desire to 'be big' has therefore an enormous influence upon his actions, life, and character. The captain of a rugby team, wanting a front-row forward, may prefer a hefty, though perhaps less intelligent boy, whereas he may choose a smaller but smart quick boy as stand-off half, for the latter has to make more important and quicker decisions.

Even boys do not regard size as *all*-important. They will give more credit to a small boy who is plucky in football, or a smart wicket-keeper, than a lout whose weight is useful in the scrum but who gets in everybody's way. Equally they may have more respect for a small boy who puts up a good fight against a bully than the bully who by brute force beats him.

Amongst girls a large size may stand them in good stead at school, but is rather a disadvantage when they later look for boy friends. For, on the whole, the latter prefer someone whom they can protect and master, not a hefty lass who can pick them up by the scruff of the neck.

The question of physique may seriously affect the mental health and happiness of boys and girls. Lack of size may give a boy or girl a bad inferiority complex. The boy or girl of small stature starts off with a disadvantage, say in the picking of a side in games : it does not improve their morale always to be chosen last. All the same they can make up in abilities in other directions – in scholarship or in skill at games or hobbies, which compensate for lack of size. That is partly why so often small men reach the top.

But their ambition does not always stand them in good stead. For instance, in their effort to compensate by learning for their quite unjustified feelings of inferiority regarding size, they often go to the extreme and at school work themselves to a nervous breakdown, which is put down to 'overwork'; but it is their anxiety which has driven them to overwork. Others assume an attitude of compensatory self-importance and become pompous, a characteristic of many small people. Other children of small size find their place in the sun by becoming the 'little pet' of other boys and girls, a most unfortunate attitude with which to go out to meet the world.

Adler's general theory of 'organ inferiority' is thus vindicated in that a large number of people certainly have breakdowns because of 'organ inferiority'. Their attempt to compensate for their physical inferiority proves too much for them.*

Physical over-development is often a cause of disturbance. A girl or boy of thirteen may have the physique of one of seventeen with all the emotional development that goes with it, while the intellectual development remains at thirteen. You cannot expect a girl of thirteen who has the physical development of a girl of seventeen to be devoted to algebra, when her emotional life is absorbed with interest in boys and her time spent in looking out of the window in the hopes of catching sight of one of them. A boy who is physically overdeveloped has strong sexual and aggressive tendencies without the proportionate powers of self-control. There is little to be done in such cases except to wait until his age, intellectual development, and control catch up with his physical

* See the *British Medical Journal* of 14 February 1959 for an article on the cure of delinquents by surgical operation on deformities like squints.

development and hope nothing drastic will happen in the meantime.

Where, on the contrary, there is physical *immaturity* with intellectual over-development, there is also likely to be trouble, because a boy of thirteen with the intelligence of a sixteen-year-old, although put in a class of older children who are his intellectual equals, will have more immature emotional interests than his class-mates. He may be brilliant at Latin or mathematics, but still like playing with his Meccano. This is particularly awkward in boarding schools, where all pupils live together and take part in the same activities *outside* school work. In day schools the intellectually advanced boy (or girl) can still find at home outlets for emotional development in interests and hobbies appropriate to his real age.

Apart from anything else these variations in growth and development make a child 'odd', and if there is one thing above all others that a growing boy or girl dislikes it is being 'different', whether in clothes, diet, interests, physique, or intellectual ability. Many children suffer silent torments and misery because of the scorn and laughter of others. Children, like animals, tend to attack the weak, wounded, and deformed. It is the function of teachers and parents to check this natural propensity.

Other difficulties arise because of a disproportionate development of one part of the body as against another. A *normal* instance of this is the disproportionate development of the pelvis and breasts in a girl as she matures; but, although quite normal, this often causes distress and embarrassment. Other girls develop rapidly and mature early. They are usually small in size and stockier than the girl who matures late, the latter being more lanky. This is because there is an opposing action between the growth hormones and the sex hormones, so that a lanky boy or girl is usually less sexually mature than the stockier one. The lanky boy whose long bones (arms and legs) grow quickly often suffers great injustice at school, for his over-growth makes him lethargic, both in mind and body, so that in neither can he keep up with the other boys. Thus he is bad at games because he is clumsy, for reasons we shall mention later (p. 188). PT instructors should understand this and make allowances for such boys without making them conspicuous.

It is an unfortunate fact that although children may out-grow these physical oddities (many fat girls in adolescence become normally slim as they develop), the inferiority com-plex and self-consciousness may follow them through life. I have known ugly girls turn into beautiful women, but the idea of being ugly still remains deeply embedded in their minds, and even when boys make natural advances to them, they still feel they are making fun of them.

Let us not then underestimate the importance of the child's physique, whether of growth or development, for both have a profound effect on his mental health as well as on his happiness.

The question of handicapped children here arises. These children require expert handling because of the emotional problems involved.

Some years ago I had two patients each suffering from a paralysed arm from birth. In the one case the mother, herself an athlete, trained the boy to ignore his partially paralysed arm, to do all that other boys did; and in fact he became very skilled at games and was even able to catch a cricket ball. But the constant strain and effort were too much for him, and he broke down.

The other, apart from his paralysed arm, suffered from fits, and his anxious mother was always impressing on him that he was not as other boys, that he could never marry and so on. To him life was made to look terrifying and over-whelming. The perpetual suggestion of his incompetence to face life, together with the feeling of frustration and anxiety it gave him, produced in him a breakdown. In fact, he later married and he and his wife kept a successful boarding house, where his occasional fits did not matter, as he was usually below stairs.

Both these breakdowns could have been prevented. In both cases the mother by her attitude – in the one case by ignoring, in the other case by over-emphasis – gave the child a sense of insecurity. The breakdowns could have been avoided by getting the child in each case to accept his disability as a matter of fact (as another child does his short-sightedness), and giving him confidence by encouraging him to do what he *was* capable of doing without stress or anxiety; to get him to realize that there were plenty of things to be done in life in spite of his disability.

DEFINITION AND NATURE OF MATURATION

Parents have always recognized in a general way that the child grows up, and that in doing so he not only becomes bigger, but develops new capacities and new interests, so that at each stage of development he is a different entity, a different being. They also recognize that such maturation is an innate process, and that he will naturally grow from infancy to childhood, from childhood to adolescence, from adolescence to adult life without any effort or training on anyone's part.

But in recent years this process of maturation has come under the scrutiny of scientific observers, who have thrown a great deal of light upon the principles by which maturation proceeds.

Definition of maturation. McGraw defines maturation as 'the unfolding and ripening of the abilities, characteristics, traits, and potentialities present at birth but only later coming to maturity in a developing organism' – an excellent and clear definition. *Maturation is the development of innate patterns of behaviour in ordered sequence.* This, though simple, contains the necessary facts about maturation, namely that the behaviour patterns are innate and follow one another in specific order.

First of all then we shall ask ourselves *what proof we have of the fact of maturation* – in contradistinction to the behaviourists, who regard environmental influences as all-important (p. 28).

Experimental evidence of maturation. An excellent method of studying maturation is by testing identical twins, for such twins have exactly the same hereditary and innate qualities. Arnold Gesell was a pioneer in such studies. Here is one of the numerous experiments he has made.* A cube is put on the table before each of the twins. There are, of course, infinite possibilities as to how each twin will react towards the cube. But what do we find? At sixteen weeks *both* independently watched it being put on the table, but made no effort to reach it. At twenty weeks, *both* reached out, but clumsily, and pushed it out of reach. At twenty-four to twenty-eight weeks each put both hands out, scooped the cube up, took hold of it, and put it to the mouth.

The fact that the the twins did precisely the same things in the same way, in the same order, at the same age, *independently of one another and irrespective of differences of environment*, is truly remarkable and confirms us in the belief that these patterns of behaviour are due to inherent factors, and not just to circumstances. That is what we mean by maturation.

In another test with identical twins, Gesell found that, in 612 separate items of behaviour, there were 513 items which were identical or virtually identical, and only 99 items of disparity, and those of a minor type.* This again suggests that these patterns of behaviour are innate.

Other researchers have discovered the same. Dr Charlotte Bühler and her colleagues, especially Dr Danziger, experimented with Albanian children. Now Albanian infants during the first year of life are (or at any rate were) 'bound to small wooden cradles, being released only for cleansing, not even for nursing'. You would expect that, being so cramped, they would, when released, take months to catch up with the movements of the children who had had free practice for their limbs from birth. In point of fact, it was

* Carmichael, *Manual of Child Psychology*, p. 314.

found that it took them only *two hours*! In other words, in spite of the lack of practice, the *capacities* to perform certain actions were developing during all that year, although the environmental conditions in the form of swaddling clothes prevented the children from exercising them. The experiment shows, first, that this process of maturation does not depend on environmental conditions, exercise, and training, but on innate potentialities; and, secondly, that these continue to develop in spite of the complete lack of opportunity to use them.

Further experiments were made by McGraw, who also studied identical twins. One was trained and practised in sitting, grasping, crawling, and walking; the other was not. The taught twin, it was found, developed no more rapidly in these activities than his brother, in spite of the training. Maturation was all important; training had little effect.

It is interesting to find that just when the behaviourists were insisting on the paramount influence of the environment in forming behaviour, the child psychologists 'reasserted without question the importance of the role of biological inheritance in the development of behaviour performance' (McGraw).

The practical importance of the principles of maturation are well summarized by Charlotte Bühler, which we may paraphrase, with comments, as follows :

(*a*) *Capacities such as walking, talking, and numerous other activities of the child depend on maturation; that is to say, on natural, innate aptitudes and not on training.* A great deal which passes as 'teaching' is really only practice in a capacity already present. We do not need to 'teach' a child to crawl, walk, or talk, the capacity to do so is there already and he will crawl anyway if left to himself. The same applies to a child's intelligence and his moral sense. All we do is to give him *opportunities* for the exercise of these functions and *practice* in the use of them.

Indeed, it would be a very difficult matter to teach a child the movements of crawling if he had no propensity to do so. He cannot crawl in the first few weeks of life; nor can we teach him. He can only crawl when the nervous mechanism for crawling develops, which it does only at a certain stage in maturation. In the same way we do not need to teach a normal adolescent to fall in love; that indeed would be a difficult task were the potentiality not present! He will fall in love anyway, and nothing we can do will stop it. Some adolescents do not fall in love and we take this to be 'abnormal', indicating thereby that falling in love is a natural innate potentiality. No amount of coaxing will make such a youth fall in love. When a girl of fourteen begins to take an interest in boys, we don't shove her into it, for that would make her recoil; we let it come gradually and naturally.

(b) *It follows that it is impossible to teach a child, in spite of any amount of practice, those tasks for which the innate disposition is not already present, nor the stage of development reached.* It is no use trying to teach a baby of two weeks to control its bladder and bowels. It cannot do so because the nervous mechanism controlling the sphincter muscles is not yet developed. We cannot teach a child of six months to catch a ball; nor a child of ten years to appreciate abstract truth as such.

Equally, to try to teach a child to read, to be sociable, or to be reasonable before the capacity for these skills has developed is not only a waste of time, it also confuses the child and does positive harm, for to try to exercise a child in a capacity he has not developed interferes with those capacities which *are* natural to him at that particular age, and which ought to be finding proper expression at that period. A child of four to seven, as we shall see, is developing his individuality; at eight to twelve his sociability. To urge him to be sociable at four to seven not only irritates him but also interferes with the proper development of his individuality; such frustration will show itself in his becoming ill-tempered.

(c) *When a period of maturation starts, the more ad-*

vanced the period the more advantage the child can take of training. We ought not to be in a hurry even when a phase of maturation such as talking, or the gang spirit, has arrived. Even when the various nervous mechanisms for these functions have started, they need time to develop – just as you get the best out of your car in the end if you run it in gently. Many a child's development has been ruined by his being *pressed*, say, to talk when he is naturally only beginning to talk. This is regarded by some experts as the main cause of stammering. Pressing often causes a nervous breakdown, which is another form of revolt and refusal to carry on. How often people lament, 'He showed such promise!' whereas it was only the parent or teacher who did the promising – the child is made to try and fulfil the promise.

(*d*) *There is therefore an optimum in maturation which, if we could discover it, is the best time for giving such training and practice as we deem necessary and have at our disposal.* 'There is a tide in the affairs of men which, taken at the *flood*, leads on to fortune,' and, in the child, that is not necessarily at the first appearance of any capacity.

(*e*) *Lack of practice in natural functions does not check the development of a maturing pattern.* If the opportunity of this maturation period is not seized or if, say, the child has been ill or delicate and has not had the opportunity to exercise any particular phase, we do not need to worry too much, because, as we have seen with the Albanian children, he soon 'catches up'. Children who go late to school often turn out to be more brilliant than the others. We do not put a girl we are training to be a singer on the operatic stage as soon as she can sing. We wait until her throat and vocal cords are fully developed, otherwise she is liable to strain both, and ruin her voice for ever. Thus it is that there is an optimum point for sociability, individuality, falling in love, and idealism, at which training and teaching are most effective, if we could but find it out.

I am not sure, however, that at this point we do not need to modify this general principle. It has been shown by experiments, like that on the Albanian children, that lack of practice does not hinder the maturation of the more basic, and therefore the more stable, biological functions such as crawling and talking. But it does not necessarily apply to the later developed, and therefore less stable, functions, like reasoning, social habits, and moral behaviour. In these cases the functions are more feebly established, and environmental factors may have a greater influence. It may therefore be that lack of opportunity means their disappearance altogether. A boy who has not the opportunity, perhaps because he is an invalid, to exercise the gang spirit at the right time in puberty may later make up for it by becoming a Scoutmaster or running a boys' club. But it may be that, never having had the opportunity to develop qualities of loyalty, comradeship, and cooperation which the gang life develops, he may for ever be deficient in these qualities. This is particularly the case if his exclusion from the gang is because he is unwanted, or if he feels he is unwanted. He may remain an isolated and unsociable individualist all his life, an excellent back-room boy, but too 'shy' to mix. Again, if a boy of nine to twelve has no opportunity to play with those of the opposite sex, he may miss the 'companionable' age, which is lost for ever, and when he does meet girls, say at eighteen or nineteen, he may then regard girls simply as sex objects. These results are often seen in patients.

It may be true therefore that while 'There is a tide in the affairs of men which taken at the flood leads on to fortune', nevertheless, 'Omitted, all the voyage of their lives is spent in shallows and in miseries.'

Such being the principles of maturation, it is important that those who bring up children should place far more faith in this process of maturation or natural development than they usually do.

Let us take the simple case of a child's eating. An infant naturally eats with its fingers. If we let it do so it enjoys its food and digests better. (Incidentally, it will make no more mess eating with its fingers than making boss shots at its mouth with a spoon.) All in good time, when imitation takes the place of reflex action, it will see others using a spoon and by imitation it will want to do likewise. The normal child learns its 'manners' best by observation and imitation of its parents, not by teaching. That is why mothers who fuss least often get the best results. Similarly, let a thirteen-year-old boy or girl mix naturally with other children; there is no need to ram the 'team spirit' down their throats, as is sometimes done in schools. They require *some* room for the development of their individuality. Many of them fortunately find it in their hobbies.

MATURATION AND ENVIRONMENT

From what has been said about the paramount import-ance of the process of maturation and the emergence of patterns of behaviour irrespective of environmental con-ditions, it might be assumed that there is nothing for parents to do except to leave well alone and let maturation take its course along its own lines. That would be a mistaken view. Environmental conditions play an important part in en-couraging or retarding this development, and that is where the parent comes in.

It is common practice to say that heredity and environ-ment cannot be separated and therefore to ignore the differ-ence between them. It is true that you cannot separate them, but you can distinguish them, and it is necessary to do so if you are to deal adequately with the child. If a plant in your garden is doing badly, it is important to know whether the *seed* is poor, or whether it is the *soil* which is at fault. If an adopted child becomes beyond control, it may be necessary to discover whether it is its heredity that is at fault (for which little can be done) or whether it is the way it was treated, perhaps before adoption (for which a great deal can be done).

It is not even enough to say that heredity and environment interact; we must discover which of a child's characteristics and how much of each are due to the hereditary factors and how much due to training, early experience, and other environmental factors.

The bee is an extraordinary example of instinct and maturation; yet a queen bee who lives for years and lays thousands of eggs differs from a worker bee who lives only a few weeks simply by the fact that as a grub she is fed on 'royal jelly'.

Let us therefore consider the *relationship* of heredity to environment. Maturation represents the innate and heredity factors. What part does environment play?

In the first place, an environment of some sort is necessary for the expression of a child's native capacities. A child has a natural capacity to crawl; but obviously he can not crawl unless he has a floor to crawl on. He has later a natural tendency to fall in with groups, but he cannot do this unless he has other children to play with. *The environment and the material world around are the medium in and through which the potentialities in the child's nature are expressed and developed.* The conditions the parents provide very largely determine what a child is going to be.

When therefore we say that capacities are innate and that patterns of behaviour appear 'irrespective of environmental conditions', we do not mean that they can do *without* an environment, but only that it is not the environmental conditions which produce the particular capacity; for training would not make anyone walk or talk in whom the capacity was not already present.

Secondly, the more suitable the environment, the better the development. A child learns to crawl and walk much better on a carpeted floor than on a slippery or uneven floor. Small children will eat almost anything, but obviously they will thrive better with wholesome food than with beer and cheese, to which some evacuated children became accustomed during the war and which they later demanded.

A child has the gift of speaking, and the more he is spoken to the sooner he learns to speak. That is why mothers naturally chatter away to their infants although the infant 'can't understand a word they are saying'. No! and they never will if they are never spoken to by a mother who is too busy to talk to them. Their speech will remain a babble or screech like that of the wolf children, found some years ago, who had lacked contact with humans.

Thirdly, although capacities like crawling and talking are innate and will inevitably emerge irrespective of teaching, *practice and training make all the difference between skilled and clumsy performance.*

A child walks by nature and without training; nevertheless we delight to give the child encouragement to practise his first steps. A child climbs naturally, but a child of two may need to be taught how to perform the complicated process of climbing into a high chair, not to speak of the still more complicated process of climbing down again.* Every normal child has the capacity to be sociable, but whether he develops sociable attitudes depends on the environment in which he is brought up and the practice he is given. Not only practice but the right *sort* of practice is required. A man may practise hours a day at his golf or his piano, but if he is practising the wrong way, if his technique is false, he is not likely to make an efficient golfer or musician. A slight suggestion from a professional in either sphere may correct a fault, which will make him efficient. No amount of practice will make an opera singer of someone with poor vocal chords; but equally no one can become an opera singer without diligent practice and proper tuition in the right way to use his vocal chords. An adolescent girl needs practice in dealing with boys, and therefore at first she indulges in flirtation, which is an innate form of practice without serious intent, necessary for the average girl. But she may still need advice in order to deal with all kinds of boys, those who are

---

* McGraw (Carmichael, p. 345) says that activities of ontogenetic origin can be greatly accelerated through exercise in the performance, though this is dependent on the state of maturation of the behaviour pattern.

self-opinionated, those who are hostile, those who are in-gratiating, and those who are boorish.

(*d*) The environment is of further importance in that it determines *which of the child's native potentialities are developed or exaggerated, which left in abeyance, and which are repressed*. A child who grows up in an atmosphere of fear is likely (though not necessarily) to grow up timid, that is to say to have his fear accentuated. A child constantly subjected to irritation and frustration will probably grow up as aggressive and ill-tempered as the child who is always given his own way. A child who is perpetually fondled and cosseted will have his sensuousness exaggerated, so that this may become his one preoccupation when he reaches adoles-cence. In an intellectual home where questions are answered and his curiosity stimulated, he will develop a wide and intelligent interest in life.

(*e*) Further, the environment determines *the direction* of our capacities. Nature provides us with the potentialities; our environment, training, and ourselves determine the end to which they are directed. As we have said, nature enables us to walk, but it does not decide where we walk *to*; to talk, but not what we talk *about*. Every child has a craving for know-ledge (what is this? why is that?) but the end or *purpose* for which he uses his knowledge is all-important. Charm and the desire to be pleasing are valuable and natural qualities in life. But there are those who use charm to become successful confidence tricksters. A mother may be fascinated by the wheedling charm of her child, who by his winning ways can get anything out of her; she says she 'simply can't refuse him, he is such a darling'. She perhaps needs to be warned that encouragement of the child to get things by putting on his charm rather than by hard work may later lead to dishonesty when he finds his charm does not work, as surely he will, for self-conscious charm in adult life often fails.

To demonstrate the relation of the innate to the environ-mental factors, we may take the analogy of the tree, say of the oak and the pine. An oak is an oak not on account of anything in the soil but because of genetic factors in its seed, the acorn; and so with the pine whose specific characteristics develop from the pine cone. By no effort of skill, imagination, or change of environment can an acorn be made to develop into a pine tree, or the pine cone into an oak. They always 'breed true', because the distinctive characteristics of each are dependent upon the hereditary genes contained in the seed, each to its kind, and not on environmental conditions, or on the way they are treated.

But neither the oak nor the pine will grow unless it has a suitable environment of soil, of light, and of air. So it is that a child inherits many patterns of behaviour, but it needs an atmosphere of love and freedom for them to develop.

(f) From the analogy of the tree we may draw a further conclusion. Both oak and pine require soil, moisture, and sunlight. But whereas the oak requires a stiff clay soil to be at its best, the pine requires a lighter soil. So with children. They differ both in their temperaments and in their capacities, and therefore *each child requires individual treatment according to his temperament*. The mother who says 'I treat all my children exactly alike' may be wrong. The studious, sensitive child requires different treatment from the sturdy, romping, full-blooded, tough type. Parents who have opposite types in the same family (as well they might, since one child may take after the father, another the mother) recognize the necessity of providing for each the environment suitable to his temperament. A sergeant-major recently remarked that in dealing with recruits he says to one, 'Clean those cans'; to another, 'What about cleaning up those cans'; to a third, 'See if you can get those cans cleaned up before you turn in, will you?' So marked may be the influence of the environment that it can completely change and transform the hereditary factors. So environment triumphs over heredity!

A striking illustration of this is found in embryology. Normally the eye cells in an embryo produce eyes, and gill cells produce gills. But if cells which normally produce eyes are transplanted at the right time and in the right place the 'miracle' occurs and the eye cells produce gills.

We can produce similar tricks with children. A boy naturally aggressive may be made timid by conditions in childhood; a temperamentally gentle child may be made aggressive and ill-tempered. The mother-instinct in a girl may be stamped out by hatred of a baby brother who gets all the attention. This may turn into hate of all children and even of her own child. The different contributions of innate and environmental factors are of importance in the sphere of mental disorders. Mental deficiency is almost entirely, and the psychoses (insanity) are very largely, due to innate and often hereditary factors, whereas the psychoneuroses are mainly due to environmental conditions originating in childhood and are therefore more preventable.

But there are many mixed conditions in which we need to discover how much of a child's disorder is due to innate or constitutional causes and how much to his conditions of life; for the degree to which he can be treated largely depends on the answer to this inquiry.

PHYSIOLOGICAL BASIS OF MATURATION

Maturation depends on the development of the physiological nervous system. It is constitutional.

When we speak of a characteristic as being 'innate' or 'constitutional', we mean that it is determined by the physiological organism. Thus when we say that some children are innately or constitutionally aggressive, others sensitive, or intelligent, we mean that these characteristics are determined by their physiological make-up. Others, though constitutionally gentle, may be *made* aggressive by environmental influences.

A child's *temperament* is constitutional and comes from the influence of the body on the mind; his *disposition* is determined by environmental conditions. The child's *character*, on the other hand, depends on his aims, purposes, and ideals.*

The capacity to walk, to talk, and later to be sociable and reasonable are all dependent on the development of the corresponding part of the nervous system, and only when this matures does the capacity come into play.

This physiological basis of maturation provides us with an explanation of the characteristics previously discussed.

It explains, in the first place, why it is that capacities like crawling, walking, talking, and venturesomeness emerge *irrespective of environment*. They emerge as and when the physiological processes with which they are associated develop. As the centre for sight in the brain develops, so the child can see, and not before.

It makes it clear also why *it is no use trying to force a child to do something for which his natural mechanism is not yet developed*, for instance, to control his bladder before the nervous mechanism for this has been formed, or to be reasonable before the full development of his brain makes it possible for him. It also explains how the phases of maturation emerge in *ordered sequence* : for they emerge and become active as the anatomical and physiological processes mature.

It further explains why *we get better results if we wait until the phase of maturation is well forward* before starting to exercise it; for the further the physiological processes have advanced the more capable they are of performing their functions adequately and the more effective their training and practice.

This physiological basis of maturation also explains two other interesting facts of child behaviour, frequently noticed by parents, namely, repetitiveness and anticipation, but they are of such importance that we must accord them separate description.

* See *Psychology and Mental Health*, p. 587.

THE PRINCIPLE OF ANTICIPATION

Put in its simplest terms, the principle of anticipation is that *the physiological capacity for any function anticipates the biological necessity for its use*. To take an illustration : the foetus, in the ordinary course of things, does not need to breath or to suck until it is time for it to be separated from its mother. That normally takes place at nine months. But supposing the foetus is born at seven or eight months, a premature child; we nevertheless find that the breathing and sucking apparatus are all ready and prepared for action. Thus even a premature child is capable of survival in spite of that unfortunate accident. Nature takes no chances, but prepares for these functions in good time and long before they are ordinarily needed. An infant as early as the second day makes walking movements,* although it will not actually walk for several months. It makes chewing movements long before it is called upon to chew, but it *can* chew if called upon to do so. The capacity to perform these functions is laid down well in advance of the normal need to use them.

A very interesting instance of this principle of anticipation is in regard to a girl's reproductive functions. She develops menstrual periods, which are of course a prelude to child-bearing, but it is not until a year or two afterwards that she is capable of bearing children (p. 193).

Boys and girls of eight or nine are quite capable of having sexual intercourse with one another, and in undisciplined communities often have intercourse long before the natural age of procreation arrives.

But the fact that nature anticipates the need does not mean that the precocious exercise of any such function is desirable. It is there in case of emergency. It is undesirable that a child should be born prematurely, although nature prepares for that eventuality. Premature arousal of sex can do no good; it often does harm. Medical psychologists

* Valentine, *The Normal Child*, p. 115.

frequently have to see cases of neurotic disorder arising from premature sex relations, although it would not be true to say that such activities in themselves always produce neuroses. A case in point is that of a very attractive young woman who suffered from excessive self-consciousness because of such an episode when she was six, the memory of which so embarrassed her with any young man that he in turn shied off, and she could not get married, although she longed to be – and now is.

The fact that we call such activities 'precocious' implies that we recognize that there is a 'right' or optimum time for their exercise, which is not necessarily at their first appearance (p. 52). It is therefore well to let nature take her time and not to encourage the premature arousal of any of her functions.

This principle applies to most patterns of behaviour, many of which find their expression in play during childhood, long before they are required. A boy, as we shall see (p. 162), at first collects things for the sake of collecting, without finding any use for the things he collects. So the girl in adolescence is coquettish and desires to attract long before the need or even the desire for sexual intercourse is developed; at the moment she wants only to attract. We, of course, know that this attraction is, in fact, in anticipation of marriage and reproduction, but at this stage that is not the idea of the adolescent girl herself (p. 228). To interpret her behaviour in terms of what we understand to be its meaning is to commit the psychologist's fallacy (p. 12).

THE PRINCIPLE OF REPETITIVENESS

One of the most fascinating features of a child's life, which every parent has observed, is the way he repeats actions and sounds over and over again. He makes kicking movements in the bath and goes on making the same kicking movements. He will say 'Ba !' and, having discovered that he can, goes on repeating the same sound by a sort of compulsion to repeat. Later on, when he has learnt a nursery rhyme, he will go on repeating it over and over again. A character- istic of these repetitions is that if they are not without rhyme, they certainly appear to be without reason; the child utters these sounds and makes these movements irrespective of any aim or purpose and often apparently independently of any external stimulus. He crawls, without wanting to get any- where in particular, just from the impulse to crawl, and goes on crawling; he utters sounds without wanting to say any- thing in particular; he kicks without wanting to kick anybody but just for the urge of kicking, and he goes on repeating these actions.

Every parent is fully and often painfully aware of the repetitive process! If we start playing Peep-bo! with a two- year-old, or fling him up in the air, or play 'lions' with him, he will cry 'again' until *you* are worn out, even if *he* isn't.

The repetition of a child's actions is nature's method of giving the child practice in the performance of its neces- sary biological functions.

We have already mentioned the importance of our giving the child practice for the development of its emerging capabilities – walking is natural but we encourage a child to walk, and we help it to talk. What we have now to realize is that *nature has devised its own method of giving the child practice*, by giving him the urge to repeat a function over and over again.

This repetitive action is no doubt in the first place merely *the result of a nervous impulse*. A group of nerve cells in the brain is like an accumulator : when it is fully charged, it begins to *dis*charge, and the impulse passes down to the cor- responding group of muscles. If these muscles are those of the vocal chords, the impulse results in a sound; if of the arms and legs, the child kicks or crawls. The *stimulation* of the discharge may come from without, or it may come from within the organism.

But once this has taken place the child feels *pleasure in the activity*. For tension produces discomfort, whereas the release of tension is associated with relief and pleasure.

You may see the look of pleasure on the child's face when it makes these sounds; when it brings up wind; when it passes a motion; and when it takes its first steps. At first, it performs these actions in response to a nervous impulse and then, with great trepidation, it ventures to repeat the process and, finding that nothing disastrous happens, laughs with pleasure at its achievement, at the effect it has produced. It then goes on doing the action, no longer merely in response to the accumulation of energy, but *because of the pleasure the action gives*.

So the repetitive action, now encouraged by the pleasure derived from it, gives the child a further practice in the performance of its biological functions.

The child's activity goes a stage further. Having given expression to a native capacity and having, by repeating it, had practice in its performance, it then begins to use it *for some useful purpose*. A child at first crawls simply because of the discharge of nervous energy along that path. Then it crawls for the pleasure this gives, not for any other object. Finally, it finds that by crawling it can get a toy it wants, or go to its mother, or out into the garden. The action is now performed, not merely as the result of a physiological urge, or for the pleasure it gives, but for an object. *Its action is now purposive* (p. 38).

So it is with talking. The first sounds are probably just spontaneous outbursts of accumulated energy in cells whose nerves serve the vocal chords. So the child makes sounds like Mmm-m-m or Ba-a-a – quite useless sounds, but indirectly giving exercise to its vocal chords. Then different sounds begin to express different feelings and emotions, so that the child crows when it is contented and happy, cries when it is in distress, shrieks when it is angry.

But now it discovers that when it crows the mother is pleased and that by crying it can call the attention of its mother, and so it begins to *use* crowing or crying to please the mother or to gain her attention.

Apart from giving practice to useful biological functions, the repetitive process helps to establish 'habits'. Habits are repetitive actions. Developing habits in dressing, washing hands before meals, attending to the toilet at certain times, saves a lot of unnecessary thought and worry. Likewise a child can develop the *habit* of being courteous, of not losing his temper, and of being generous. Such forms of behaviour are really useful, and, once formed, cause the child no distress.

The repetitive process further develops into moral qualities like *persistence* and *perseverance*. The child in his efforts to crawl or to walk or to make a boat or to mend a lock goes on and on with extraordinary persistence. If he fails, he tries over and over again until he may succeed. Continuous failure will however ultimately produce discouragement; that is why we need to help him over difficulties.

Play. The most dramatic illustration of both the principle of anticipation and that of repetitiveness is found in play.

In a game such as hide-and-seek a child is engaged in activities which will be serviceable to him in later life, but long before he needs to use them for their ultimate purpose. That is anticipation. Also, as he continues to play the same game over and over again, he becomes more practised in both hiding and observing.

So far we have dealt with repetition of action. Repetition is also an aid to understanding. In adult life when we hear something surprising, the significance of which we have failed fully to grasp, we say 'Say that again!', although, in fact, we heard perfectly well what was said. We heard but did not fully comprehend, so we want it repeated so as to grasp it.

As every parent knows, the child wants the same story over and over again. He asks for 'Little Black Sambo' or 'Bre'er Rabbit' or 'Rupert the Little Bear' every night and sits enthralled as you read it, although he has heard it so often that he could himself almost say it backwards – indeed, woe betide you if you make the slightest mistake! There are times when we surely sympathize with the nanny who, with a total disregard for final prepositions, said to the little girl, 'What do you want that book to be read to out of for?'*

Why this craving to have something repeated? There is some sense in it after all. For just as repetitive actions serve the purpose of giving *practice to a function*, so the desire to have things repeated enables the child to *grasp* and *understand* a problem.

For these favourite stories frequently represent some problem existing in the child's own mind. By listening to the story over and over again he comes to understand his own problems and is better able to deal with them. Cinderella deals with the problem of the child being left out and un-wanted – a common experience in childhood. The story gives a child reassurance, and he wants the story repeated over and over again so as to establish him in that reassurance. When the child has got all he wants from the stories, he ceases to be interested, for the problem is solved.

So a boy of five or six beginning to feel his independence and strength, with the desire to throw off authority, likes to hear over and over again how Jack the Giant Killer managed it; or how David, small as he was, slew Goliath. He wants the story repeated so that it can sink in. Later on he loses interest; for he has now established his self-confidence; he is convinced that Jack, that is himself, *is* capable of killing giants. As he grows older, biographies of famous people serve the same purpose as his childhood fairy-tales.

Fairy Tales. Many people object to fairy stories because they so often deal with frightening situations. It is true that some sensitive children are much too frightened by them and have nightmares, which is a sure indication that the parent should stop telling such stories. But the ordinary child likes them and even likes to be frightened! A morbid taste? Not at all; for by these means the child is acclimatizing

*Quoted in *Plain Words*, by Gowers.

himself to frightening situations in phantasy, so that when he meets them in reality, he will be able to cope with them. He 'plays' with the idea of witches and danger, while all the time he has the reassurance that he is in fact quite safe and that the fairy story is only a fairy story.

The repetitive process is thus one of the principal methods a child has of adaptation to life.

3

THE PHASES OF EARLY DEVELOPMENT

THE NEED TO RECOGNIZE THE PHASES

MATURATION, as we have defined it, is the development of innate potentialities in ordered sequence. The child passes through various phases of development, each differing from the last. For various reasons it is necessary for the parents to recognize these phases.

First, the child must be given the *fullest opportunity for the development of each phase as it emerges.* Every phase has its specific contribution to make to the full development of the personality. The phase of suggestibility (about the age of two and a half), in which the child takes over the moods and behaviour of the adult, is as necessary as the phase of individuality at four to seven, when he strikes out on his own. The gang phase in which the child mixes with the herd of his own sex is as important and necessary for his development as the later phase when he or she falls in love with one of the opposite sex.

Secondly, we need to know the phases of development *in order not to take for abnormal what is normal for that phase.* A child of two is self-willed. Many parents are concerned at this and say, 'He *has* got a will of his own! We can't let him grow up like this!' – and set about breaking his will. Self-will is *normal* at that age and must not be treated as abnormal. He will not 'grow up like that' if treated intelligently : he is more likely to grow up 'like that' if you attempt to 'break his will'.

Thirdly, we should have some knowledge of the stages of development *so as to recognize the abnormal as soon as it occurs.* Let us say that it is normal for a boy of thirteen to belong to a gang of boys. If, then, we find him interested only in one girl friend, we suspect something abnormal; he may, for instance, have been badly bullied by boys earlier and so shuns them. On the other hand, a boy of eighteen who avoids girls is also abnormal. We can judge of the abnormal only by reference to the normal.

If a child has had every opportunity for the full development of one phase he will *naturally pass on to the next phase*. We need not be afraid, therefore, as many parents are, that if a phase of development, say that of self-will at two or individuality at four to seven, appears very pronounced it will remain so.

Individuality will normally give way to sociability, in its own good time. That is why no sensible parent takes the 'showing off' of their boy or girl of five seriously because they know he or she will soon pass out of it. Even such a phase, when allowed expression, makes its own contribution to the development of the whole personality.

On the other hand, if a phase is *not* given its opportunity for development, it tends to persist into the next stage. As a result a conflict takes place between the earlier phase, which refuses to give way because it has not been satisfied, and the later emerging phase whose turn has now come. This leads to confusion and unhappiness. It is pathetic, for instance, to see a boy of sixteen, who, not having acquired a sense of security in his earlier years, now wants to go out into the world but at the same time feels tied to his mother's apron strings and still clings to the earlier phase of dependence.

When in later life infantile tendencies persist which the individual should have grown out of, it is not because these tendencies have simply been exaggerated : on the contrary, it is because they have been repressed at a period in the past when they should have been given expression. So the adult person may suffer from childish fears or childish tempers or childish auto-erotic practices which he should long ago have outgrown.

Various theories of the phases of development have been suggested.

The *theory of recapitulation* is a very tempting one. It

holds that the individual develops as the race – 'Ontogeny (the development of the individual) reproduces phylogeny (the development of the races).' 'Every individual climbs up his own genealogical tree.' So, it is said, the race passes through the root and grub stage, then the hunting or fishing stage, then the nomadic stage, the pastoral stage in which they domesticate animals (like sheep) for food, then the agricultural phase when they are sedentary, and finally the industrial and commercial stage. There are those who see these various phases in the child's development – such as his interest in pets (domestic), in gardening (agriculture), and in swapping (commerce). There can be little doubt that *physiologically* we develop through many of the stages of evolution (every individual has gills at one stage). But as applied to the child's interests and behaviour, the theory that the individual develops along the same lines as the race does not hold water. There is no race of man which has passed through these stages of development in such an orderly fashion. How nice it would be if we could describe the stages of development in a child by this simple analogy. What determines whether a tribe consists of fishermen or of agriculturalists depends on circumstances, whether they live by the sea or inland !

The stages we shall describe are not so dramatic as this, but were derived mainly by direct observation of the children in the Leytonstone Homes, corrected and corroborated by our investigation into the mind of the child in analysis.

What I shall give is not a complete account of the child's psychology at any particular age, but of what appeared to be the *dominant* characteristic of that phase. When we speak of the self-will phase, for instance, we do not mean that self-will is confined to the age of two; nor, on the other hand, that other characteristics, such as dependence, do not appear then, but that self-will is dominant at that age. A child of six months can be very self-willed, but dependence is its dominant characteristic at this age.

Basically speaking most of the phases I shall describe I

believe to be the result of maturation, and to be innate. That is why we find them in most children.

The ages we shall give are, of course, only approximate, since one child develops more rapidly than another and reaches a stage sooner. Nevertheless it will probably be found that the phases I describe follow the same *order* in each individual.

There are many influences which come to disturb the appearance of the natural stage of development. Thus imitation is very strongly developed in every child. A girl of thirteen may like to ape older girls by putting on lipstick and behaving in a coquettish way, but that does not mean that she has the same heterosexual motivation as the older girl. She is only playing at being grown up.

If, therefore, you fail to find these phases in your child, it may be that we are wrong in our descriptions; but it may equally be that something has intervened in the particular case of your child.

*

The main purpose of this book is the promotion of mental health, and if there are readers who dispute that the stages mentioned are phases of innate maturation (as they are perfectly at liberty to do), what I write may be taken simply as descriptive of what happens to a child in our culture. But if they reject even that, the phenomena I have described may simply be taken as illustrative of the principles of mental health. The age of two may or may not be the phase of self-will, but the way in which a child's self-will can be dealt with in conformity with the principles of mental health, as described in this chapter, still holds good. The 'gang spirit' at puberty may or may not be a phase of innate maturation; but at least it is a very common thing, and we may discover its value for the development of loyalty and cooperation. I should, therefore, like the intelligent parent to apply what is printed in this book just as and to the degree that he or she thinks fit.

THE FIRST THREE YEARS

The first three years of life are concerned with *the organization of the child's personality*. Of these, the first two years are engaged in the emergence of the primitive biological impulses necessary to the pursuit of life, such as curiosity, assertiveness, and fear : the third and fourth years are engaged in the organization and harmonization of these various impulses under the control of the will. The foundations of the personality are thus laid down in those early years.

If the child's personality is well organized, if, that is, the impulses are fully expressed and usefully directed, then it will be strong in will, happy in disposition, and of good character. If, on the other hand, there is a failure in organization in the early years, then the individual is incapable of facing up to the responsibilities of life and may fall victim to various disorders. That is why we find, as most psychopathologists would agree, that the predisposing causes of neurotic disorders originate in the first three or four years of life.

There may, it is true, be later events, such as shocks, illness, or an unhappy marriage, which *precipitate* the actual breakdown, but these experiences would not have produced such illness unless the individual was *predisposed* by unhappy conditions in early childhood.

Indeed, we may go so far as to say that, given a soundly organized personality in these early years, it is virtually impossible for an individual to have a nervous breakdown; for such a personality is capable of facing up to any emergency in life. There were many men who spent years in meeting the hazards of war and came out stronger men than they went in. On the other hand, if you analyse a man with 'shell-shock' or other traumatic neurosis you always find that there were factors in early childhood rendering him incapable of coping with his present situation.

We shall, therefore, not hesitate to describe in some detail how the child's personality is organized in these first three years because upon that depend the whole future health, happiness, and efficiency of the adult's personality.

The first year of life is characterized by three main phases: dependence, control over bodily movements, and sensuous pleasure.

DEPENDENCE

The baby of a few months, lying in its cot, is a picture of complete helplessness. It is entirely dependent upon the mother for food, for warmth, for protection, and for security; without her it would rapidly perish. It would not be true to say it can do nothing for itself; for it can breathe, suck, swallow, digest, and excrete, and protest by crying when uncomfortable or hungry. But that is about all.

Indeed, in the early months of life, it can be said to have hardly emerged from the womb. It dislikes being born and dislikes the world into which it has been rudely catapulted.

The fear experienced at birth later recurs in nightmares in which one passes through a narrow tunnel with a sense of suffocation, and in feelings of claustrophobia. This has been proved in analysis by tracing back such nightmares and symptoms to their origin. Similarly, the horror of the wide open space confronting the new-born child recurs in nightmares of being alone, and in agoraphobia.

The infant, disliking the cold, uncomfortable world into which it has been so rudely thrust, turns away from it as soon as possible, and sinks again on to its mother's bosom to recover the state of passivity. It wants to be left at peace, it wants to stay put. If it could, it would put up a notice, 'Not to be disturbed!' It does not like to be moved. That is why it is quite content to be in the cot, or in the mother's arms; all it asks is that it shall not be moved from the one to the other. It is *transition* to which an infant objects, relapsing into calmness only when restored to quiescence.

But while the infant does not like to be moved from place to place, it welcomes movement of a sort; it likes to be gently rocked, whether in the mother's arms or in the cot. Indeed, the infant of the South Sea Islands will sleep peacefully, bound by a shawl to the mother's back while she works in the plantation. Why is this? Because movement means that someone is near and is, therefore, reassuring, whereas absolute silence and stillness may signify aloneness and desertion. Quite frequently, then, when the infant is crying in the cot, a mere rocking, indicating the presence of the mother, or, still more, the mother's voice is enough to reassure it, and it stops crying.

Evidence of the infant's dependence and helplessness is easy to find.

Sleep. In the first month the infant sleeps sixty per cent of its time, and of the remaining forty per cent, ninety-nine per cent is spent in dozing (Bühler); so that we may say it spends practically the whole of its first month in sleep and dozing. That is as near the pre-natal state as it can get. By the time it is twelve months old it sleeps and dozes *half* its time, and spends a *quarter* in quiet displeasure.

Close contact. The infant's dependence is also shown in its need to be in close contact with the mother. This need has its origin in the deep-rooted tropistic urge which makes an organism keep in close contact with another body. This urge makes it snuggle close to its mother, and want to be cosy, to be nursed and cuddled.

This contact gives it the sense of protection and security. It also gives it sensuous pleasure, which further encourages the activity. But the biological urge is more primitive than the sensuous pleasure which comes to be associated with it. The old-fashioned nannies understood this need and tucked up an infant in its cot, in which state it felt more secure and slept more peacefully.

Clinging. The dependency is also shown by an infant's tendency to cling. One of the first reflexes, no matter where a stimulus is applied, is a movement of its arms outwards, and then towards its chest and head, as though drawing something towards itself – an embracing movement. The infant of three weeks has such abnormal powers of clinging that it can support its own body weight when hanging by its arms. This may well be an atavistic tendency, a reverberation of that stage in evolution when our simian ancestors lived in trees and had to cling to branches – but even the infant monkey clings to its mother before it clings to the branch!

These movements of clinging in situations of distress have been observed even in adult apes.* 'An ape who was punished uttered one or two heartbroken wails as she stared at me horror-struck. The next moment she had flung her arms round my neck, quite beside herself, and was only comforted by degrees, when I stroked her.' Again he tells of apes being shut out in the cold rain, who, when the door of the cage was ultimately opened, instead of going straight in, 'put their arms round me, one round my body, the other round my knees in a frenzy of joy'. How very like a child! These clinging tendencies of ape or child express their dependence upon others for their security.

The cry of distress. The helplessness of an infant is also illustrated by its cry of distress – for instance when it falls, or is disturbed by a loud noise, or is separated from its mother. The function of the cry is to call the attention of the mother to relieve its distress. It is, therefore, well to remind parents that an infant does not cry unless something is wrong. It is not (certainly at this stage) pure cussedness, nor intended simply to annoy the mother. If the mother gets annoyed, her irritation may stop the child crying because it finds that crying makes things worse by calling the attention of evil hostile forces to itself. Then, instead of crying, the child may fall into a silent anxiety. The mother is then satisfied by its quietness; the infant is not. It lies in a state of terror.

Omnipotence. Some psychologists maintain that infancy is characterized by omnipotence. It is true that an infant demands immediate satisfaction for its needs, and creates a rumpus if they are not satisfied; and no doubt if it is always immediately satisfied, it gets the *illusion* of omnipotence –

* Wolfgang Kohler, *The Mentality of Apes.*

that it has only to express its wish, to have the wish satisfied. But it is its very feeling of helplessness and need, not its omnipotence, which causes it to make these demands on others.

Analysis. This sense of dependence constantly crops up in analysis, when we take our patients back under hypnosis, or by free association, to re-live their infantile experiences. Let me quote one instance from a woman doctor under hypnosis who, going back to soon after birth, re-lives the feelings she experienced as follows : 'I have a burrowy feeling – everything is so big and open and I hate everything; I hate being alive. I want somebody close with their arms right round me so that I feel protected and close. I want to be all inside something so that I can be protected. I don't like the light or the noise or anything. If somebody would allow me to burrow in their arms and let me be close properly! I do hate everything! I'm so cold and miserable and lonely. Everything is like a pandemonium, like a nightmare.'

In analysis a patient often describes a *feeling of identity*, the baby feeling that it is one with the mother, part of the mother; or the mother being a larger part of itself. Separate from the mother it therefore feels incomplete, as though a part of itself were severed off.

This feeling of oneness with the mother is reflected later in religious mysticism, in the ceremonial eating of the token animal in primitive tribes, and in drinking with someone as a symbol of friendship.

These facts then are sufficient to establish the first year of life as the phase of dependence.

*

In describing this and other phases I shall try to recount (*a*) its natural biological form and function; (*b*) its development into higher forms; (*c*) its fixations due to arrest of development; (*d*) its perversions into abnormal character traits; and (*e*) its emergence as neurotic disorders. Then will follow a discussion of the mental hygiene of each phase, which, in brief, means how to deal with each phase so as to give it full and healthy development and thus avoid disorders.

Development of dependence. The feeling of dependence, having served its purpose of securing protection, does not disappear, but develops into higher forms. The *physical* dependence of infancy, for food and warmth, develops at about the age of two and a half into *suggestibility*, which is *psychic* dependence, dependence upon the mood and feelings of those around the child. After an interlude at the age of four to seven, when the child is developing his sense of individuality, dependence returns in the form of *companionship* with other children, at the age of eight to twelve.

The dependent tendency then takes on a still more strongly social form, at puberty, with *loyalty to the gang*, a strong sense of comradeship, obedience, and dependence upon a leader. In later adolescence (sixteen to eighteen), it appears as devotion, first in hero-worship, then to some person with whom he (or she) is in love; or as devotion to *idealism*, whether social, patriotic, aesthetic, or religious; or as devotion to truth, scientific or philosophic. So strong may be this devotion to a cause and so completely subservient may the individual be to his ideal that he may be prepared to sacrifice life itself for it, as many patriots, religious men and women, and scientists have done.

Later on in adult life the dependence finds its expression in *social life*, which we may call *inter*dependence.*

Dependent character traits. There are some children who, by nature and constitutionally, are more dependent than

* An attempt has been made by Dr Flügel, following the Freudian preoccupation with sex, to show that social life is derived from sexual life. We agree with Freud that the earliest 'society' is that of mother and child, but the basis of this is not sexual. The basis of all these activities – of the clinging of the infant to the mother, of the devotion of the soldier to his leader, on whose skill his life depends, and of our family and communal life – is the need for security, not for sex. The sensuous or sexual pleasure the infant derives from the mother is secondary, although serving to *enhance* the biological function.

others, and need to rely more upon others, just as there are children by nature more independent and self-sufficient. The former conform to the herbivorous type, like the horse, who depends for its safety on flight; the latter are of the carnivorous type which depends for its existence on attack.

Such children are of dependent *temperament*; they tend to be timid, to shrink from life. It is no use pushing them into positions of responsibility; they can't take it. But they may be made very loyal servants such as secretaries who will do anything for those in whom they put their trust and whom they wish to serve.

Exaggeration of dependence. Some children are *over-*dependent and later become over-suggestible. This is generally considered to result from a child's being over-protected, over-petted, over-indulged, having everything done for him, so that he can do nothing for himself. This may be the case, especially if he is already of a dependent *temperament*. But the most common cause of abnormal dependence is not being coddled too much, but just the opposite. It is the child who feels insecure, that is to say, who has not had its need of dependence satisfied, who clings to his parents or who gets a neurosis to escape from life.

Neurosis. The most characteristic neurosis relating back to this phase of infancy is 'anxiety neurosis'. When in analysis we trace phobias back to their origin we usually find their root causes lie in experiences of fear in infancy, Which is, of course, why these phobias are commonly called 'infantile'.

Separation anxiety may take the form of fear of leaving home or travelling. Both actions revive the infant's need to cling to the mother. *Agoraphobia* is another striking illustration : it is said to be a fear of open space, but is in reality a fear of loss of contact with someone. Similarly with *claustrophobia* and some causes of asthma, which are often found to derive from a feeling of suffocation at birth.

When, for any reason, the child is over-dependent, he may become like Peter Pan (and his author James Barrie), mother-fixed and unwilling to grow up. He may then end in becoming a Mary Rose, a 'ghost', with a feeling of unreality, a condition psychiatrists often have to treat.

In analysis it is necessary to discover and revive infantile forgotten experiences, the prototype of adult disorders. In reliving the infantile prototypes the patient re-adjusts himself to them, as he could not do in infancy, and so is cured of his neurosis.

Mental Hygiene. The mental hygiene of every phase of development requires that the characteristics of the phase should be given full and complete expression, enabling them to make their full contribution to the development of the child. It means that, in this phase, the infant's feelings of dependence should be fully satisfied by being given security, so that the later developments of social life, already described, should evolve naturally, and neurosis be avoided.

It is, therefore, of the utmost importance, especially in the first year or two of life, that we should give the child the sense of protection, and avoid, as far as possible, all forms of shock and fear. Or, if these are unavoidable, as indeed they often are, as in the case of illness, the child should be given all the comfort and assurance necessary. A bad birth or severe illnesses, like whooping cough with its feeling of suffocation, may produce a *life-long* feeling of insecurity, unless reassurance is forthcoming.

BODY CONTROL

The first year of life is also engaged in the infant's exercise of its muscles and of bodily control. It kicks its legs, it exercises its arms, it twists its body, it jerks its head. These movements are without object and apparently without purpose. But in point of fact the child is limbering up its muscles for future endeavour – like a boxer before a fight. This is the period of *physical preparedness,* after which it puts its muscles to good use.

For there follows in the second year, the phase of

exploration when it begins to travel around and to investigate the world in which it is going to live.

Characteristically enough, these movements, as Gesell has shown, take place, in order, from the head downwards.*

One of the first regular movements is that of the eyes. The infant opens its eyes to the world with wonder. It cannot as yet focus, but looks vaguely around, sometimes knitting its brows as it exercises the eye muscles, to get a clearer view of its strange surroundings. As it feeds, it gazes wonderingly and peacefully at the mother's face. It cannot at first accommodate its two eyes together and therefore often squints, putting the anxious mother into a flap. With a little practice, it learns to accommodate its two eyes, and instead of vaguely looking into space, it can focus both at one object.

At sixteen weeks it focuses and follows round the movements of the mother, or watches the older children play, but without taking part itself. At sixteen weeks also the infant will respond to the mother; it smiles in response to her smile and frowns when she frowns. Thus it develops social response. By its mouth also it learns about the outside world. It discriminates between things by putting them into its mouth, accepting the friendly nipple, but rejecting the father's hard and not too clean finger, which tastes nasty. After its eye and mouth movements, it uses its hands and arms, at first in quite aimless movements, 'lashing the air with more or less symmetric windmill movements of the arms' (Gesell). It then develops the capacity to *coordinate* its eyes with its hands, so that when it sees an object it can now reach towards it and take hold of it. At sixteen weeks also the infant exercises its lungs and vocal chords by burbling, cooing, and laughing, and so prepares for the function of speech.

Then it develops its abdominal muscles so that it can sit up, first with support, then, at about forty weeks, without support.

Its legs then come into action, but at first are exercised

* *The First Five Years of Life*, p. 13.

merely in kicking movements due to the discharge of nerve tension. These movements, like those of the arms, then become expressive of emotions, whether of excitement or of anger, and finally are used purposively.

At twenty weeks an infant can roll over; crawl at forty-four weeks; creep on hands and feet at fifty weeks; stand temporarily at fifty-two weeks; stand independently at fifteen months; and walk alone at eighteen months. All these are illustrative of maturation – the development of innate activities in ordered sequence.

While all this is taking place the child is also establishing control over its internal muscles of bowels and bladder. At first it has no power over its excretions, defecation and urination. But as the nervous mechanisms for these develop, so the power over the sphincter muscles which control them comes into action Only then, and not before, can the infant control these functions, however much it is coaxed, scolded, and punished.

Children vary as to the age when they develop bladder control. About one-third do so at eighteen months, about three-quarters at two years, and the great majority are fully controlled by the time they are three. But don't worry; it will come right. There is an 'optimum' for the training of these functions and that is *not* in the first year.

The biological significance of all these bodily activities is of great importance, because they are exercising muscles for future action. They illustrate the principles of both repetitiveness and anticipation. Before the infant can use its arms and legs and other functions in voluntary activity, it must exercise them in readiness to do so.

When the infant has, by these spontaneous outbursts of nerve energy, got some voluntary control over its movements, it then begins to experience pleasure in controlling them. It is exciting for it to find that it can itself make a noise with its lungs or by crumpling a piece of paper. It is later thrilled when it finds it can venture a few steps from the chair to its mother. In all this it is building up a series of adaptations which will serve it in good stead in later life. Childhood is a phase in which the child, in an atmosphere of security, can practise its skills.

The *mental hygiene* of this phase is very simple; it is to allow free play to all these bodily activities.

Abnormalities. A common *perversion* of this period is the exercise of this manipulative function upon its own genital organs when it is not given material to play with. Very commonly we find in analysis that such masturbation starts by simply 'wanting something to play with' (for the urge to do something with the hands is a natural one), and this is the only object available. This 'innocent' type of masturbation can usually be overcome by giving the child some counter-attraction. But the time may come when it finds that it gets more pleasure from the masturbation than from the toy, and the problem is then more difficult, for it encourages the child in sensuous lethargy and discourages it in its natural propensity to do things. The 'pleasure principle' overrides the 'reality principle'.

THE SENSUOUS PHASE

The physiological activities and bodily functions just described are commonly associated with sensuous pleasure. It gives pleasure for the infant to suck; it finds pleasure in moving its limbs and in kicking and crowing; it finds sensuous pleasure in urination and in defecation. In fact its first smile often comes after passing its motions.

The biological value of pleasure. From this we may infer what is the biological function of pleasure; it is *to encourage and enhance the physiological functions*. It is pleasant for the infant to suck; and the pleasure encourages the sucking process. If it were unpleasant for it to suck (as indeed it is sometimes, when the milk is hard to get or of an unpleasant taste), it would be discouraged from sucking, and that of course is biologically harmful. Mothers sometimes take unfair advantage of this by putting bitter aloes on the nipple in order to wean the child, for that has the effect of discouraging the sucking. Incidentally, it also has the effect of making the child distrust the mother, and dislike her, since she is now associated with a nasty taste.

This, which I may call the 'biological theory of pleasure', differs from the *ascetic view* so commonly held by parents, in practice if not in theory, that it is wrong to enjoy oneself. Children are so often punished for things they enjoy that they grow up with the idea that if they are enjoying themselves they are doing wrong, and will at some time have to pay for it. Others get the idea that since all enjoyable things appear to be wrong it is only wrong things that are enjoyable, and they will enjoy doing wrong simply because it is wrong. One child, rebelling against this principle, said, 'I'm going to do what I want, even if I don't want to!'

This biological theory of pleasure clashes equally with the *libertine view*, which regards pleasure as alone desirable and the main pursuit of life. The function of pleasure in nature is to enhance the activity which gives the pleasure, not to be a substitute for it.

This biological theory of pleasure is also opposed to the Freudian view, that these sensuous activities like sucking are sexual, and that there is an essential antagonism between the 'pleasure principle and the reality principle'. There is no essential antagonism between these principles, for the pleasure involved, say in sucking or in movements of the limbs, encourages the functions of reality and self-preservation.

They may, however, and often do, *become* antagonistic (as in activities like thumb-sucking and masturbation) when pleasure is sought for its own sake, and apart from any biological function. In such a case the pursuit of pleasure for its own sake may prevent the child facing his responsibilities in life. It was the Land of the Lotus Eaters from which Ulysses's companions were so unwilling to part.

Development of sensuousness. If infantile activities, such as defecation, are given normal expression they become

established as *habits*, whereupon the pleasure associated with
them tends to pass and becomes *transferred to other activities.*

(*a*) In the first place, the child who is allowed to find
pleasure in these early activities develops a *joyous attitude
towards life.* He enjoys everything he does, and turns even
hardship into the joy of achievement. We may use the term
'sensuousness' of physical pleasure, 'joy' of the satisfaction
of the emotions, and 'happiness' of the whole personality in
the pursuit of its aim.

On the whole, the happy child will be the healthy child,
both in body and mind. For pleasure, joy, and happiness
stimulate the metabolism of the body – the appetite and
digestive processes, the storing up and releasing of energy;
whereas the unhappy, gloomy, discontented, grumbling, or
frightened child tends to suffer from indigestion and depression of spirits. That is why we pay our comedians more
than our Prime Ministers! Happiness also conduces to efficiency because it gives the child an interest and an incentive
in all that he does.

Generally speaking, then, the happy child will be the
healthy child, and the happy child will be the good child,
for he is contented.

(*b*) But there are more specific developments of these
infantile sensuous activities; they become *transformed into
adult sexuality.* As Freud has shown, adult sexuality consists
of two forms : the preliminary wooing activities, like kissing
and fondling, and coitus or intercourse. The wooing tendencies are largely infantile sensuous activities transferred
to the uses of adult sexuality. Kissing, for instance, is little
else than sucking, and the parts of the body we like to kiss
are the soft rounded parts reminiscent of the breast, like the
cheeks and, especially, the lips, the mucous membrane of
which is reminiscent of the nipple, and physiologically highly
sensitive.

There are other specific developments of infantile sensuous activities. The infant loves to fondle and squeeze the

mother's breast. This manipulation of soft yielding material is later transferred to the pleasure in manipulating Plasticine, clay, and other materials.*

Over-stimulation of the sex organs in infancy is not to be encouraged, for it commonly leads to masturbation, and masturbation is not nearly as harmless as many of the 'modern' school maintain. The old idea that it may produce a mental deficiency or insanity is, of course, an old wives' tale. But there are other harmful effects.

Physiologically the child who constantly masturbates becomes nervous from the persistent over-excitation of its nervous system. The most striking case of a nervous wreck I have seen was that of the son of a famous literary man who allowed him to masturbate as much as he liked on the principle that to 'repress' him was harmful.

Secondly, persistent masturbation encourages self-love (for it means having sex intercourse with oneself), instead of object love, whether of the mother in infancy or of the mate in marriage. Those who threaten that masturbation produces sex impotence are in some cases right; not physiologically, but the self-love which it encourages may preclude love for anyone else and so lead to impotence.

Thirdly, masturbation commonly results in the repression of sexuality, and the repression of sexual activities in infancy may result either in impotence or in perversions. This repression may come from (*a*) external or (*b*) internal causes.

(*a*) *External*. The mother, seeing the erection of her little boy, or seeing her little girl giving herself pleasure by putting her hand between her legs, is scandalized, and, not realizing that sexual activities of this kind are common in infancy, scolds or smacks the child. This produces in the child a sense of fear and 'guilt' for something it regards as

---

* Freud says this manipulative tendency comes from manipulation of the faeces. That is only secondary. There is no biological reason why the infant should manipulate faeces; there is a biological reason why it manipulates the breasts, namely to squeeze out the milk. I have seen lambs do the same with the ewe.

perfectly normal and natural, and it also produces resentment. It may then continue masturbation secretly and defiantly. Such guilt may then develop into an *anxiety neurosis,* especially in adolescence; or lead to *sex impotence* because the guilt arrests development, or to *sex perversion* because the guilt misdirects the sexual impulse to abnormal activities or wrong objects, such as sadism, exhibitionism, or fetishism.

(*b*) The repression may also come from *internal* causes, even if the child is never scolded or restrained. For masturbation often produces an orgasm even in infancy, and this to the infant is so overwhelming that it is terrified of its own emotion. Orgasms are often objectified and personalized as an overwhelming monster, of which the child is terrified but against which it is helpless. This, as I have demonstrated in *Dreams and Nightmares,** is the origin of the nightmares of vampires and other terrifying monsters. We see then the curious fact that *sexuality can be repressed by the terrifying consequences of its own exaggeration.*

It will be obvious then why I do not subscribe to the view that sexual stimulation and masturbation in early childhood do no harm. To hold that view implies ignorance of the pathological results which may follow, and it is surprising that so many psychologists have ignored this fact.

What then are the *causes of masturbation*? They may be cossetting, accidental stimulation, and boredom, for want of something to play with. These often pass when other interests are forthcoming.

The most common and serious cause of persistent masturbation in infancy is undoubtedly the feeling of deprivation of love. The child, feeling deprived of love, resorts to masturbation as a solace. This is a natural substitute; for in infancy protective love is experienced in close contact with the mother's body and also gives sensuous pleasure. When, therefore, it feels deprived of its mother's love it naturally resorts to the sensuous and sexual pleasure as a solace, in an

* Penguin Books, 1954.

attempt to recapture the sense of security. You may often see a child who is frightened press its hands to its sex organs.

But sometimes this deprivation produces a more persistent and harmful result. The child, feeling deprived of love, perhaps because of the arrival of another baby, may resort to masturbation as a solace, and then say, 'I don't want my mother any more; I have something I can have at any time, which is much better.' That is to say he *represses* his love of his mother in favour of self-love.

This is the beginning of true perversion. For one thing, the sexual pleasure is sought for its own sake, *apart from its biological function*. Secondly, the child's love-life is *turned into itself*, instead of to object love for its mother; it is completely auto-erotic. Thirdly, *the whole of love is concentrated upon its sexual aspect*, which is therefore exaggerated, while true love is pushed aside. We find most exaggerated forms of sexuality in adolescence are due to such deprivation in incoming love, followed by repression of outgoing love.

Mental hygiene. This consists in allowing the child the normal pleasure in its physiological and biological functions of sucking, defecation, and the rest; but to keep the pleasure attached to these functions, and not encourage their exaggeration by excessive cossetting or by sexual stimulation.

If sensuous pleasure does become exaggerated, and leads to masturbation (as well it may, especially if a child feels deprived of love, or is depressed or ill), it is harmful to repress the action by threats of punishment. The repression of these activities does more harm than their simple expression; for, while their expression may lead to exaggerated sexuality later on, their repression whether by threats or by consequent nightmares is more likely to produce either impotence or perversions.

The normal and sensible mother who loves her child will avoid most of these difficulties. For if he has her love, he will love her, and will not need to resort to these pleasures as a substitute. If there is lack of love, he is driven to find

solace in these perversities, and his rebellion against her will
make him cling to them more obstinately. Some conditions
require expert treatment from a child psychologist, since the
child's break with the mother may be too severe for the
mother to deal with, however well-intentioned she may be.

SELF-DISPLAY

The characteristics of the *first* year of life so far described
are all centred on the infant itself : its protection and security, which it finds by its dependence on the mother; its sensuous pleasure; and the exercise of its bodily functions.

In the second year, having prepared itself, it goes out to
meet life and to take a more active interest in the world
of people and events. Far from wanting, like the new-born
infant, to be left in peace, it begins actively to call attention
to itself in *self-display*, and begins to move out to meet the
world in *curiosity and exploration*. Far from wanting to be
quiescent, it will not leave the mother a moment's peace
but wants to do everything in *imitation* of her. Let us consider these phases.

Self-display and desire for attention. Most parents have
noticed that the small child of about one year loves to
attract attention to himself. Sitting up in his pram he will
shout out to passers-by, and call all the men 'Da-Da'. He is
jealous of the attention others receive, and if you pet the
dog or the cat or another child he immediately pushes his
way in to get attention – and this he does although previously he was playing happily by himself on the floor.

This is confirmed by Gesell who says : 'The one-year-old
child ... frequently is at the very centre of the group. He
shows a significant tendency to repeat performances laughed
at. He pleases himself thereby as much as he does his
audience.'*

This phase of self-display represents a transition from
the security of the first year to the exploration of the

* *The First Five Years of Life*, p. 28.

second. The child still has a need for attention, as in the first year, but uses different methods, and goes further afield, to get such attention. There is a biological significance in the emergence of self-display at this particular moment. For during the breast-feeding time the mother is more closely attached to the infant, both because of the lactogenic hormone which fills her with tenderness and care towards it; and also because she needs to feed it for her own physical comfort, if for nothing else. After the breast-feeding period she tends to be somewhat more casual with the infant – there is so much housework to be made up – so the baby is put in the pram, wheeled out into the garden, and left more to itself. Feeling cut off from its base, and therefore less secure, it must call attention to itself for its own security.

The self-display tendencies like any others may be developed, exaggerated, perverted, or take neurotic forms.

Development. While self-display primarily serves the function of self-preservation, since it seeks the attention of others, it incidentally develops social contacts; for in its efforts to gain people's attention, the child discovers what pleases people and what they dislike. It studies what they approve and avoids what they disapprove. This, therefore, is one of the earliest sources of social behaviour in the child.

Later the self-display develops into more specific forms. The little girl of four or five likes to look pretty and show off her dress; the little boy likes to show off his achievements : 'Look what I have made !' Later still, it takes the form of skill at games or getting prizes at school work. In adult life it takes such forms as acting, public speaking, painting, writing, teaching and preaching, and being a good story-teller; or is revealed in ambition that is needed for gaining positions of prestige. The desire for admiration and the desire for approval are, in fact, incentives in any walk of life. For most people want to count, to be recognized as somebody, to be noticed for something. To be ignored is one of the most cruel forms of torture.

Indeed, in the pursuit of admiration some people are

prepared to undergo many sacrifices. Many men lost their lives in their determination to be the first to fly the Atlantic.

Exaggeration. Exaggeration may come about because the parents are always showing their children off, the real motive, of course, being to show themselves off, to demonstrate what wonderful parents they are to have such a marvellous child; for woe betide the child if it does not show up well, letting the parents down by crying or petulance! The fact is that many a child intuitively recognizes that the mother is showing herself off through him. He resents it and so refuses to cooperate.

This simple form of exaggeration by encouragement does little harm, for the healthy child soon grows out of it, and wants admiration for something more worth while, for its own achievements. 'I wish', said a boy of my acquaintance, 'that people would admire *me* and not just my curls!' Even if the child himself does not tire of it, other boys and girls at school will see to it that he doesn't get away with it. Therefore this kind of simple showing off by encouragement is harmful only in that it almost inevitably causes the child himself a good deal of distress in unlearning the idea his mother gave him of his being wonderful. Disillusion is painful, but necessary.

But the real 'lime-light' child, who must show off, in spite of all rebuffs, is very different from a child that suffers from a simple form of exaggerated self-display. The typical 'lime-light' child is not one who has had his self-display exaggerated simply by being shown off; he is, on the contrary, the one who feels left out and unwanted, deprived of protective love and attention. He therefore *must* call attention to himself for his very security. It is anxiety and insecurity, not praise, which produce the 'lime-light' child. To snub such a child – which is what most people have the impulse to do – is to do him a most grievous hurt, for this throws him still further into insecurity.

If, on the other hand, the snubbing or humiliation succeeds in making him repress his showing off, such a child then may suffer from shyness, blushing, stammering, and other forms of morbid self-consciousness; for every time he has the impulse to call attention to himself, this is accompanied by the sense of humiliation with which it is associated.

Another form of exaggeration is what I have elsewhere called 'exaggeration by thwarting'. A typical example is that of a mother who is so anxious that her little girl should not be vain that she dresses her in shabby clothes and leaves her hair untidy. The real cause is often jealousy of her child, who is taking away some of the father's love. Such a child, seeing others prettily dressed, yearns for the same. Later she must have pretty clothes at all cost, and the cost is sometimes very great !

There are also *perversions of self-display*. There are children who, failing to get attention in any other way, get it by making a nuisance of themselves, by annoying the baby or by bed-wetting. Better to be scolded and beaten than to be ignored : at any rate, the mother then knows you are there !

But the most typical perversion is *sexual exhibitionism*. The child who feels left out and unloved looks around to discover how he may get attention. He naturally assumes that what gives pleasure to himself, namely his sex organs, will give pleasure to others. So he displays his sex organs in a pathetic appeal for the attention he craves. If this is repressed by being punished it may become fixated and arrested, and later emerge as a full-blown sex perversion of exhibitionism, in which there may be no desire for sexual intercourse at all, and the whole of the sexual urge is concentrated on the desire to expose oneself. In analysis we find such perversions to relate back to such early causes.

The *mental hygiene* of this phase is simple. As with all other natural tendencies, the child should be allowed the expression of self-display and encouraged to direct this in desirable forms. It is, after all, quite natural that a one-year-old should want personal attention, that a little girl should like to be prettily dressed – how else is she to develop social graces? It is natural that a boy should like to be praised for the model boat he has made, and not to be told by the father what is wrong with it or how much better *he* made boats!

The parent who is so afraid of making the child conceited that he disparages what the child has done is likely to produce the very effect he wants to avoid. For the child naturally desires attention and approval, and if he does not get it by encouragement from others he will get it from himself. If no one else thinks anything of him, he will think a hell of a lot of himself. He becomes both anti-social and arrogant. The conceited child, like the 'lime-light' child, is not usually the one who is over-praised, but the one who is denied the praise and love of others and so must needs boost himself.

CURIOSITY AND EXPLORATION

From the very beginning the infant has an interest in the outside world. In the first few weeks you can see it gazing at things, especially at its mother when it is being fed. At sixteen weeks it will follow objects around; later it will pick things up, examine them, and at twenty-eight weeks put them into its mouth. This last no doubt is nature's method of spontaneous feeding, but it also gives the infant a knowledge of objects of the outside world. But this interest in the outside world during the first year is mostly passive; the child *takes things in*.

In the second year he *goes out to meet* the world, and to investigate everything and anything. This phase of curiosity and exploration may be contrasted with the phase of self-display which it has just superseded. In self-display a child calls the attention of others to himself; in the phase of exploration his attention is outward-going, extraverted, concentrated on interest in the outside world, and not on himself.

At first he does not go too far afield. He still likes to be near his mother, to play in the same room, although on his own. We may see the same pattern of development in young animals. In my morning walks in the spring, I notice that when the ducklings are first hatched out, they swim *after* the mother, following her wherever she goes. But after a short time, perhaps a week or two, they all begin to swim *in front* of her : they take the lead and she follows them, seeing that they come to no harm. But you still see the ducklings turning round from time to time. Later on they go farther afield until they are entirely independent, out of sight of the mother, who now, herself, couldn't care less ! Similarly the child at first explores, but likes to explore in an atmosphere of security : later he feels entirely independent, constantly breaking away, and the mother is always losing sight of him. She finds that he has slipped away into the cellar or into the street to befriend the milkman.

The child is very largely helped in this exploration by his ability to walk on two legs, for this enlarges his sphere of operations. He can now travel much farther, and much faster. Not only this, but now that he can walk and not simply crawl on hands and knees, his hands are free to pick up things, pull them to pieces, and generally investigate them – an achievement of which he takes full advantage ! Leave a child of eighteen months alone in a kitchen or sitting-room and there is hardly an object within reach that he will not have touched, handled, and examined. This avid curiosity never seems to be satisfied. No sooner has he examined one thing than he goes on to another; he leaves no stone unturned, no avenue unexplored.

He does this examination rather cursorily at first; but a little later he settles down for longer periods, examining this or that toy and playing with it for a more prolonged period. Spontaneous attention turns to voluntary attention, as the psychologist would put it.

Biological value. This curiosity and exploration is a natural phase of maturation appearing in all ordinary infants at this age. Its biological value is obvious; for this is the way in which the child gets naturally acquainted with the world in which he is going to live, and learns to discriminate between the various objects he sees and examines. *Such discrimination is an essential feature of all learning.* At first, to the infant, all people are alike, but then he distinguishes his mother from others, his family from strangers, the cat from the dog, a tractor from a car.

Development. The spirit of curiosity changes its form as the child develops. About the age of two or three it takes the more intellectual form of asking questions : 'What is this? What is that?' At the age of four, as we shall see, the child wants to know the *reason* for things. 'What is the use of that? Why does Daddy go to work? Why does Mummy put powder on her face?' His questions should, of course, be answered, for it is well to encourage his curiosity and thirst for knowledge. But if we do not know the answer we should say so; or, better still, find out together with the child by looking it up. To do this not only improves our own knowledge but forms a good habit in the child. Do not try to bluff him with your reply; his intuition can detect your bluff by the tone of voice, however you try to disguise it.

In later life this curiosity and exploration take specific forms, such as scientific research. One boy explores the earth and becomes a geologist; another is interested in plants and becomes a botanist; while yet another is more interested in human nature and becomes a psychologist.

Many a child's later interest and even work in later life is determined by the things which interested him in these early years. A little boy whose mother liked dressing him up in pretty frocks became a dress designer, and another whose interest was in Meccano and carpentry became an orthopaedic surgeon. (I base this on definite cases.)

One value of a prolonged and protected childhood, such as is found in human beings, as against lower animals, is that it gives the child the opportunity to explore *in an atmosphere of security,* and therefore to gain a great deal of knowledge and experience before launching out into life.

Abnormalities. If the child is denied outlets for his natural curiosity and exploration, for instance by being constantly scolded for touching things, his interest in life may be inhibited. The result is boredom. Then the mother says, 'Why don't you get something to do?' The child's reply, if he dared, would be, 'Because when I do something really interesting, you stop me!' Another common result of such thwarting of his interests is that a child 'regresses' to an earlier phase and becomes lethargic, perhaps clings to his mother's skirt, finds consolation in thumb-sucking.

There are also *perversions*, the most typical of which is *morbid curiosity*. The gossip is an instance; his interest in human nature takes the form of prying. We call this 'abnormal', for the typical gossip pries into the lives of other people, not out of a desire for knowledge, but to satisfy his or her own frustrated emotional desires, whether sexual or otherwise. Sexual curiosity is natural, like all forms of curiosity, and should be satisfied. There is nothing prurient about such curiosity to a child. He is interested in this as in everything else. But if the sexual curiosity is aroused in childhood (say, by seeing the mother undressing) and then repressed by punishment, we may get the typical 'observationist' or Peeping Tom type whose proclivities may completely exclude any desire for normal sexuality.

The *mental hygiene* of this phase of curiosity and exploration is simple : it is, in the first place, to give the child plenty of material and scope for his curiosity, to help him to find out things for himself, which he will do if given the material, and to let him explore. A roomful of rubbish, old battered toys, or a shed in the garden of discarded stuff will give him the spirit of adventure as exciting as that of the Argonauts. Bombed sites are a good second, but the police frustrate the opportunities thus provided by Providence.

It is as well for parents and teachers to recognize that the desire to know and to learn is natural to a child. The successful educator, whether teacher or parent, is one who can make use of the child's natural thirst for knowledge in order to teach him the things the educator wants him to learn. It is a high art.

IMITATION

One of the strongest and most deeply rooted instincts which help the infant to adapt itself to life is imitation. One of the earliest child psychologists, Baldwin, laid great stress on this.

Imitation is an innate propensity. The child is not taught to imitate : it does so naturally. So do many animals : a very young wild rabbit is not afraid of you – it runs away only in imitation of its mother; parrots and other birds can even be made to imitate man's speech. The *propensity* is innate : *what* the child imitates depends on environmental influences.

Imitation commences a few weeks after birth. A child crying in a cot makes other children cry, till in a home for infants there is a hullabaloo.

But imitation does not come into full force until this phase, between one and two. If you are planting, the child wants to plant too; if you are sweeping up, he wants to sweep up. A child given a chocolate covered with silver paper would eat the lot; but seeing the mother unwrapping it, does the same. If you are shelling peas, he must have peas to shell. If you smack him, he would like to smack you, but that being precluded he will smack the baby.

We are apt to take this process of imitation for granted, whereas, in fact, it is most mysterious. How and why does the infant do exactly what the mother does? Presumably when it sees its mother smile, frown, or become anxious, the impulse passes from the eye to the brain, and in some mysterious fashion finds its way to the *very same centre* in the motor area of the brain that activated the mother's action; from which the impulse then passes down to perform the same action. But by what process of selection the incoming impulses are transmitted to exactly the same spot in the brain, and so make the child smile or frown instead of, perhaps, making it hit out at the mother, is a mystery.

The *biological value* of this capacity to imitate is less mysterious. Like conditioned reflexes, imitation enables an infant *to acquire adaptation to life for which it has no innate or hereditary responses.*

But imitation is a great advance on conditioned reflexes; for in order to form a conditioned reflex a child has to go through the experience – it has to be burnt before it avoids the fire – and in the process may come to serious harm. In imitation it does not need to go through the experience, but directly does what the mother does – if it sees her avoiding the fire it does so too.

So a child not only learns to avoid danger, but learns how to do things like building up bricks in imitation of the mother. He later takes over the mother's attitude towards other people, and so learns the social graces. By imitation, therefore, the child acquires healthy modes of reaction and adaptation to life.

One of the most valuable acquisitions gained by imitation at this age is speech. In the first year the infant makes noises by an inner urge expressive of its nerve tension, just as the duck squawks when it feels like it. Later, having exercised its vocal chords, it imitates the *sounds* the mother makes. She says 'bottle' and the child says 'bo – le' without at first attaching any meaning to the sound. Then it learns to attach certain sounds to certain objects, associating the one with the other, so that the 'sound' becomes a 'word'. It then learns to use the word when it wants to indicate the object, that is to say it acquires 'language'. Now, it says 'bo – le' when it *wants* a bottle and when it wants a spade it asks for a 'pade'. Imitation is a transition from the dependence of infancy to the independence of later childhood. The child needs to be independent and do things for himself, and he learns *what* to do by imitation of his mother, that is to say, by dependence on her. A child, seeing the mother change her shoes when they are wet, will begin to take off his own wet shoes. Later on, this, by that repetitive process, turns into a habit;

he will take off his shoes when they are wet independently of the mother by the age of three or four, because he understands the reason for it. The child likes to go out for walks with his father, and do gardening in imitation of him. Then he likes going out for walks or gardening on his own. Thus, by *dependence* upon his parents and imitation of them, the child develops *independence* and adaptation to life. A child of three got a nettle sting, which was rubbed by his father with a dock leaf. The next day the child receiving a knock on the knee picked a leaf off a tree and started to rub it! This was the phase of imitation, but not yet of reasoning.

Because he learns through imitation a child finds it much easier to do a thing when *shown* how to do it than by being *told* how to do it, whether it is how to mend a fuse, cook a steak, or, later, row a boat or learn to dance. He will imitate even when he cannot understand your verbal explanations. Most of us can learn to dance much more easily by watching others dance than by being told how to take steps or being shown diagrams of feet.

Imitation is far more effective than teaching at this age. If you tell a child not to cross the road in heavy traffic and then do so yourself, which do you think the child will do? It will almost certainly follow your example, not your precept. 'Mummy does it, why shouldn't I?' is its logic.

This principle has its converse side. You must often have seen a child imitate you, perhaps by mopping the table, and, when told to stop, listen in mild surprise or indifference, and promptly do the same thing again! The teaching has not sunk in because if *you* do it, it must be right. To counter the child's natural impulse to imitate needs a lot of effort; it is easier to show the child what you want him to do.

Later on, say at the age of four when he can reason, you can explain why *you* can dive into deep water and *he* cannot until he learns to swim. He will then do as you say, not just because you say so, but because he sees the reason for it. But between one and two he has no power of reasoning.

Imitation is a subconscious process. So much so that if a

child is following his natural bent to imitate, he does not like the intrusion of being told. Indeed, if you deliberately *try* to get a child to imitate you in some action, and say, 'Do as Mummy does!' he will as likely as not resent it and refuse. But he will do so if you don't tell him to! This is not pure cussedness, but because imitation is primarily a subconscious and not a conscious or deliberate process, and to make it deliberate confuses the child.

Development. Imitation is a process which persists throughout life, and a most valuable one. We cannot all find out by personal experience which is the soundest of several courses, and a very strong motive for our actions is that 'Everybody's doing it!' Our fashions, our social habits, our traditions, and our morals largely depend on it.

Mental hygiene. We should allow the fullest scope to the child's propensity to imitate as far as possible, being careful to be and do what we want the child to be and do. A practical illustration of this was that of the child's eating (p. 53). That is how he learns. Later on he likes to have a try *himself* and without interference. But he finds it beyond him and he is willing to be *shown* how to do it, because by that means he achieves and gains power over nature.

Abnormalities arise first of all from a child imitating a parent's bad example. An arrogant parent will produce an arrogant child. Secondly, the parents may expect a child of this age to do other than they are doing without explanation. I am at the moment treating a boy of fourteen, who is anti-social and gets into violent tempers with other boys at school, as well as being subject to fits of weeping. This arose because he was constantly frustrated in the things he wanted to do, mainly what his parents were doing. His mother is of the bull-dog breed and will stand no nonsense. But so is the boy, and because he would therefore not give in lightly, there was constant warfare and rebellion. When she was planting he was ordered off the flower-bed. He refused, was beaten, and thereafter hated his mother and everyone else. How easily such a case could have been *avoided* had the mother let him do what she was doing and shown him how to avoid the plants when he wanted to dig as she was digging! How difficult in later life to cure a boy so obstinate!

THE SELF-WILLED PHASE

The age of two is the age of self-will – as most parents are all too aware! It is the age of tantrums. The child must have his own way : if he wants to go somewhere, he insists on going; if he wants to do something, nothing must prevent him. He is the Eastern potentate who cannot brook frustration or interference.

This phase is in direct contrast to the phase of dependence in infancy when the child prefers to be passive, to shut out the world and turn away from it. He is now excessively active and wants to give expression to whatever impulse is aroused in him. He is prepared to take on all comers, to act on his own.

It is also different from the previous phase of exploration. In exploration the child goes out to the world in order to find out about the world, examine it, investigate it. In the self-willed phase, having found out about the world, he is now prepared to exercise his will upon it and to make it conform to his will.

The biological value of this phrase is that it leads to the child's beginning to learn to *control the world* in which he is to live and shape his own life.

Aggressive self-will is, of course, not confined to this age, but it is now the dominant characteristic. Even the infant of ten or twelve days has its outbursts of uncontrollable rage, especially when, for instance, its head, arms, or legs are held. But in infancy the rage is short-lived, soon giving way to misery and despair, whereas at the age of two it is frequent, strong, and persistent. Charlotte Bühler, for instance, found that a six-month-old had only ·07 outbursts per hour, a two-year-old ·12, and a six-year-old only ·08.

These outbursts, of course, depend on the degree of frustration, but the point is that the two-year-old *demands* much more than the two-month-old. On the other hand, the six-year-old has developed a will, and can control his impulses and tolerate frustration more easily.

Now, what are we to do about these tantrums? In many cases the parents, seeing the child's outbursts of temper, say : 'He *has* got a will of his own! He can't be allowed to grow up like that! We must break his will'; and, unfortunately, too often succeed in doing so. By means of punishment and threats, that is to say by an appeal to fear, they compel the child to be good and docile, and then are surprised that he grows up to be sapless, easily led astray by others, wanting in strength of will, and lacking in initiative! He has learnt that initiative does not pay, that he only gets the worst of it and has to give in in the end! By crushing his assertiveness, such parents rob the child of strength of character. After all, this assertiveness was provided by nature for the child to use in his adaptation to life and to enable him to overcome obstacles. Denied it, he is incapable of fending for himself and may take refuge in indolence or neurosis.

Development. Aggressiveness normally develops into self-confidence; self-will is transformed into the will. Indeed, *self-will is the raw material of the will*; it is the source of determination, confidence, resolution, perseverance, and all the qualities which make for a strong character.

The difference between self-will and will is that in self-will the child is completely dominated by his *impulses*. The will, on the other hand, is the function and activity of the *personality as a whole, in the pursuit of its ends*.

Abnormalities of aggressiveness. If the child's natural aggressiveness is frustrated, the first result is the perversion of aggressiveness into sullenness and sulkiness, by means of which the child registers its protest without actively being aggressive. Sullenness and resentment are frustrated aggressiveness.

Secondly, since the biological function of assertiveness and aggressiveness is to enable the child to cope with life, the child who is deprived of these forces will be unable to meet his responsibilities. He becomes sapless, spineless, a good boy, but without initiative.

Thirdly, the child whose assertiveness is suppressed, and who is thereby deprived of the wherewithal to meet life, falls into a state of insecurity, anxiety, and fear.

Finally, he may take refuge in a neurosis, as the only means of getting protection and being cared for; as a means of escaping from his responsibilities; or as a means of getting his own way – some neurotics are tyrants.

Mental hygiene. What then are we to do about the self-willed child? The simple answer is not to repress but to *find the right outlets for the aggressiveness.* This is the secret of developing a strong will and character.

If you observe your neighbours and the way they bring up their child, you will come to the conclusion that nine out of ten of the things which he is forbidden to do could be allowed with no great harm to anybody. 'Don't climb up on that sofa, you might fall off'; 'Don't touch that knife, you might cut yourself!'; 'Don't put the coal on the fire, you might burn yourself!' – and so forth!

Now, in the majority of cases, there is really no reason at all why he should not be allowed to do these things. Supposing he did fall off the sofa – a little cry, a little comfort, and what does he do then? He will go straight to the sofa and will try again! The repetitive process comes into play and he learns how to do it *without* falling off, and so develops skill at climbing as well as perseverance. Do not say, 'Naughty sofa!', as some parents do. This may be comforting, but it teaches the child to put the blame of his own acts on something else or on other people.

Take the example of the knife. If a child sees his mother cutting a loaf of bread, he wants to do the same. The alarmed mother cries, 'Don't do that! You'll cut yourself!' Not with any bread knives I have come across! But even if the child did cut himself, what harm is there? He learns from experience how to avoid cuts and also how to deal with them if the worst happens. But if forbidden, he will later on get hold of a sharper knife when the mother is not there and may do real damage to himself. Or take lighting a gas fire : a child of three, of ordinary intelligence, is capable of being taught how to light a gas fire – first how to strike a match, put it into the jets, and only then turn on the gas. Taught how to do these things, he is thrilled at his achievement.

Moreover, a child so taught does not break the rules. Indeed, on one occasion when I was in a hurry and told a child to 'turn on the gas', he reproved me for not striking the match first. 'No! Match!' he said. It is the frustrated child who gets into mischief : the child who is allowed to do things, learns how to do them.

In all such activities therefore I have a slogan : *If a child wants to do anything 'naughty', teach him how to do it!*

If he wants to cut the loaf, teach him to cut downwards and not across as Granny does; if he wants to climb the apple tree, teach him *how* to climb and he will climb with safety and be thrilled at the achievement.

In such ways you may deal with nine out of the ten things the child is ordinarily forbidden to do. It takes time, but it is the function of the parent who regards parenthood as a vocation to take time to help the child to develop. It *saves* time in the end, because the child who has been taught to do such things will be of great help to the mother, and will be happy and contented in doing them. A child of ten, for instance, can be taught to start up your car and have it nicely warmed up on winter mornings by the time you need it. Your little girl of four or five will enjoy learning to bake a cake. An adolescent will mend your fuses, repair your burst pipes, or make loose covers for you. But the ultimate aim of letting a child do these things is not, of course, for our own convenience, but to give him confidence by supplying opportunities for his development; for in doing these things he becomes efficient, learns discipline, and finds happiness.

We have said that probably nine out of ten ordinarily

forbidden things can be allowed, treated in this way. What about the odd one out of ten? For there are some things which a child cannot be allowed to do, things that are too dangerous. I have no doubt some of us might say about the lighting of the gas fire, 'I should not like to take such a risk with my child' – and not because of any lack of intelligence in the child, but simply because of the danger. Very well! In that case do not do so; for parents must decide for themselves. A boy of three was allowed to climb an apple tree, but when he wanted to climb a ladder set up by workmen to the roof of the house, I said, 'No!' – not that he *could* not do it, but that the consequences of an accident if he did happen to fall were too serious to take the risk.

If a child is allowed to do the nine out of ten things, he usually accepts the discipline in the one case without demur. His natural assertiveness is satisfied by outlets in all these other activities and he realizes that there must be a good reason for not being allowed to do the one. When you tell your boy not to go up the ladder on to the roof, he just accepts it. He recognizes that you are not being fussy or pig-headed about it, for, after all, *you* taught him to climb. He does not protest, because there are lots of other things to do. It is the child who is *consistently* told not to do this, that, or the other, in whom the repeated frustration works up into an outburst of tantrums or foolhardiness.

But there is another important natural corrective to these tantrums, namely that of imitation, which has already been described. Look at it this way : a child only gets into a tantrum when frustrated in what he wants to do. But at this age what he wants to do is mostly what the mother is doing. He sees the mother dressing, eating with knife and fork, washing the dishes, scrubbing the floor, peeling the potatoes, putting up wall-paper. The child loves to imitate the mother and to do these things *with* the mother, and if she lets him do so and shows him how to do them, he is perfectly contented. It is, after all, right and proper that the child *should* want to imitate all that the mother does, for this is the way in which he acquires skill in doing these things, and the discipline exercised in the doing of them comes naturally to him. It is all in the day's work.

There are, therefore, many children who show no signs of tantrums at this age since they are given plenty of outlets for their assertiveness : it is the age of assertiveness but not necessarily of tantrums.

For the purpose of experiment, I took a little girl friend of two and a half to my country cottage where I had a lot of spring-cleaning to do. When we arrived, and indeed throughout the day, she wanted to do everything I did. She helped to bring the things in from the car; she swept the floor with her little brush; she carried in wood for the fire; she didn't want to chop the wood up because she knew she couldn't and simply said 'No! you do it!' But she helped to lay the table for lunch, and so on, through the day. Now in all those six hours she was perfectly happy and contented doing as I did, and in all that time there were only four protests. When we had swept the dust into little piles I carried mine away, but she clung to hers and wanted it left. After all, it was *her* pile, and at this point her sense of possession was stronger than her imitativeness. So, of course, I left it and removed it later when her interest had faded. The second instance was when we had got lunch ready and I proposed lifting her on to her chair; but 'No-o-o!' she said, she could get up herself and, of course, she was right. The third was when we were going to wash up, and I said I would wash and she could dry. But 'No-o-o!' once more, she wanted to wash up with me. So I put up a chair by the sink and then both of us washed up and both dried. It was not that she objected to drying, but only that she wanted to do what I was doing. The last protest was when she wanted to 'go somewhere' and I offered to take her panties down. 'No-o-o!' she protested – but after all, that is a thing that any young lady would object to !

On the other hand I would not let her spread the rat poison on bread to kill the rats, for a small quantity might have got on her fingers, and two grains of poison can kill a rat and harm a child. But she made no demur at this.

But there are times when the child does demur. In the case where a tantrum is imminent, what are we to do then?

The golden rule is *calmness and firmness*. Calmness is necessary, for if a child is in a tantrum it does not help matters for the mother to get into a tantrum as well. The child is suggestible and if the mother keeps calm and speaks quietly he will soon become calm. But, unfortunately, the mother is also suggestible, and when the child gets into a tantrum she often follows suit! When that occurs, the situation rapidly deteriorates until war breaks out in a crisis of smackings, kickings, and tempers. The mother, of course, gets the best of it because her smackings are more painful than the child's kicks, but it does not solve the problem at issue. It leaves a deep feeling of resentment as well as of fear in the child's mind. The confident relationship between mother and child is lost – perhaps for ever.

Firmness is also required – for if a thing must not be done (like spreading the rat poison, or climbing the ladder), then it must not be done, and that's an end to it. If it is too dangerous, then it must be forbidden. You can be firm without being cross! The child soon gets to know that when his mother says 'No!' she means it. But let her 'No!' be as infrequent as possible. Give your child reasons for things, by all means, but at this age he is not as much affected by reasons as by your own mood. For instance, if you give him your reasons for not doing something he is likely to reply: 'But I want to!' That is the one and only sufficient 'reason' he knows or will accept.

But there are certain rules in the enforcement of such principles which are helpful.

The first is *not to command what you cannot enforce*. You can make a child go to bed by carrying him there, because you are stronger. You can make him eat by forcing something into his mouth and holding his mouth shut until he has to swallow, and so make yourself his enemy for life.

But you can't make him pass water or pass motions. A child often delights in defying his mother or nurse by obstinately refusing to perform these acts, or in performing them at the wrong time, and he is successful in his defiance. There are few points in which a child can effectively defy a parent, and this is one; some children make the most of it. Indeed a patient of mine used to spend a long time in the closet because it was the only place where he got peace and quiet !

Incidentally that is why excretions are said to be connected with obstinacy, which Freud emphasizes; but it is not the anal activities which produce the obstinacy, but the obstinacy which makes use of the anal activity – or lack of activity.

Obstinacy is also a common cause of constipation in children. You can bring a child to the pot, but you can't make him pass a motion. You can say, 'You'll sit there till you do!' but he can still defy you and will delight in doing so! Californian Syrup of Figs is not the best cure for obstinacy.

It is then that the mother resorts to other threats and makes the second rule necessary.

This rule is that if you demand anything of a child *do not then insist on more than you have demanded*. A mother says he must eat up his bacon. His reasons for not wanting to may be quite justified. He may not want to, because like many children he can't digest fats and it makes him sick, or simply because he has had enough, and more would nauseate him, or because he is emotionally upset and has no appetite. Short of forcing the food down his throat the mother can't make him eat it. She then resorts to argument : 'There are plenty of poor children who would be only too glad of that bacon !' His response (although he does not say so for fear of getting a smack from Dad), is 'Very well! By all means let them have it !' Since her appeal has met with a blank, the mother hits on a bright idea. 'Very well, if you don't eat up your bacon you won't go to the circus on Saturday, as I promised !' (adding under her breath, 'I'm not

going to let the little brat get the better of *me*!'). But still
he refuses. What is the mother's next move? She may relent
and, having already got the tickets, or having cooled down,
she says 'I'll take you *this* time – but don't let us have any
more nonsense of that sort again!' That, of course, has given
him a good lesson in obstinacy : it has taught him that if he
holds out long enough he will get his own way. On the other
hand, the mother may be adamant, carry out her threats,
and cancel the circus. The child is, of course, disappointed
and the mother considers she has won the day and taught
him a lesson. But that is not as the child sees it! His point
of view is, 'That is all right, you can stop me going to the
circus, but *you did not make me eat the bacon*!' In other
words, he considers himself the victor. Not only so, but he
feels that the mother has broken her promise, and so he not
only loses confidence in her, but by example learns that it
is not necessary to keep promises; they can be broken when
it suits.

What is the remedy for all this? It is simple. Don't insist
on what you can't enforce! Discretion is much better than
valour in dealing with the child.

The other rule is that when you do command something
do not accept a compromise. If you think it necessary to tell
a child to go to bed at a certain time and he says, 'Oh just
five minutes more!', it is a mistake to yield unless, of course,
there are good reasons for the delay. If there was no good
reason why he should go to bed at that time, then why
tell him to? For the mother to vacillate only encourages
the child to be vacillating. It is therefore advisable for the
mother not to tell a child to go to bed when he is in the
middle of doing something interesting, or making something. It is most irritating to him and teaches him to give
up doing things instead of persevering. Far better to give him
warning, 'Finish what you are doing and then it is bedtime!'
– and then be firm. Or if he wants a story read to him say,
'I'll read you a story when you are in bed.' That is a positive
incentive.

This approach of quiet firmness has an even more import-ant effect than merely controlling his actions. *The quiet firmness of the parent enables the child to be quiet and firm with himself.* At this age he has not yet developed a will in the true sense, though he has plenty of self-will, and he has little control of his impulses. In such a case *the will of the parent stands in the place of the will of the child.* This helps him in the building up of his own will. If, therefore, the parent is quiet and firm with the child, he will in turn be quiet and firm with himself, and so develop a strong will and the power to control his impulses. This saves a lot of trouble later on. Life is much easier for the child if, when he says 'No!' to himself, he, like the parent, means 'No!'

On the other hand if the parent is vacillating, the child will have no stable principle to guide him and so remains prey to his uncontrolled passions – and wretchedly unhappy.

As to corporal punishment at this stage, it is an undoubted fact that when a child is being thoroughly naughty with out-bursts of tantrums, a good smack will often settle the matter. And this is not necessarily out of fear, for he will afterwards be quite happy and play contentedly with you. Nor is it masochism, the sexual pleasure from being smacked. Why is it then? It is simply that the child has got into a state where he is completely possessed by his ill-temper and wants to get rid of it, but cannot of his own accord – he cannot solve the problem himself at all. A smack settles the matter and the child is glad of the intervention. But, even so, there is no need for smacks; quietness and firmness are all that is re-quired, and they avoid the harm that often results from severe punishment.

FREEDOM AND DISCIPLINE

The discussion of the self-willed period gives us an appro-priate opportunity to say something about the principles of freedom and discipline. Some parents say, 'I bring my child up to freedom!' Others say, 'I believe in discipline!' The

Victorians said, 'Spare the rod and spoil the child' – they believed that to train a child you must start at the bottom! The Neo-Georgians said, 'Let a child do what he likes; if you frustrate him he will become neurotic.'

What is the unfortunate parent to think? More urgently, what is the parent to do? The two principles seem incompatible. But are they? On the contrary, rightly considered, discipline is necessary to true freedom; and freedom is necessary to true discipline.

An illustration already given should make this clear. Take the child wanting to climb a tree. If he is allowed to 'do as he likes', the time will come when he seizes a rotten branch and comes a cropper, and that is the end of his 'freedom'. If, on the other hand, he is altogether forbidden to climb, he will become rebellious and will climb when no one is watching, which is just as likely to end in disaster. The freedom of the first, and the too rigid 'discipline' of the second, may have equally disastrous results.

But if he is taught *how* to climb, to test each branch before trusting himself to it, never to trust to one limb (arm or leg), but always to two, in case he slips – he is then *free* to climb, and as high as he likes. All such skills require discipline, and *only by such discipline does the child have freedom to climb* and to go on climbing. The undisciplined fool who tries to climb an Alpine mountain without training will soon pay for his foolhardiness.

It is only by discipline that we can learn to do things properly; and it is only by learning how to do things properly that we have real freedom to do them.

Take the case of the gas fire. The child is only free to light it *as long as he keeps to the rules*. No amount of self-will or petulance, or claiming to 'do as he likes', will prevent the gas exploding.

In general it is only in so far as we understand *and obey* the laws of nature that we can make use of her powers. The sailor must understand the laws of the winds and obey them : he must be highly disciplined if he is to be free to sail

THE PHASES OF EARLY DEVELOPMENT III

the seas. The scientist has to go through a very rigid discipline before he can make use of atomic power, or of hydro-electric schemes to give him heat and light. The bee-keeper needs to understand and obey the laws of the hive, and he will then get an abundant harvest of honey. If he 'does what he likes' with the hive he gets badly stung!

These illustrations show that only by discipline do we have the freedom to achieve our ends; that discipline is necessary to true freedom.

The same applies to a child's social relationships. The spoilt and undisciplined child wants his own way, wants to do as he likes; he knocks over other children's bricks, runs away with their toys, and spoils the game. But he soon finds that if he behaves like that, other children will not play with him, and will not allow him to play with their toys. He finds himself unpopular, ostracized, isolated, lonely. He *wants* to play with them; but what do they say? 'If you want to play with us you must stop knocking over our bricks, stop snatching our toys, and keep to the rules of the game.' In brief, if he wants to be free to play with them he must be socially disciplined.

Social life demands discipline, and if we are to be free to take advantage of communal life we must recognize the rights of others and our obligations to the community. If we do not want others to snatch from us we must not snatch from them. It is the law-abiding community whose members have the greatest freedom. Any confusion that arises is because we are not clear in our minds as to what we mean by freedom, and what we mean by discipline.

What do we mean by freedom? Freedom for what? When we speak of freedom we can mean freedom for our native instincts and impulses; or we may mean freedom for our personality as a whole. The two 'freedoms' are very different and to a certain extent incompatible.

Freedom of the impulses means that we do as we like: give way to our anger when it is aroused, indulge our sex passions when we want to, become indolent when we feel like it, take things belonging to other people when we want them, and resent other people interfering with what we do.

Apart from social and moral considerations, this behaviour does not work. After all, nature has developed a cortex of the brain, one of whose main functions is that of inhibition and control, and there must be some good reason for its existence. The truth is that if the primitive impulses are given unbridled freedom, they clash with one another and with the aims of the personality as a whole. For if the impulses are strong enough they will make the will of no effect. That indeed is the state of mind of the two-year-old. Since the cortex of his brain is not yet fully developed, the child is the slave of his impulses, the victim of his passions. That is why, as we have seen, the child requires the help of his parents to establish his control, and that cannot be done by the parents losing their temper with the child, but by quiet firmness, the will of the parent taking the place, for the time being, of the will of the child.

Neurotic conditions in later life are characterized by lack of freedom for the personality as a whole. One man is obsessed by a fear of hurting people; another by a compulsion to perform propitiatory acts. One comes for treatment because he suffers from irrational and unnecessary lying about the most trivial things; a woman comes for treatment because she cannot resist sexually any man who comes along; others suffer from irrational jealousies which threaten their married life. Such people cannot pursue their real aims in life because their passions prevent them. Their 'freedom' has brought them no happiness, because thereby their personalities are enslaved.

A patient describing such a condition in his childhood put it well : 'I feel as if I have been thrown into a den of lions [his impulses] who are tearing at one another [the impulses conflicting with one another] and then turn upon me ! [against his personality as a whole]'.

The child who has tantrums usually ends up in misery. Even if children get their own way in the end, they are unhappy because they have thereby forfeited the parents' approval. This is a condition often described by patients in analysis.

It is obvious, then, that when we speak of being free, we mean, or should mean, not freedom of the impulses to do as one likes but *freedom for the personality as a whole*. This means that the *personality* should be free to pursue its ends and aims, unhampered either by uncontrollable impulses or by complexes. That is what we mean by 'freedom of will'.

What, therefore, do we mean by discipline? There is confusion about this term also. The old idea of discipline was the crushing of any natural desire, for all natural desires are evil. Discipline meant suppression. This was encouraged by the theological doctrine of 'original sin' and the 'old Adam'. The modern counterpart of original sin persists in the Freudian theory of the Oedipus (or Electra) complex, an inevitable taint from which all suffer, and from which we can be saved only by psychoanalysis. The modern view of discipline, whether of child or adult, is that its aim is *the right use and direction of the native impulses*.

To refer again to a simple illustration. The child has a native impulse to climb. If he is taught how to climb, he is free to exercise this propensity. By such discipline he avoids danger and is free to go on climbing. There is no incompatibility between the freedom to exercise the propensity and the discipline necessary to do so skilfully and safely. Discipline means 'learning', as in the word 'disciple', and means learning to make proper use of our native capacities. That is what childhood is for. Childhood gives us time for the organization of our personality, so that we can then go forth to meet the demands of life.

By discipline, as it is here understood, we also give greater freedom, not only to the personality but to the native impulses. For in directing them we are not repressing them, but giving them freedom of expression, without conflict.

A child can be given as great a sense of achievement by

cutting *out* a paper duck as by cutting *up* the picture of a duck; by beating the carpet as by beating the dog; by exploring an attic as by upsetting your drawers. His love of his mother can be just as well expressed in doing things for her as in being fondled by her. It is not a question of how much or how little of any propensity is expressed, but of the way in which it is expressed. If used in the right direction it does not matter how much of it is used. Virtue and mental health both depend on the way we use the capacities with which nature has endowed us. By such discipline, then, not only do we have freedom and strength for the personality which uses all its impulses, but freedom for the impulses which are so used.

But just as discipline is necessary to freedom of the personality, so *freedom is necessary to discipline*. Moralists tell us that an act is not truly moral unless we are free to choose to do the wrong as well as the right. This is no less true with the child.

The only discipline worth while is *self-discipline*; and for self-discipline a child must have freedom to act and freedom to choose. If a child is always *made* to do this or that he cannot learn self-discipline, and when he goes out into the world he will be hopelessly at sea, the victim of every wave of temptation or wind of adversity.

There is, therefore, a true and a false 'discipline'. The false discipline crushes and represses; the true discipline controls and directs. The former leads to rebellion – or to neurosis; the latter gives freedom, both to the personality which uses the native potentialities and to the potentialities thus used, and it makes for both efficiency and happiness.

If when you ask me, therefore, whether I believe in discipline or freedom, my reply is that you cannot truly have one without the other.

How this discipline is naturally developed we shall see in the next chapter.

4

THE ORGANIZATION OF THE
CHILD'S PERSONALITY

IMITATION AND SUGGESTIBILITY

THE first two years of life, as we have seen, are engaged in the emergence of the primitive instincts and potentialities : the next phase, from two and a half to four, is concerned with the *organization of the personality*. I make no apology for dealing in considerable detail with this period, because the child's whole future life and happiness depend upon it.

We have said that mental health consists in the full development of the whole personality and all its potentialities, directed to a common aim or purpose. In this way the personality is organized, coordinated, and harmonized.

The question then is in what way and by what means the child develops such aims and ends.

This is a perfectly natural process; for there is in every child the natural tendency to take over the personalities and standards of behaviour of others by identification with them, and incorporate these standards and ideals into himself as a guiding principle in life. By this means the child's personality is coordinated and his impulses brought under the control of the will.

When a little boy says, 'I am Daddy tidying the garden!'; when the little girl says, 'I am Mummy cooking the dinner!', they are not merely imitating the parent but taking over the parent's personality into their own, and so establishing within themselves principles by which to regulate their lives.

Upon the nature and quality of these ideals and standards of behaviour thus incorporated, whether good or bad, depend not only the child's morals, but his mental health and future happiness. Healthy ideals are those which are *capable* of so coordinating the personality.

The process of organization takes place in four well-defined stages :

(a) The phase of imitation.
(b) The phase of suggestibility.
(c) The phase of identification.
(d) The formation of the Ego ideal.

(a) *Imitation* by the child means taking over the *actions* of others, especially of his parents. We have already described this and so need say no more. It is the first stage in the take-over of a child's standards of behaviour. If a parent acts cruelly, the child will act cruelly; if kindly, he acts kindly.

(b) *Suggestibility* goes further; it means that the child takes over, not only the actions of others, but the *moods, feelings, and ideas* of those around him.

(c) In *identification* the child goes further still : he takes over the entire personality of the other person. 'I *am* Daddy tidying the garden.' He impersonates the other person so completely that his own personality is absorbed in the personality of the other. For the time being he *is* that other person.

(d) In the *Ego ideal* phase, the child, having taken over the personality of the others with whom he identifies himself, now adopts their standards *as his own*; so that thereafter he has a guiding principle *within his own personality* by which to regulate his life and conduct.

To illustrate these phases and their differences. A boy is out for a walk with his father. A dog rushes up and barks at them. The father stands his ground and remains calm and unafraid, whereupon the boy takes over the action of the father and stands unmoved. That is *imitation*. Not only that, but he takes over his father's mood, his attitude of mind, and remains calm. That is *suggestibility*. In the next stage the boy goes further and adopts the personality of his father and says : 'I'm a brave boy like Daddy !' That is *iden-*

tification. Finally comes the stage of the *Ego ideal* when he forgets his fathers but keeps the ideal and says, 'I'm a brave boy.' He has now established in his personality a standard of courage *for himself*, quite apart from his father. Indeed, having adopted this standard, he may turn and criticize his father, from whom he originally got the ideal, for *not* being brave. 'Oh! you were afraid!' he may say. Children have a way of criticizing in this fashion, much to the discomfiture of the parents. They say, 'You didn't say "Thank you"!' and 'You didn't wipe your feet when you came in!' They are simply applying the standards they have derived *from* their parents *to* their parents who, of course, have no defence! It is better for the parents to admit the fault. Do not tell the child not to be cheeky. That is pompous – and unfair.

Suggestibility. In this phase, which most commonly takes place about the age of two and a half to three, the child takes over the moods, feelings, and attitudes of minds of those about him. It is in dramatic contrast to the self-willed phase through which he has just passed. Indeed, it is sometimes almost miraculous the way in which a child changes from being headstrong and passionate to being acquiescent, anxious to please, and cooperative; in brief, he has become suggestible. As I began by saying, every phase of development, if given full expression, passes into the next phase.

Suggestibility is psychic dependence. Just as in infancy the child is *physically* dependent for food, warmth, and security upon those around, so now he becomes *mentally and emotionally* dependent upon others, absorbing their feelings and emotions. If the mother is irritable, he will be irritable; if the mother is anxious, he senses her anxiety and becomes anxious too; if she is calm and quiet he will take over the same mood. If the father is domineering and arrogant, the little boy will be found to follow suit and become arrogant, bullying those weaker than himself. If the father is cynical and superior, the boy will be scornful of others. If the father is unselfish and considerate, the boy, in spite of natural tendencies to the contrary, will share his toys and be thoughtful of others.

In the blitz on London during the war, it was found that children were not afraid of the bombs as such, but were afraid in two sets of circumstances : separation from the mother, and the anxiety of the mother. If in the bombing the mother remained calm and serene, the child took over her mood and had no fear.

The phase of suggestibility may be demonstrated by any parent or teacher, as in the following instance. A boy of two and a half was wheeling a barrow from the garden through a french window into the sitting room. Adopting a domineering tone, I said 'Take that barrow out !' He stamped his foot and said 'I won't !' I then changed my tone and said, 'That is a very dirty barrow and you would not like to bring it into a nice clean room like this, would you?' He quietly said, 'No !', turned round, and took it away. This was true suggestibility. When I was apparently angry, he took over my mood and was angry too : when I was conciliatory, he was prepared to be conciliatory too.

Some people might regard this as reasoning, but that is not so. The boy did not care at all about the carpet. What induced him to take the barrow out was not my reasoning but my tone. If I had given my reasons for not dirtying the carpet in an angry tone he would certainly have replied truculently; it was my change of mood which made him change his attitude.

Though suggestibility seems to be characteristic of all normal children about this age and is probably a phase of maturation, we must not expect to find it in the same degree in all children; for this, like any phase of maturation, may be modified or interfered with by other factors.

Suggestibility, for instance, may be overridden by the persistence of the earlier aggressive phase. The child who is made excessively rebellious or aggressive by wrong discipline in the self-willed period may continue to be the 'difficult child' even when he ought to have developed into this suggestible phase. He thereby loses the contribution this phase has to make to his personality and pays for it – or his parents do – later on.

Similarly if the child is constantly provoked he will be truculent and not amenable, even in the suggestible phase. But even in this he is being suggestible, for he is still taking over the moods and feelings of those around – the mother's impatience or the father's grumbling.

To be suggestible is not necessarily to be amenable : if what is suggested is irritability or impatience, the child will adopt it.

That leads on to another important feature of suggestibility.

Suggestibility is a subconscious process. The child is not aware that he is taking over the moods and ideas of the mother; he does so automatically. This is because suggestibility is a function of the sub-cortical centres of the brain, whereas the higher cortex of the brain is concerned with reasoning and criticism.

That is why in treatment by suggestion, whether hypnotic or otherwise, we put the patient into a non-critical state of passivity or 'sleep'. For by doing so we abolish for the time being his critical faculties, so that he now accepts without question all that we tell him, and responds accordingly. If we say to him that all his anxiety is gone and he is full of confidence, he does not criticize or reason about what we say, but will respond by losing his anxiety and feeling confident.

The subconscious nature of suggestibility is a point for parents and teachers to remember : to insinuate an idea is often more effective than deliberately to teach it.

Take the following illustration. At a seaside resort I observed two fathers, newly arrived, each with a son, taking them down to the sea for a bathe. To reach the water from the huts they had to pass over some shingle, and as they did so on the first day each of the boys said 'Oh, it hurts !' One of the fathers replied, 'Yes, it does hurt, doesn't it ?' and walked on. The other father said 'Nonsense, it doesn't hurt at all!' Now what would you consider would be the result of each of these suggestions? I watched for the next three mornings. The boy whose father said 'Nonsense, it doesn't hurt!' complained each morning of its hurting. The boy whose father said 'Yes, it does hurt!' never once complained again. Now, of course, there are differences in boys, but that apart, why this result? It is because suggestibility is a sub-conscious and not a conscious process. The father who *said* it did hurt was really *suggesting* to the boy that despite the pain they must nevertheless stick it and walk on because they wanted to swim. The father who said 'Nonsense!' no doubt thought he was giving his son a good suggestion, but all that it really suggested to the boy was that the father was a fool, because obviously it did hurt. In fact the father himself was walking very gingerly!

A child is about to go into hospital for an operation for removal of tonsils. The mother anxiously says, 'You'll be *quite* all right! And it will make your throat better!' And so on. To the mother that is a good suggestion. But the child *senses* that there must be something terrible going to happen for the mother to be so anxiously reassuring! The sub-conscious inference the child draws from the reassurance is more potent than the reassurance! Under such conditions a mother's quiet calm is far more reassuring than her words.

From these illustrations, we learn that subconscious suggestion is more potent that conscious suggestion, and it is well to bear this in mind in the treatment of children. That is why, at the phase of suggestibility, if you are mopping up, the child will do the same; but if you deliberately *try* to get him to imitate you in some action and say, 'Do as Mummy does!', he will as likely as not refuse. He will do it if you don't tell him to; not if you do! This resistance is not pure cussedness; it arises because suggestion is primarily and *naturally* a subconscious process, and if you try to make it a conscious one you interfere with the *natural* process. Little

Bo Peep discovered that if you 'leave them alone, they'll come home'.

The same applies not only to actions and moods, but to matters of moral conduct : the child will take over persistence, patience, consideration for others, friendliness for strangers, and most other moods. These he catches automatically from the mother without being told, and often all the better if he is not told.

Development. Suggestibility is itself a development of the dependence of infantile life; it is psychic dependence. Its development follows the same lines as physical dependence (pp. 73 f.). It develops (after a period of individuality at four to seven) into *sociability* in the 'primitive man' period of eight to twelve; and still more into the 'gang spirit' of puberty. In both these periods children are very concerned to do as others do, to be as others are. Woe betide the schoolboy whose mother makes him wear corduroy shorts when the others are wearing flannel trousers !

Suggestibility is the essence of the so-called 'herd instinct'. A crowd of people is very subject to suggestion : it can easily be aroused by an orator to anger, to enthusiasm, to cruelty, or to sacrifice, whereas the same arguments would leave the individuals unaffected. Similarly boys and girls of school age in a crowd can be viciously cruel to a wretched new boy or girl, a cruelty of which they would be quite incapable as individuals; but they can also be aroused to great heroism – as witness the boys of thirteen and fourteen in the blitz on a Bristol Hospital, whose one desire was to help with the younger ones.

In adult life suggestibility develops into *social life,* in which we are *dependent* on one another. We adopt prevailing opinions in literature, follow fashions in art or dress, and accept rumours from the prevailing gossip, for no other reason than that it is what others are doing.*

Suggestibility is also at the basis of good characteristics of social behaviour such as politeness. The essence of politeness

* See Trotter, *The Herd Instinct in Peace and War.*

is consideration for others. So too with morals. In so far as we have within us this tendency to do as others do, so we adopt the *mores* or customs of the society in which we live. At a very early age the child adopts these customs and in a simple way can be led to realize these moral obligations, by, for instance, sharing his toys, or keeping to the rules in games, or letting others have their turn.

The biological value of suggestibility, like that of imitation, is that it saves the child the necessity of going through a great deal of experience by the dangerous process of trial and error; for the 'error' may be fatal. But whereas imitation is of actions, suggestibility is of words and attitudes of mind.

The child cannot prove everything for himself, nor experience all the vicissitudes of life; and if he is to get on at all, he must needs take advantage of the experiences of others. Nature provides him with the capacity to do this. Suggestibility is thus an *innate* capacity which enables the child to take over the *acquired* experiences of others, and enables him to profit by their experiences. This is an incalculable advantage in the struggle for existence.

Suggestibility, therefore, primarily subserves the function of security : it is a means of adaptation to life.

Abnormalities. (a) *Wrong suggestions*. By this we mean suggestions which are harmful to our adjustment to life or to our social obligations. The mother who has a morbid fear of illness or is morbidly shy or suspicious of strangers will transfer these attitudes to the child who has enough to cope with in life without having to adjust himself to his mother's complexes. That is why the neurotic mother so often has a neurotic child.

(b) *Over-suggestibility*. Some children are by nature more dependent and, therefore, more suggestible, but that is not in itself an abnormality. Such people later often do excellent work under others who are natural leaders. We cannot all be leaders. But when a person is over-suggestible, he loses individuality and character. He is spineless; he has no opinions of his own; his opinions and moods reflect those of the last person he has talked to; his actions follow what everyone else is doing. Some children are weak and spineless by nature; others are made so.

The most common cause of this spineless and weak character is the breaking of the child's will in the previous self-willed period. The parents are determined to crush his will, and succeed in doing so to such an extent that he dare not do anything on his own initiative but must wait to see what others are doing and mould his actions, moods, and thoughts upon theirs. Then the parents complain that he has no guts or initiative, that he never makes decisions of his own or takes responsibilities on his own. Of course not. He has been taught not to!

Later on he is of the type who is 'easily led' by more robust and often undesirable characters who 'take the lead'. Amongst delinquents and criminals you often find that of a pair one is dominant, the other suggestible.

As we have seen, dependence and suggestibility play an important part in the psychoneuroses, especially hysteria, among the main characteristics of which are dependence and helplessness. This applies to all kinds of hysteria, whether it is 'hysterics' in which the individual gives way to uncontrollable emotion, weeping, or laughing; or 'anxiety hysteria' in which he gets into a panic; or 'conversion hysteria' in which he appeals for help and sympathy by developing a physical illness. (See *Psychology and Mental Health*, Chapter 8.)

Hysterical reaction may be observed in the simplest form in any child who feels left out or unloved, perhaps because a new baby is getting all the attention. He cannot *ask* for affection because either he is too 'grown up' or he fears he will get a snub; so he represses the desire for sympathy, which emerges in a hysteric form. He says, 'I've got a sore knee!' or 'I don't feel well!'

This child is a potential hysteric, although, of course, he does not necessarily develop into one. A lot depends on how he is treated. If you say, 'Nonsense! you haven't got a pain at all!', he gets even more anxious, for he then feels, 'But suppose I am *really* ill, mother won't help me.' If you fuss too much over the supposed pain he says 'Splendid!', for he has now discovered how he can always get attention and plays up to it! How then are we to treat him? Obviously by treating the cause and making him feel less left out and more loved and secure. He will forget all about the pain. The hysteric child does not want sympathy because he is ill; he is ill because he wants sympathy; and he wants sympathy because he feels left out.

Mental hygiene. At this age the mother can appeal to a child's suggestibility as a means of directing his behaviour into right and helpful channels. The most effective way of doing this is by herself doing and being what she wants the child to do and be. His natural suggestibility will lead him to do likewise. If a mother gets irritable with a child of two and snatches something from him with a slap, he will at once do likewise with the baby saying 'Naughty baby!' in exactly the same tone and with the same show of irritation.

But parents may use suggestibility more positively with children of this age. 'I wouldn't do that if I were you' is far more effective than 'Don't do that!' By all means give your reasons, why or why not. The child will probably not be influenced by your reasons at this phase, but will certainly be influenced by the reasonableness of your tone of voice and attitude. A great compliment to any mother is that she 'never raises her voice'!

But parents should not take too great advantage of this suggestibility or exploit it. The nurse or the mother who is persistently saying to the child, 'You *would* like to do this, wouldn't you?' (and like Pilate does not wait for an answer), is ultimately going to force him into a rebellious frame of mind instead of calling forth natural suggestibility. He can have a surfeit even of suggestibility from a well-meaning parent. Suggestibility is natural to a child and should be allowed to take its natural course; it should not be forced upon him.

The essence of suggestion treatment, as we have said, is to get the patient into a non-critical state of mind, for it is found that when criticism is abolished the suggestions penetrate to the subconscious area, and the mind passively accepts and acts upon the suggestions given to it. Suggestion is also of the greatest value in the treatment of children's disorders, such as bed-wetting, nail-biting, anxiety, or jealousy.

IDENTIFICATION

Suggestibility leads to identification. In suggestibility the child takes over the moods, feelings, and ideas of those around : in identification he takes over their whole personality. He not only imitates his father driving the car, but says, 'I *am* Daddy driving the car!' He *impersonates* his father; he *incorporates* his father into his own personality, taking over his father's arrogance or kindness. He acts and thinks and feels as if he were his father.

So the child says, 'I am the charlady' and cleans the floor; 'I am the gardener' and spits on the path; 'I am Mummy cooking the dinner!' In these cases so absolutely does he absorb the personalities of others that he entirely loses his identity in theirs. He is not merely *like* the person with whom he identifies himself – he *is* that person. Indeed, for the time being he is *more that person than he is himself*. He is no longer a little boy; he is an engine driver, a captain of a ship.

This characteristic of the child has long been recognized by parents, who find it very entertaining. A boy of four and a half spent his whole day watching some men working in the road, coming in only for meals. One morning he came back earlier than usual, and his mother, entering into the spirit of the thing said, 'Hello! have you knocked off early today?' 'Yes,' he said, wearily throwing his cap on the chair. 'We have to; we're buggered for bricks!'

This identification is confirmed in analytic treatment in the revival of early memories. A boy whose mother was distinctly unkind to him recalled, 'I would dream of being the great and big man, which, of course, was my father; and I would feel my chin and wish there was a beard there!'

These early identifications are so strongly embedded that they persist into adult life. A doctor patient of mine had a predilection for wearing large flap collars, being untidy, wearing patched trousers, and bolting his food – all of which idiosyncrasies he recognized as irrational and detrimental to his professional work. They were all derived from his father, a busy practitioner, whom he looked up to as the most important man in the populous district in which they lived, and who was too busy to attend to his food and clothing. So completely did the son identify himself with his father that he took over his father's patched trousers. Indeed, we may often observe our own mannerisms, ways of speaking and laughing, and the way we behave to strangers, by watching our children.

These characteristics transmitted from father to son are often taken as hereditary. There are, of course, many temperamental characteristics which are inherited : some children are more sensitive, some more phlegmatic, some full of energy, following their parents' constitutional make-up. But the wearing of patched trousers can hardly come in that category.

Most of the idiosyncrasies which are passed from father to son, mother to daughter, or mother to son are not transmitted by heredity but by this process of identification with the parent.

We see then that while the *capacity* for identification is inherited, *what* we inherit is acquired from others by the exercise of that capacity. So it is with the boy who struts about the house like his pompous father. He does not inherit this, he acquires it by identification. If the mother is vain, the daughter becomes vain. The vanity is not inherited, although the good looks which justify it may be, but the daughter imitates the mother by looking at herself admiringly in the mirror saying tacitly, 'I'm beautiful like Mummy!'

Identification, therefore, like suggestibility, is an inherited capacity for taking over the acquired characteristics of those around, but it goes a stage further in that it takes over not only individual characteristics but the whole personality with all its characteristics. Identification itself is a development of an earlier experience, that of identity. The infant before birth is physically one with the mother, a part of her body. Later this oneness persists in identification. A patient reviving her infantile feelings says : 'In infancy I drew no distinction between my mother and myself. So when I hated her it was the same feeling as hating myself – there was no difference. There is such a great understanding between my feelings and my mother that when I want to romp about with my mother she smiles and is responsive. When I am actively affectionate and clasp her round the neck and kiss her she does the same to me.'

Identification may take two forms. A child may take over the personalities of others as we have illustrated : that is 'introjection'. He may also ascribe his own characteristics to others : that is 'projection'. By projection a child ascribes all kinds of feelings and desires to his toys. He says, 'My teddy bear is sick and wants a drink.' The little girl is anxious and concerned about the moral welfare of her doll who is 'naughty'. It is the age of 'animism', when all inanimate things are given life and personality, which in itself is a projection of the child's own personality. A child learns a lot about both himself and others by means of such play.

Identification serves a very important biological function; for by putting ourselves in the place of another we develop mutual understanding and sympathy, and this enhances social life and behaviour. Identification is present even in adult life and explains why we feel embarrassed for a man who is making a fool of himself reciting, even though he himself is not in the least embarrassed !

Motives for identification. With whom does the child

normally identify himself. Mostly with two groups of people – those he loves and those he admires. There are thus two motives for identification – love and power, which are the two qualities a child most desires and needs. He identifies himself with those he loves because he still needs protection and security; he must, therefore, keep in with those who give him this protective love and must conform with their demands and be like them.

The motive of love is a very healthy form of identification, because it gives the initial sense of security and also tends to give him the right *kind* of identification; for those who are loving and lovable usually have the more desirable characteristics.

The motive of power is also of value because it encourages the child to grow up and adapt himself to the world.

Every boy wants to be an engine driver because of the immense power he would control. The very tone in which he declares himself to be a bus driver or captain of a ship reveals the tones of strong manhood. The little girl wants to be a nurse, not only because of sympathy with those in need, but because the nurse is the most important person in the house, even bossing the mother about when someone is ill – and the little girl in her make-believe leaves us with no doubt that she is determined to 'boss the show' with her 'sick children'.

The motives of both love and power are confirmed in analysis. A boy says, 'I wanted to be big so that I could get away and push my mother out of the way.' (Not big, let it be observed, so as to possess the mother.) 'Then my father came in, and he started to show me how to put up the bricks, and had me on his knee and showed me books; and he would wait for me when we were out for a walk. He was so nice to me; and when I put up my bricks, I would put them up to show him. I felt he was definitely superior to my mother. My mother was annoyed with me; but my father was pleased that I was there. Then I would often dream that I was as big as he was and as good as he was.'

The transition from the security motive to the power motive is well illustrated in this infantile memory from an Oxford don. 'I seem to be lying in bed with my mother : but now I don't seem to be enjoying it much. I have a feeling of dissatisfaction with my mother; I want to be more active and the picture I get is of myself creeping away from my mother on the bed and playing by myself. My mother has wanted me to stay with her but I don't want to, and am running up and down at the foot of the bed and letting off energy in that way. Then I go to my father and try to climb up his leg and on to his chest – the man rather than the woman – he is big and strong. The idea is to escape from being a baby. If I stay with my father I shall develop like him and grow strong and big.'

Development. The tendency to identification does not pass with childhood, but continues throughout life. One of the forms it takes in early adolescence is, as we have seen, that of hero-worship, in which boys or girls admire some character, historical or fictitious, and mould their whole lives on him, taking him as their standard. It is very obvious in the worship of film stars. In later adolescence identification takes the form of identification with ideals, whether social, political, or scholastic, to which the youth or girl gives complete devotion.

The tendency of identification also plays an important, though unconscious, part in adult life. For instance, there is the mother who is so identified with her family that all their joys are literally hers; the shame of her wayward son becomes her shame. She may mind little how she is herself dressed but finds joy in her daughter's being attractively and tastefully dressed; on the other hand the distress of any one of her brood fills her with a pain more poignant than any disaster to her own person.

Love and power are both healthy motives for identification, for they make for security and adaptation to life.

Abnormalities of identification. But things do not always work out in the best way, for although the child may identify himself with desirable people whom he admires, he may also admire those with undesirable characters, because they are strong and ruthless, as, for example, gangsters in films. Thus a boy may admire a father who is big and strong, but a bully, and himself becomes a bully. A girl may admire her mother because she is pretty and gets much attention from men, and so becomes a courtesan.

It is also possible for a child to identify himself with someone whose standards of life are excellent but not appropriate for himself. An extreme instance I know was that of a dull and backward girl who had a 'pash' on a school mistress and wanted to be a mathematics teacher like her! It was sad to have to disillusion her.

Another abnormal form of identification is that in which the child identifies himself with a great person and imagines himself to *be* that person and lives in a phantasy world. Instead of this being an incentive to action and endeavour, it prevents him from doing anything since he is already there, in imagination. Such children are described as being 'always in a dream'.

Such extravagant self-fantasies may have the opposite effect and produce *self-depreciation* because of the feeling of failure at not achieving complete identification with the ideal. ('I've played golf for forty years, and never been on my game yet!')

There are also false motives of identification. By false, I mean that unlike those of love and power they do not conduce to healthy development of the child, but retard it.

One of these is the identification which is based on *fear*. A mother can *make* a child do what she tells him by threats and punishment and compel him to identify himself with her, to be as she is, to do as she does. ('You must do as I tell you, or else . . .') Such an identification, instead of acting as an incentive, is apt to be paralysing. It leaves no room for spontaneity, initiative, or self-discipline, and later often ends in rebellion and delinquency. Or the child may take over his mother's severe personality and condemn himself as his mother condemned him, which may end in obsessional compulsions and neuroses.

There is another false form of identification, namely the sexual, and it is not surprising that the Freudians maintain that it is the root of all neurotic evil. It is 'false' because it does not serve any useful biological purpose, as do those of protective love and the search for power.*

'Double identification', that is to say conditions where the child identifies itself with two *conflicting* characters at once, are not uncommon and very confusing. A boy identified himself with his mother, who was artistic, and with his father, who was a big business man. The two conflicted in him. After treatment he combined the two in the art of theatrical decor!

Identifications may persist unconsciously, and have peculiar consequences. This is illustrated in the common experience where a child feels ill-used by her mother and says, 'I'll never treat *my* children as my mother treated me!' But so strong is the identification that when the child herself becomes a mother, in spite of herself and her intentions to the contrary, she treats her child in exactly the same way as her mother treated her. She is usually quite unaware of doing so unless it is pointed out to her, and even then she will probably deny it or claim that circumstances justify her.

A case in point from a mother in analysis : 'I find myself letting fly at my son nowadays. I act just as my father did to me and rage at my little boy; then I feel afraid, as I did as a child, because I had made him part of my hostile world. Then I identify myself with my son and have an exaggerated pity and sympathy for him for being treated so ! This makes me furious with myself for being such a brute, as I felt furious towards my father.' The complications of such identification take some unravelling.

Mental hygiene. This innate tendency to impersonate, to

* For a new explanation of the Oedipus complex see *Psychology and Mental Health,* p. 127.

live in the lives of other people (which Pippa did in Browning's *Pippa Passes*), is of great value in building up the personality of the child, who can thus gather nectar from many flowers. It is good for the child to mix with a variety of children for the enrichment of his personality and to give him, within limits, the opportunity of incorporating into himself those characteristics and interests most suited to his temperament. By this means a child develops a character and personality distinctly his own; he develops *individuality*. William James says that we have as many selves as there are people who recognize us; we may reverse the dictum and say 'we have as many selves as there are people with whom we identify ourselves'. It is therefore undesirable that the child should live with one person alone, say a nurse or a devoted mother, or still worse a grandmother, for in that case he tends to identify himself with her alone without the opportunity of that variety of identifications with others which is the essence of individuality.

Identification is also of value in developing skill, and this should be encouraged. When the child says, 'I'm a carpenter', he sets about making things – in play at first, seriously afterwards. So by living the lives of a large variety of people and enjoying their activities, the child learns housekeeping, gardening, carpentering, shopping, buying and selling, sailing ships, and delivering coal, and so becomes handy in tackling any job. Identification, by helping the child to see what he can and cannot do, also enables him to choose a career which is suited to him.

If a boy forms a bad identification during this period of childhood, does he necessarily carry it through life? Fortunately not, for though these early ones are of the greatest moment, he may abandon them if they turn out to be unsatisfactory and accept others which may have a greater appeal. So a boy who is brought up in a bad home with bad example and imitates his bullying father may join a club or the Scouts and identify himself with the leader, from whom he derives an entirely different character. This is particularly likely to happen, since he finds in the leader more to love and admire than in his father and so readily attaches himself to the former. This may change the whole course of his life. That is why it is so necessary to have the right type of men and women to run these clubs, since the boys and girls almost inevitably identify themselves with them and take over their characteristics.

You sometimes, therefore, find a child brought up in a bad home who turns out well in life. In such cases you often discover that although the parents were neither lovable nor admirable, there was someone else, a kindly neighbour or a school teacher, to whom the child was attached and with whom he identified himself.

Sometimes, therefore, a change of environment for a 'difficult child' from a bad home to a foster home, in which he receives love and affection, changes his whole life and character, because of the formation of new and healthier identification.

THE EGO IDEAL

The fourth stage in the organization of the child's personality is the formation of the Ego ideal. This is a direct outcome of the earlier phases. In imitation he takes over the action of others; in suggestibility he takes over the moods and feelings of those around; in identification he goes further and identifies his whole personality with that of another person.

In the last stage, that of the Ego ideal, the child *scraps the person but keeps the character,* which now becomes a part of his own personality.

No longer does he say, 'I'm a brave boy *like Daddy*', but, having incorporated his father's standards of behaviour, says, '*I'm* a brave boy.' He has now *established within himself a guiding principle of life* by which he can control and direct all his native impulses, and so harmonize his personality. The centre of gravity of his behaviour has shifted from the other person to within himself. From being disciplined from without, he now disciplines himself; from being told what to do, he tells himself what to do. The transition from identification is well illustrated from this case in analysis. A boy had been bullying his sister until his father came and scolded him. The boy felt morose and desolate, and then, identifying himself with his father, turned against himself and spoke with his father's voice against himself. 'I look at my own hands,' he says in analysis, 'and the idea strikes me to do to myself what my father has been doing to me. I say to myself, "Now you sit there and don't move, and if you bully your sister, my God! I'll wring your neck." When I do that, things look up. I join my father and say to myself, "Go on, you little sweep, you grovel." I do the same with myself in relation to my sister. "I'll take this little devil (myself) and make him grovel to her" – just what my father has been trying to make me do. I become as sadistic to myself as I was to my sister. So it works all right. I say to myself, "Now you get out into the garden," and then I say, "Now you damn well go in again." But that leads to complications; for when my father now tells me to do something, I get under his thumb, instead of under my own.' That creates a conflict in his personality, because he is confused between being the child again and being his newly acquired personality, which he has got from his father. It is a conflict between his natural self or Ego, and his Super-Ego, which he gets by adoption from his father.

We see from these illustrations that it is by a perfectly natural process that the child develops standards of behaviour and a moral sense. So that *if you never taught a child one single moral maxim, he would nevertheless develop moral – or immoral – standards of right and wrong by the process of identification.*

The mental health of the child depends more than anything else on the nature of the Ego ideal the child adopts.

An Ego ideal which is too severe, by identification with a severe parent, will repress the native impulses and weaken character. A too easy-going Ego ideal has not the power to control and guide the impulse. A healthy ideal is of such a nature that it is capable of directing all the forces of the personality to a common end.

Let us consider more specifically some of the results of this incorporation of the Ego ideal into the child's personality. These are :

(a) The formation of a duality in the personality.
(b) Self-consciousness.
(c) Self-criticism.
(d) Self-control and development of the will.

(a) In the first place the incorporation of the Ego ideal obviously forms *a duality in the personality*. On the one side there is the Ego or natural self with its innate impulses and desires : on the other side there is the Ego ideal or moral self which the child has got by identification with the personalities of other people and incorporated into his own personality. This duality of personality is probably one of the most characteristic features of human psychology as distinct from animal life.

In extreme cases this duality takes the form of a 'dual personality'. Like Jekyll and Hyde, there is a split between the two sides of the personality, which operate alternately.

Now that the child has incorporated his new Ego ideal, he has to contend with a fight on a double front. Not only has he to cope with the problems and difficulties of objective life and preserve himself from external dangers, but he is now confronted with dangers from within, from his own impulses. The child is the unhappy battle-ground of all these conflicting forces. It does not make things easier for the mother to scold him for his failure in this difficult task. He needs help, not rebuke.

This duality is responsible for the age-long conflict between impulse and will; between the self as we naturally are, and the self we ought to be; between the natural and spiritual self. Long before Freud, St Paul put this psychological truth very dramatically when he said, 'For the good that I would, I do not : but the evil which I would not, that

I do . . . I see another law in my members, warring against the law of my mind, and bringing me into captivity.'

(*b*) The second result of the incorporation of the Ego ideal in the personality is *self-consciousness*. This simply means that one part of the personality is conscious of the other part of the personality.

Anyone may observe self-consciousness emerging in a child about three years of age. A little girl of two will walk up to two old ladies chattering in the park, and stand in front of them watching them and their funny ways for minutes at a time. She is absorbed, but quite oblivious of herself or even of their talking about her – and then she runs off when she has had enough. Not so the child of four; for if you look at such a child, say in the train, she will soon get uncomfortable and shuffle about self-consciously. As likely as not she will be wondering what is wrong with her dress, or herself, or she may feel that you can 'see through her', feels guilty and blushes. The reason for self-consciousness developing at this age is that this new 'self' has now been established into her personality : so the child becomes conscious of herself. Prior to this, in infancy, the child is aware of sensations in its body, but he regards these as external objects. A tummy ache is felt as an object, a hated, disagreeable, threatening object. But at three the child is aware of himself *as* himself.

It is at this stage of self-consciousness that the child begins to talk of 'I' instead of saying 'Peter does this', 'Kathy wants that.' He now says, 'I have a tummy-ache !', 'I am hungry !', 'I feel good !'

The biological value of self-consciousness is that it enables the child to see himself as others see him, to observe his behaviour and match it against what he *should* be, and what others desire him to be.

It is, therefore, one of the most important assets in the development of social and communal life, and also the basis of moral life, in that it sets up within the child *conscious* standards and ideals to follow and live up to. Self-consciousness is thus one of the qualities which sets man above the lower animals.

Morbid self-consciousness. Unfortunately, like most valuable qualities in human nature, it can bring its train of abnormalities. When we speak of a child as being 'self-conscious' we usually mean that he is morbidly or excessively self-conscious.

This arises when he has at some time been made, by his mother or others, to feel shameful, wicked, disgusting, stupid, selfish, or clumsy, and the idea becomes so deeply embedded in his mind that he cannot get rid of this idea of himself although it may later be contrary to the fact. The result is that instead of his self-consciousness helping to regulate his life, the morbid idea becomes an obsession which robs him of all self-confidence : instead of making him sociably minded, it debars him from ordinary social intercourse with his fellows. 'Self-conscious' persons often become recluses; excessive blushing has led even to suicide.

Contrast these children with the child who is self-conscious in that he is *conscious* of himself as being loved, cared for, and capable of doing things. Such a child starts off in life with self-confidence, and his very confidence in himself makes him succeed.

Mental hygiene. Self-consciousness is a natural and desirable quality developed as the result of the incorporation by identification of the standards of those around. It can, therefore, largely be left to itself. As it is a natural quality we should avoid making a child self-conscious by constantly calling attention to it. We should be as *objective* as possible.

Take as a practical example an activity like washing up. It is far better to say to the child, 'There is a bit of dirt left on that fork', than to say, 'You have not washed that fork properly' – which is personal and makes him resentful. If he has made something badly, you do not need to scold him and say how silly, clumsy, or stupid *he* is; rather, you can draw attention to what is wrong with the *object*, or show why it won't work the way he is doing it, and help the child to do it correctly. This method keeps the child's attention focused on the object to be achieved rather than on himself. It may seem a quibble, but it makes all the difference in dealing with children.

After all, the same applies in dealing with mothers. We do not say, 'You shouldn't do that with your child', for that puts her back up. We say, 'If you do this with your child, you will probably find that this will happen'; 'If you do that, the result will probably be so and so.' It is the scientific approach rather than the moral.

(c) *Self-criticism and conscience*. Self-consciousness in-evitably leads to self-criticism, for the one follows the other. Just as the mother or father criticized the child, so when the child incorporates them into his own personality he criticizes himself. This was very clearly brought out in the case of a boy who bullied his sister and then adopted his father's severe attitude towards himself. If a boy adopts from his father the standard of being brave, he blames himself if he falls short of this. If a girl adopts an attitude of being un-selfish because her mother is, she will feel ashamed when she has snatched some cake from the baby, quite apart from her fear of the consequences. A boy of this age may still get into tantrums, but afterwards he is ashamed, feels how silly it is, and hopes nobody noticed. In all these cases, the child com-pares his or her behaviour with what are now his own stan-dards, and approves or disapproves as the case may be. So one boy of three said, 'Paul now a good boy; this morning Paul bad boy!'

This function of self-criticism constitutes conscience. Psychologically speaking, *conscience is the judgement which the Ego ideal or moral self passes on the Ego or natural self*. Its biological function is to put a check upon the impulses of the natural self, so that the actions of the personality should be rightly directed and harmonized.

The question is often asked whether the 'moral sense' is innate. As far as psychological evidence shows, it suggests that the moral sense *as such* is not innate, but that *the ingredients* which go to the formation of a moral conscience are innate, namely, the processes of suggestibility and identification, and, as a consequence, the adoption of an Ego ideal.

Morbid conscience. Conscience, though a most valuable asset in correcting our conduct, is by no means an infallible guide, and history proves that the most cruel things have been done in the name of conscience, even by Christian churches, whose religion professes to be one of love.

Self-criticism can be very irksome; it is unpleasant to be criticized, even by oneself. Indeed we may say *especially* by oneself, for we carry our critic about everywhere. Certain measures are therefore adopted by the child to evade this. The simplest is to turn the criticism upon others, the object being to pull others down to his level, which makes him feel more comfortable. This is particularly characteristic of the child of six or seven who tends to depreciate the action or work of others.

But the *repression* of self-criticism may have an opposite effect, namely that the child projects its self-criticism on to others and thinks that they are perpetually criticizing him, that they are thinking what a fool he is or how wicked he is, when, in fact, they are thinking nothing of the sort, for they are much too absorbed with thinking of themselves. It is he who is critical of himself, but since self-criticism is so unpleasant and he can't get away from it, he accuses others of being so.

(*d*) *Self-control.* The establishment of the Ego ideal within the personality also gives the child self-control. The boy says, 'I'm a brave boy!' – and therefore controls his fears; he says, 'I'm a big boy!' and therefore does not cry! This requires restraint, but not repression, for the boy is *aware* that he is afraid, but controls it; whereas in repression he would deny that he was afraid.

True self-control is established about the age of three to four when the child adopts his own Ego ideal. That explains why there are far fewer tantrums at this age. Instead of getting into a tantrum the child is much more likely to set about trying to master the thing he wants to do.

The healthy Ego ideal. What then should we consider to be a right and healthy Ego ideal? From the *social* point of view it is one which is in conformity with social customs and behaviour and avoids breaking the law. But many children break down with neurosis because of a too great conformity to social demands, which crushes their individuality. From the *moral* point of view, it may be said to be one which obeys the eternal laws of right and wrong. But how are we to determine what these are? From the point of view of *mental health*, the Ego ideal should be of such a nature that it is capable of utilizing, directing, and coordinating all the energies and capacities of the personality; and this it does by directing them all towards the common aim.

Some ideals are obviously more capable of achieving coordination than others. Ruthlessness, for instance, which a boy may take over from his father as 'the stuff to give 'em', is not a healthy ideal because it suppresses the impulses of tenderness and affection which are also part of his nature. Licentiousness and self-indulgence are also incompatible with mental health because they are divorced from the demands of reality and life. To the psychologist such ideals are 'wrong', not because they are incompatible with social or moral demands, but because they fail to bring about that coordination of the personality which is the criterion of mental health.

The pursuit of ends also enables a child to exercise self-control. If a boy has set his heart on buying a toy engine, he controls his immediate natural desire to buy sweets, and saves his money for the engine instead. This is all the more effective because it is voluntary; it is his own doing. Another boy says: 'I'm going to be a farmer, like Uncle George!' This gives him an incentive, something to work *for*. He wants to be a good farmer, or maybe a lawyer, doctor, parson, or business man, so he works hard and directs all his energies to that end. He does this by the exercise of his will, which is his personality functioning in pursuit of his aims. The little girl says, 'I'm going to have lots of children', and that makes her careful with her dolls in health and sickness.

It takes time for the child to coordinate his personality and to get all his impulses under control. But the ingredients of self-control and the means of adopting standards and ideals by which to control and direct his impulses are all provided by nature. The child is trying, even though he may not appear to be, for coordination is a natural process. Let us then be patient with him when he does not always succeed, and not make the task more difficult for him by making excessive demands on him.

The will. When the Ego ideal is well established in the personality and directs its impulses, it constitutes the will. *The will is the function and activity of personality as a whole in the pursuit of its ends and aims.* A free will is one which is free to do this unhindered by uncontrollable impulses or neurotic complexes. But where these impulses and complexes dominate, the individual cannot carry out what he desires or intends, and his will is not free.

The will derives its *strength* from the native impulses which constitute its driving force; it derives its *direction* from the ideals and standards it develops mainly by identification but also from experience. A strong will and personality is one in which the maximum of native forces has been mobilized towards healthy aims in life for the use of the personality as a whole.

THE CHILD'S MORALITY

We are now in a position to look into the question of a child's morality. How does it come about? Why *should* a child be moral?

There are two broad meanings of the term morality. The one is that morality is conformity to the *mores* and customs of the community; the other meaning is that morality is the pursuit of right ends and aims.

The first type makes us automatically follow the fashion, observe the customs, and conform to the behaviour of our social set.

According to the other, right ends and aims, like generosity, loyalty, and honesty, are regarded as good in themselves and to be pursued irrespective of the customs and standards of the community.

The origin of both types can be observed in the child's development as already described.

In the phase of suggestibility, the child automatically reflects the behaviour of his parents and those around. This is morality in the sense of conformity to the *mores* and customs of the community.

According to this meaning, morality changes from one community to another, and from one age to another. In the early years of this century in the west of Canada, horse stealing was regarded as almost a worse crime than murder.

Morality in this sense depends on circumstances. This is epitomized in the jingle of the last war when goods were in short supply and rationed :

> Bertie cut his father's throat;
> Stained with blood his Sunday coat.
> His mother cried in tones impassioned,
> 'Naughty boy! when clothes are rationed!'

The higher conception of morality – the pursuit of right ends and aims – is awakened at the age when the child adopts his own Ego ideal and standards of behaviour, which he pursues, and by which he regulates his actions.

In either case we observe that *morality is the outcome of natural processes*, and inevitably takes its place in the course of a child's development.

It is often asked, 'Is there a moral sense in the child? Is the child born with a sense of right and wrong?'

Many religious people maintain that conscience and moral sense are implanted by God. If so, they can get very badly smirched, for not only are many people's consciences most ineffective, but many cruel things have been done, even by religious people, in the name of conscience.

It would be truer to say that the moral sense as such is not inborn, but that the ingredients of a moral sense are present in every child. A moral sense of some sort is *inevitable*, because of the natural processes of suggestibility and identification. But the *nature* of the moral sense depends on the environment in which the child is brought up and the people with whom it identifies itself. Unfortunately a child can adopt a mother's irritability as well as her kindliness, a father's disillusionment as well as his sense of humour.

That is why, as we have said, conscience, like all the functions of the human personality, requires both exercise and educating.

But why be moral? Why should not we, and the child, do as we like?

The main reason is that man achieves his highest fulfilment as a member of a community. Man is a social animal, and must necessarily live in a community. As a member of a community he enjoys many privileges. Only in a community can man find *safety and security*. Being a member of a community provides him with armies to defend him from his foes, police to protect his property, food from far-off lands when his crops fail, and a hospital to care for him in times of sickness. As an isolated individual he would soon fall victim to enemies, starvation, and disease. Again, it is only through contact with our fellows that our horizons are widened. Communal life gives us the delights of culture, of literature and the arts; schools and universities to broaden our minds and teach us about the world; clubs to meet our fellows; pubs and cafés where we have freedom of speech to discuss all aspects of human life. As solitary individuals we would enjoy none of these.

The community is the medium through which man's life is developed and his happiness made complete. In other words, and contrary to general opinion, only as a member

of a community can a man attain true freedom and fulfilment of his personality.

But if we enjoy the *privileges* which society provides, we
also have *obligations* towards others in the community who
also want to enjoy the same rights and privileges. If we do
not want others to steal our possessions, we must not steal
from them. If we do not want other men to run off with our
wives we must not run off with theirs. Laws are generally
regarded as restrictive; but *laws are made so that all should
enjoy freedom*.

A child can be led very early on to accept this simple
principle. We say to a child, 'If you want to play with other
children's toys, you must let them play with yours.' This
implies restraint and inhibition, but in the end it gives him
greater freedom in having the toys of others to play with,
and leads to communal games, which all enjoy.

Again, a child is given a bow and arrow and shoots it
towards people in a garden. If he persists, the parent is quite
justified in removing his bow and arrow. If he protests, 'But
the bow and arrow are mine! I can do what I like with
them!', the best retort is, 'But other persons' eyes are theirs
and they have as much right to their sight as you have to
shoot.'

In the pursuit of *his* freedom he has no right to rob others
of *their* freedom. If he persists, he is put out of circulation –
when a child, in another room; in adult life, in prison. If he
is not sociable, he must be deprived of the privileges of
society. So much for morality as conformity to social
demands.

Now for morality in the higher sense, as the pursuit of
ends and aims. Only by the pursuit of some aim or end can
a person coordinate and harmonize the conflicting forces
within his personality, so that it is well-balanced and at
peace. Otherwise his life is a chaos of conflicting forces.
Ideals and aims of some sort are, therefore, as necessary to
mental health as they are to social and moral life. Once
implanted in the mind they act as a guiding principle which

gives purpose to life. Whether the moral ideals the child adopts will be sufficient for harmonizing his personality to the full will depend on the parents and others with whom he identifies himself. What about *teaching* moral principles? Certainly the teaching of principles like generosity, kindness, industry, and perseverance is of great value, because such teaching transforms the subconscious process of identification into a conscious acceptance of abstract ideas and ideals, which can then be applied to all occasions. But remember that a child will accept only the teaching of one with whom he is identified, and will reject the teaching of one he dislikes.

The appeal to *fear*, though sometimes necessary, is not a very desirable motive for morality nor is it in the long run very effective – for several reasons. In the first place, a morality based on fear may make a child well behaved; but being in a state of constant anxiety lest he incur displeasure, he will be ineffective in life; for, like many children, he will do nothing rather than do something wrong. A certain degree of fear is stimulating : an excess of fear can be paralysing. This we may observe in animal life as well as in human.

Secondly, the child who is made 'good' by fear and threats may neverthless be filled with latent hostility, resentment, and a sense of injustice. When he attains the independence of adolescence and is no longer afraid, he may throw off the restraints, kick over the traces, and become delinquent.

Our aim for the child should be not merely to produce good behaviour but to instil *right dispositions* in the child; that is to say, to produce not merely a well-behaved child but one that wishes to behave well. We aim not just to make him share his toys, but to be generous; not merely to behave politely, but to be considerate of others; not only to do daring things, for a child may do foolhardy and reckless things out of timidity, but to *be* venturesome and courageous. Similarly, we want a child to be of a kind disposition, not just to act in a kindly way, for he may do this for selfish motives. If he has a good disposition, he will naturally act according to his disposition and will spontaneously be good, generous, kindly, and courageous.

It is to be recognized, however, that a child at first does not think in abstract terms, and the way to develop a disposition, say of politeness, is to get a child to *act* politely. For the child, being polite means doing polite things, and being brave is doing brave things. But actions will lead to the formation of dispositions. The old saying 'An action makes a habit; a habit makes a character; and a character makes a destiny' has much truth in it.

NOW THAT WE ARE FOUR

By the time the child is four he has all the ingredients of a grown-up, and at this age you can with some justification call him a 'little man'. The girl is a 'little madam', ridiculously mimicking her mother as she goes shopping or entertains visitors.

Indeed, children of this age are more 'little adults' than later at nine to twelve or at puberty, the reason being that their personalities are based on identification with adults. Later they break away and have interests quite different from those of their elders, and individualities of their own.

By the time he is four years old, the child has an *organized personality*, with standards of judgement, whether of being brave, or good, of big, or tough, according to the Ego ideal he has derived from his parents. He is not as yet physically independent or capable of making his own way in the world, but he *feels* independent and able to dispense with his parents and go his own way. A boy of my acquaintance at this age got lost in a huge exhibition. A policeman saw him wandering about and said 'Are you lost, Sonny?' 'No!' he replied. '*I'm* not lost, Mummy's lost!'

The child of this age, as we have explained, also has a *will* in the true sense of the term, which means that he is now capable of using and directing his energies towards his chosen goal.

Furthermore, his behaviour is *purposive*, motivated by aims rather than by impulses. He knows what he wants to do, and sets out on his own to do it. This gives him determination, resolution, and persistence in the pursuit of his ends. No longer has he the tantrums of an earlier age (unless provoked beyond endurance by those who still treat him as a child), but is quiet and determined in his actions.

Because he has his own standards of judgement, he is *no longer suggestible* as he was previously. If you try on the old trick of saying 'Daddy doesn't do it that way!', he will reply, 'Yes, but I like doing it this way!'

He is now also possessed of *reason*; so that, though no longer suggestible, he can be appealed to by being told why.

This comes out in all kinds of ways. One is that he wants to know the reason for everything. 'Why does Daddy stop in bed all Sunday morning?' 'Why do you put that red stuff on your lips?' 'When', asked a little girl who was looking at Roman frescoes, 'did women start to wear clothes?'

This indeed is the *age of questions*. As he stands on the threshold of a psychologically independent life, the child plies you with question after question about the outside world which he is to enter.

At the earlier age of two he also asks questions, but then it is, '*What* is this?' and 'What is that?' By the time he is four he asks, '*Why* is this, and why is that?' In other words, at the age of two he is a scientist, at the age of four he is a philosopher!

He also wants reasons for the things he is told to do. 'Why should I go to bed when I am not sleepy?' 'Why should I go to see Granny when I don't like her?' 'Why do I need to wash my neck when nobody sees it?' 'Why can't I go out in the rain? I won't get rusty!'

But as he demands reasons for things, so he is prepared to listen to reason as to why he should or should not do this or that. He will listen to reason because he is treated as a reasonable being. He is flattered at being treated as a grown-up and responds accordingly.

The parent should be more than patient with the child's innumerable questions, remembering that this is his way of learning about life. Busy or tired as we may be, we should try to answer his questions, especially as to why he should do the things we demand of him. Apart from the value to the child, this is a salutory discipline for the parents themselves; for, called upon to give reasons, they must themselves *have* good reasons before telling him to do this or that, otherwise the child loses confidence in them. He may go off to do the things he is told to do, 'Because I say so', but he does so muttering, 'It's silly!' And that goes for the parent too!

At most ages in childhood we have to be careful not to regard the child as a little adult, for at each phase he is a being in himself with his own interests and aspirations. But if there is any age at which a child can be treated like a little adult, it is at this age of four.

Now he stands on the threshold between dependence and independence. He is physically dependent on his parents for food and clothes; he is also dependent upon his parents for knowledge of the world – that is why he asks questions about the world into which he is about to be launched. But that is so that he may be *independent* of them, and so rely upon his own judgement of things. He is so full of confidence in himself that he is no longer self-conscious. I remember one occasion when an acquaintance was entertaining three of his business partners to dinner at his home. In the middle of dinner the door opened and there stood his little four-year-old daughter, stark naked. Looking reprovingly at them in turn she said, 'One of you left the seat up and I fell in!' Complete self-possession!

It is obvious that the parent needs to change his attitude towards the child at each phase of the child's development. At this age we treat him as a reasoning being.

THE AGE OF INDIVIDUALITY: FOUR TO SEVEN

The child, having organized his personality in the first three years of life, now begins to *develop* it, to consolidate and build up his individuality. This he does from four to seven. We therefore call this the age of individuality: it is the age of self-assurance.

It is an egocentric age in which the child is more concerned with himself and what he does than anything else. Sociability is at a discount.

In this phase the child is all out for achievement, to develop his sense of power, to assert his personality, to prove his worth – all in preparation for meeting the difficulties of later life.

This characteristic of individuality and egocentricity is very evident in his behaviour. He calls out, 'Watch me do this !', 'Look how far I can jump !', 'See what I have made !'

It is therefore an age of showing off, but very different from the self-display of the age of one to two. In both cases he is calling attention to himself, but whereas at the earlier age this was due to his insecurity and *feeling of dependence*, his fear lest he should be overlooked, now it is a demonstration of power, to show how *independent* he is. 'Look what I can do; I am a big boy ! I can dress myself !'

To the unsympathetic onlooker this may appear to be nothing more than 'showing off', and such a child is lucky if he does not get a rebuke for doing so. It was indeed a principle of parenthood a generation ago never to praise a child.

But 'showing off' is *natural* to this age, and the child should be encouraged to demonstrate his achievements, since it is his way of building up self-confidence and skill. If we say 'Well done !', 'That's good !', this encourages the child to further endeavour. On the other hand, if we snub him for 'showing off', or immediately begin to point out the faults in what he has done, or on the other hand say 'That's clever!' while continuing to read the paper, he will be discouraged and not attempt things. Alternatively he may start being cruel to the cat, in which he *can* feel effective; or he may regress further back and sit and suck his thumb disappointedly. When the mother says, 'Why don't you get something to do?', his answer should be 'Because I got no encouragement when I did.'

The child's main motive at this age is to feel that he is grown up; he is not being altruistic. A girl of four was laying the table for tea as she had seen her mother doing; the mother came in and said 'You *are* a good little girl to lay the table to help Mummy!' The child immediately threw down the spoons she held in her hand and did no more. Why? Because she was not doing it, and did not want to do it, 'to help Mummy', but because she regarded herself as grown-up like her mother – a very different thing.

Other investigators have confirmed that this is an age of individuality.

Professor Green, who has investigated children's dreams, says that the dreams of a child of this age are egoistic in nature, dreams of power. Piaget says, 'In the early years the child is very largely a naïve egoist', though he doesn't specifically mention this period.

Susan Isaacs says,* 'When a number of such young children are brought together in a given space, but left free to play and move about as they wish, they do not at first constitute a *group* in the psychological sense. They behave simply as a number of independent persons; each is mainly concerned with his own immediate ends, whether or not these ends cut across or chime in with the pursuits of others . . . [the child] may be friendly or hostile; but even when he is friendly, he will not look upon other children as ends in themselves, but always as a means to serve, or an obstacle to hinder, his particular interests.' She also says that this is most characteristic of the under fours, but also true at five or six if the child has not had much to do with other children.

* *Social Development*, p. 213.

Gesell says that 'Five is more a little man than four'. He has greater dexterity than four – in brushing his teeth, etc. He sums up the qualities of the five-year-old as 'seriousness, purposefulness, patience, persistence, carefulness, generosity; outgoing sociability, friendliness, poise, pride in accomplishment, pride in going to school, satisfaction in artistic productions, pride in possessions'. (I should suggest he is friendly rather than sociable.)

All these can be summed up in the word 'individuality'. Let us then study the child in some of his relationships.

His relation to nature is significant. He uses nature to inflate his ego, to demonstrate his power over nature. This of course prepares him for later life. That is why many of his actions take the form of sheer destructiveness. Out for a walk, he knocks off the heads of flowers, breaks off branches of trees for the sheer joy of breaking them off. He throws stones at birds, is cruel to animals, teases the cat, kills for the joy of killing, pulls his sister's hair, kicks stones along the road, bullies those younger and weaker than himself. It is not that he hates the cat, or his sister for that matter, or that he has anything against flowers. These actions express his sense of power. He destroys in order to prove his strength, and to build up his self-confidence.

Not that he should be encouraged to indulge in these destructive activities, for his sense of power should be directed to more positive achievements. He can build up his individuality equally well if he is given creative ways of expressing it. Indeed, cruelty and wanton destructiveness are usually resorted to when the child is frustrated in other forms of achievement, or has a feeling of inferiority. It is a last resort whereby he demonstrates his power.

Therefore our function as parents is to provide him with the materials and opportunity whereby he may direct his energies and powers in more *constructive* directions, by helping him to make things, to excel at games, and to take up hobbies, always giving him due praise for his achievements.

Relationship to himself. He is *self*-confident at this age.

A man walking by a country stream was fascinated by the skill of a fisherman who was casting his fly exactly where he wanted, matching his skill against the wary trout. The stranger approached him and congratulated him on being so skilful. 'Well, I ought to be,' said the fisherman, 'I have been fishing half my life.' 'How old are you, then?' the stranger asked. 'Six,' replied the fisherman ! There you have as typical a picture as you can want of the six-year-old, independent, self-sufficient, proud of his achievements. Compare a similar incident concerning a patient of mine who, as a boy of this age, spent weeks trying to catch a particularly large salmon in a Devonshire stream and, when at last he had succeeded, brought his trophy back and slapped it down on the kitchen table with pride – only to be met by his mother's 'Take that messy thing off my table !' It is not surprising that the boy, full of natural buoyance but brought up in such an atmosphere, became a frustrated neurotic patient.

By such achievements the child of this age also builds up his *self-control*. For in his efforts to subdue and master nature, he is not merely exercising skill in the use of his material, but exercising infinite patience and control over his impulses. The young fisherman of my story needed to exercise patience and perseverance, suffer much disappointment, and exercise a great deal of self-discipline in his efforts to outwit the trout. No tantrums here ! – the fish would not stand for it ! Failure had to be met, not with temper, but with greater skill and more patience and endurance. Thus, to discourage activities and hobbies such as fishing is to deprive the child of much useful exercise in self-discipline. The *moral qualities* thus developed in the pursuit of these natural interests remain long after the interest in them has declined.

Self-confidence must not be confused with bumptiousness, for the bumptious child is one who *doubts* his ability and so must hide his sense of inferiority by bluff. He sets out to do things which he cannot do, and generally makes a mess of it. Self-confidence is built up on achievement.

In the initial stages, it is true, this newly-discovered sense of power, often takes the form of *boasting*. 'I can do this better than you can!' or less pleasantly, 'I'm going to hit you!' or, apropos of nothing, he will say, 'You are a naughty man!', the purpose being to demean you and inflate himself. It may relate to possessions – 'I've got a better boat (or a prettier dress) than you have!', 'My father has a bigger car than yours has!' But it is usually the child with a feeling of inferiority and without confidence, because he is not given enough to do, who boasts in this way. It is because he has no achievements of his own to boast of that he resorts to these forms of showing off. We rightly regard this as undesirable, but it is not the child's fault.

The way to deal with these gestures, therefore, is not to snub him for showing off or boasting, for that only increases the feeling of inferiority and may produce morbid self-consciousness. One way to deal with this temporarily is to turn it into a game and if the child says, 'I'll hit you!', reply, 'Oh! Will you!' and romp with him. If he boasts of what he can do, say to him, 'Show me what you can do!' or 'Let me see you do it!', then praise him for what he has done, but, when he fails, as probably he will, help him to do it properly. This turns his attention to the achievement, and away from his person.

Since they are egocentric and preoccupied with individual power and self-sufficiency, children of this age are *not* suggestible, as we have illustrated with the three-year-old (p. 117). When a father said to his little boy, 'I'll show you how to do it properly,' the boy replied, 'I don't want to do it properly, I want to do it myself!' On the other hand, if you appeal to his sense of power, 'You are a strong boy; will you empty the bucket for me?' he will probably respond. But don't overdo it – or he will look at you from the corner of his eye to see what you are up to!

Because of their egocentricity *children of this age are not particularly affectionate*. But the child will feel grateful, if not affectionate, towards parents who provide him with the materials he needs for carrying out the jobs he wants to do. One must therefore not expect a boy of this age to be particularly kind to his little sister, although he may be so spontaneously, especially if he is playing the role of 'big brother' which emphasizes his importance. A girl of six can be left in the house by herself while her mother goes shopping, and can even be left to look after a younger child and feel proud of it, not necessarily because she loves the child or the mother, but because she feels proud of the responsibility.

Relationship with other children. Whilst we call this the phase of individuality, for such it is, that does not exclude simple forms of sociability, for in his very desire to give expression to his power he requires other children to play with, and this leads to a degree of cooperation and sociability. Susan Isaacs, whose school children were left entirely free to do as they liked, says : 'The other person's part is limited to a minimum role. This other person is indeed nothing more than a pivot upon which the active player's phantasy can turn.' As already quoted (p. 150), she maintains that when brought together they do not constitute a group in the psychological sense. Typical of this age was a boy of five who, when asked what he thought about his mother having another baby, said, 'I hope they are twins so that they can play together when I am busy.' He did not want to be bothered or interfered with.

Children of this age do play with others, but mainly as a means of expressing their own individuality. A boy of this age plays baseball or cricket with others, but will quite likely try to sneak off the field when he has had his innings. No team spirit there !

Susan Isaacs says, 'A child takes every opportunity to compare itself with other children who are being praised or criticized ... There is a primary tendency to depreciate the other child ... In other cases, where a child fails to solve a problem, the problem is depreciated as unimportant.' Only at about six or seven does the child begin to make depreciating remarks about his *own* achievements, and only about the eighth year does he assume an appreciative attitude towards the efforts of others. He is then in the phase of sociability.

The child's play is, therefore, essentially individualistic : he likes to play by himself with his engine, his carpentry, his Meccano, and will not let others interfere – unless they can be useful to him. If he lets others play with his toys, it is with reluctance, and he keeps a watchful eye on them to see that they do not damage his precious possessions. I cannot but admire the courage of mothers who have parties for children of this age, for as soon as a little girl arrives she makes a beeline for her hostess's doll's house or pram; and the little boy wants to monopolize his host's train for the whole afternoon.

There are games, *apparently* corporate, in which all join, but the successful games are those like 'turning the trencher' or a 'treasure hunt' which are not really group games, but depend rather on each child having his chance of being the star turn. In the treasure hunt, of course, there is also a strong element of rivalry, an opportunity of beating the others.

But though they are not social games, in the true sense, these activities are a good *introduction* to cooperation and sociability. For there is some give-and-take even in their individualistic play. When the girl says, 'I'll let you play with my doll if you'll let me play with your teddy-bear !' she is learning to be cooperative. The boy says, 'I'll bowl to you to bat, if you will bowl to me afterwards.'

This is of value, for although the motive is primarily individualistic it teaches the child that we get the best out of life by sharing and cooperating with others.

Rivalry. The desire for power naturally leads to *quarrelsomeness*, which is very characteristic of this age. You can hardly leave such children to play a game amongst themselves without its leading to quarrels : they need an umpire or parent to see fair play. The quarrelsomeness is an expression of *rivalry*, and rivalry, or the desire to do better than others, is a natural and valuable quality. Fundamentally it is for self-preservation. The fittest survive and if you do not get the other animal in the forest, it will get you.

In the next phase, that of sociability, the child's desire to excel, developed between four and seven, is used for the common good. His individuality now being established, he prides himself on being able to put up a tent quicker than others, to cook a meal, to attend to the cuts and bruises of his playmates, to run an errand more quickly. In such a community life every child is made to feel of some worth. His individuality is now used for sociability. But all this comes later.

Imagination. The imagination of the four- to seven-year-old is practical; it has to do with everyday problems, with doing things. This is not an age for fairy tales, which belong later. Gesell says, 'There is a vein of seriousness in the five-year-old which makes him less hospitable to fanciful fables and grotesque fairy tales than children of riper maturity who have a better footing in realities ... fairy tales vex him!' This, I believe, is true, though a different interpretation might be suggested. Fairy tales are really symbolic of abstract ideas, and the boy or girl of this age is concerned not with the abstract but with practical achievements. His imagination is occupied with the wonderful things he can and will do, and so he is not interested in fairy tales, except in such stories as 'Jack the Giant Killer' or the Old Testament account of how Joseph rose to great power. These stories appeal strongly to a child, who identifies himself with the heroes.

'Lies.' Pathological lying usually comes from fear of punishment. But there is a normal 'lying' which derives from imagination. So completely does the child live in an imaginary world of his own achievements that he will often relate these as facts. A boy will describe how on the way back from school he saw a child drowning and dived in to save it – and how grateful the parents were! The fact that his clothes are perfectly dry does not detract from the story – the rescue

should have happened if it didn't; it represents what he *would* do if the situation arose – so he might as well believe it to be true. These stories are often treated by the mother as 'lies', and the child is scolded. It would be better to treat them with a little mild humour. Anyway, it is boys and girls who are not given *normal* outlets for their achievements who are more likely to indulge in these imaginary ones, so the cure is obvious, namely, to encourage them towards real achievements, to teach them to swim, for instance, so that they *can* rescue others when the emergency in fact does arise.* The point is that to a child there is a very narrow margin between wish and fact: imagination can easily bridge the gap. Thus I once took a child of four to a party. She was unaccustomed to meeting people and was very shy, speaking to nobody but burying her face in my coat when spoken to. To my surprise, when I was putting on her things to go, she said, 'I would like to come to this house again!' Not only that, but when she got home she told her mother what a good time she had had, how she had spoken to everybody and played with all the babies! Now this 'lying' was certainly not out of fear, nor, I think, a desire to impress. It is to be interpreted as what she would *like* to have been doing and therefore what she imagined she *was* doing had her shyness not prevented her.

Imagination of this kind serves a useful purpose, for, after all, achievements have to be imagined before they are put into effect. The boy who imagines himself to be a hero is more likely to be a hero. The girl, when she goes to the house again, is likely to do what the shyness at first prevented. In her mind there is no clear dividing line between fact and fancy; fancy leads to fact.

There are, however, two other kinds of imagination which are not so healthy. A child who finds the world of reality too

* Recently a boy of twelve saw his brother drown and could not save him because he could not swim. He vowed he would learn, and a year after saved a girl of his own age from drowning in a canal in North London.

unhappy or too difficult escapes into a fantasy world of his own. Many children, for instance, whose parents are not all that can be desired, have daydreams of having a mother or father who is kind and understanding; or, if their own family are addicted to quarrels, of belonging to a happy family. Such a child may play by himself in this world of fantasy, and everyone remarks how happy and contented he is, but it is not a healthy content, for it removes him from the world of reality; it is an escape. If he has ability he may become a novelist, or a musician, or an artist. If he has not got ability he may become neurotic. Some, of course, manage to be both!

A very interesting form of imagination found in children a little older than this is that of the 'invisible playmate'. The child has an imaginary companion, gives him (or her) a name and a personality, and ascribes actions, likes, and dislikes to him. This is not, as we should naturally suppose, because the child is lonely and has no one to play with. The explanation lies rather in the duality of his personality (p. 135). It is often found that the playmate represents the child's rejected repressed self which is then projected on to this imaginary companion. So if a child is very good the invisible playmate is always getting into mischief, playing pranks, and being naughty – things the child would like to do and can't. If the child himself is none too good, the invisible companion is obedient, truthful, and a fine example! Regarded in this way, the fantasy of the invisible playmate is not so pretty a picture as the parent may imagine, for it indicates a dissociation of personality, not unlike a dual personality. The two sides of the personality should be united and harmonized, not divided.

First love. Before we embark on the 'primitive man' period, there is an interesting phase, noted in many children about the age of six or seven, of falling in love. This is confirmed not only by direct observation but in the recollection of adult patients in analysis. It is definitely an affection towards an individual of the opposite sex, not the same sex. After I had mentioned this in a lecture one evening, a teacher told me that a little boy of seven had come to her one day and said, 'I *do* love Sheila!' The teacher had replied, 'Oh, is she a friend of yours?' He retorted, 'Friend? No! I *love* her!' It is an age when boys and girls vow eternal devotion and say they will marry each other when they grow up. It is essentially non-sexual, characterized by friendship and devotion, but distinctly heterosexual. An amusing instance occurred when I asked a boy on his seventh birthday whom he would like to have to tea. He said, 'John B. and Betty K.' I said, 'And who else, supposing they cannot come?' He replied, 'John may not come, but Betty will', Betty being a fluffy little blonde with whom all the boys were in love. Asked why he was so sure, he replied, 'Because she likes me best!' Thinking he was a bit conceited, I asked, 'Why do you think she likes you best?' After a moment's pause, he said, 'Because all the other boys mess her around, and I don't!' – a true intuition into the psychology of feminine vanity!

It is desirable not to suppress this phase. It marks the first need for companionship and represents a movement away from the individualistic phase and towards the next social phase. It soon passes.

THE 'PRIMITIVE MAN': SEVEN TO TWELVE

By way of contrast to the age of individuality comes the 'primitive man' phase, which is the age of socialization. We call it the 'age of socialization' because at this age children like to be together and join in corporate activities for a common purpose.

We call it also the 'primitive man' period because at this age the child, boy or girl, is interested in those activities which we associate with primitive life, such as camping, hiking, fishing, climbing trees, swimming, playing at Red Indians, and 'messing about in boats'. If we believed in the theory of recapitulation, we should say that this age re-capitulates that of primitive man.

The children utter wild war whoops; they make raids on orchards; they plot amongst themselves; they go hunting; they catch birds and rabbits; they are untidy and they steal when inclined. Indeed, stealing may almost be regarded as a 'normal activity' at this age, for, belonging to a group, they regard all other groups, including adults, as hostile and therefore fair game. It represents a period in evolution when the savage was at his prime, when he successfully struggled with forces of nature and adjusted them for his own purpose.

This phase is delightfully described by Kenneth Graham in his *Golden Age*, in which the adventures of a family of children are described together with their attitude towards adults. It is a book all parents should read.

Physiologically, this period from eight to twelve is said to be the healthiest in life. It is the period of greatest vitality, of least illness : the period when the boy or girl least feels the cold, most rapidly recovers from fatigue, and sleeps most soundly at night. The death rate at this period is said to be only one-fifth of what it was in the first five years of life, and only half of what it is between twenty-five and thirty.

Children of this age have good appetites and eat well. They will eat almost anything and want plenty of it. If they need to be encouraged to eat, it means that there is some-thing wrong, either physiologically or psychologically, for many children try to get attention (this earlier phase having been denied satisfaction) by being fussy about their food. Worry, fear, or anger will put them off their food. But normally eating and drinking occupy a large part of their interest. Enough is certainly *not* as good as a feast to them – they prefer the feast.

The young married man who tells his wife about his mother's 'wonderful cooking' is paying a compliment to his early appetite rather than to mother's cooking, which may in fact have been no better than his wife's. To a boy with a healthy appetite *any* cooking is wonderful !

The large quantities of food which children at this age consume are burned up in their bodies to release both heat and energy. That is why the boy or girl hates to be bothered with overcoats and mufflers, and considers the mother a 'fusser' if she insists. The body is thermostatically controlled so that whatever climate we are in, tropics or poles, hot summer day or winter ice, the body normally retains the same temperature : it is like a furnace, burning more brightly when heat is required, slowing down when little is required. That is why a boy wants little food on a hot day. (A baker tells me he has to bake twice as much bread on a cold as on a hot day.) The child's personal comfort will therefore be the best guide to the necessary precautions against cold and fatigue.

However, there are measures to be taken, especially about getting wet. For the child is not aware that evaporation of damp from the body requires heat, which it draws from the body. He therefore gets chilled without noticing it and may develop pneumonia or rheumatic fever. The latter especially may lead to life-long invalidism.

Though, at this age, the child is full of life and vitality, his *reserves* of energy are not great. The energy which his food provides is rapidly produced and quickly expended. He goes all out in full-blooded activity but has not great staying power. On the other hand, his powers of *recuperation* are very rapid and his energy is quickly restored.

Psychologically the child's mood follows the physiological pattern. He is full of life, and full of interest in everything and in all people, on whom he passes shrewd and often humorous judgements. Teachers are often the butt of these remarks, for boys soon spot their peculiarities. It is usually all in good fun, and the teacher should feel complimented that he is noticed at all !

The child's changes of mood correspond with his physical energy; his enthusiasms are strong, though often short-lived. Hobbies are taken up enthusiastically and as soon dropped, for in a few days' time he has found other absorbing interests. The same with friends : his loves are strong and his hates are strong, but neither, as a rule, are lasting.

Relation to nature. All this is exemplified in his changed attitude towards nature. Contrast this with the previous phase. In the phase of individuality, the one desire is to get power over nature for the sake of inflating his sense of power. His actions are otherwise useless and purposeless; and are often wantonly destructive. The boy of this 'primitive man' age of seven to twelve subdues nature, but *for his own ends*. If he kills a bird or rabbit, it is not just for the love of killing or to show his prowess, but in order to get food which he takes back to his 'wigwam' for his 'squaw' to cook.

This illustrates an important principle of maturation, which was illustrated in the case of crawling, namely, that first comes the *impulse* to perform some action and then comes the *use* of that impulse for practical purposes. Children first have the impulse to destroy, then they destroy for a purpose.

Collecting. An even better example of this principle of maturation is the urge to collect, which is very common at this age. The collecting is at first useless, and only later becomes purposeful. As regards the impulse itself, I went through the pockets of a boy of ten (quite illegitimately, I confess, but purely in the interests of science !) to see what they contained. This was not a select case; I did it once only and this was the result. Ten ordinary pencils, two propelling pencils, one magnifying glass, one roll of adhesive tape, one whistle, one piece of cord, one match box, one inking pad, one wallet of stamps, one small note book, one purse, 'the little reference book', watch and chain, piece of chalk, five glass marbles, fourpence-halfpenny, foreign coins, 200 kronen notes, a key, seven pieces of rubber, a broken pencil top, a pen top, broken soldier, two matches, blotting paper, leaves of a calendar, two tram tickets, two pieces of papier-mâché, one paper bag, one rubber band, six jujubes, and a nut !

This list, which was the result of a casual investigation, shows the extent of this urge to collect, and to collect apparently useless things.

All parents must have experience of the child out for a walk who collects bits of stick from the woods, shells or bits of seaweed from the beach, insists on bringing them home, and refuses to let you throw them away. He has no special use for these things, and after a day or two takes no further interest in them. He then lets you throw them away. Obviously he is collecting just for collecting's sake.

Later on, however, he collects only things he will find useful. Indeed there are many of us who all through life collect a lot of junk and are very reluctant to throw anything away. Our excuse is that 'it might come in useful' – indeed it often does, which is the biological justification for the urge.

Primitive man, by storing up food and using means like smoking to preserve his fish, anticipates the future and therefore avoids starvation in time of scarcity. The boy in this 'primitive man' period does precisely the same.

At a seaside flat I once noticed an increasing smell in one of the bedrooms. A little research revealed a bottom drawer half full of stale bread, bits of meat, and vegetables in a state of decay, all of which was being collected by a boy of ten. It transpired he had a purpose; he was, he said, collecting it for a long sea voyage which he contemplated taking, in imagination. When the inedible qualities of the rotten food for such a voyage were explained to him and a promise to supply him with the necessary food when the time came was given, he agreed to the voluntary destruction of the precious store.

Boys and girls in towns, with nothing else to collect, will collect the numbers on railway engines or count the number of green, red, or yellow buses. A coroner recently condemned the practice (after a fatal accident on a railway bridge), as being so 'senseless'. It may be senseless to him and in itself, but it is a natural impulse which may later turn into the collection of data by the same boy turned scientist. Some of the greatest discoveries have been made by scientists working at problems which interest them, although at the time they may seem to have no earthly use. I am told by one of our great physicists that we cannot do without the kind of scientist who sets about the apparently pointless task of discovering how flies land on ceilings.

Therefore, let the boy and girl do their collecting, useless as it may seem; it is fulfilling a natural urge which later will prove useful and purposive.

The collecting impulse, primitively designed to anticipate future needs and to ensure self-preservation, is later transferred to the *procreative instinct*. Watch the birds in springtime busily collecting all kinds of twigs and leaves for the nest, for spring in nature is the time for procreation. In nature the collecting urge is also used for courting purposes. The male bower bird, a beautiful creature of Australia, builds a bower and adorns it with feathers and other pretty things to attract the mate. This is not a nest or a place to live in, but simply a place of resort. When he has attracted the female there he does an elaborate dance and finally mates with her.

Relation to himself. The child between eight and twelve is not egocentric, as he was at four to seven because he was too absorbed with his interests and activities. He is extraverted, interested in the outside world; not introverted, turned into himself.

Although this phase contrasts so markedly with the previous phase of individuality, there is a direct connexion or sequence between them. For the child, having developed his individual qualities in the earlier age, now devotes his prowess and abilities to the life of the group. That contribution consists of skills he has already developed. Previously it was, 'See how far I can jump!'; now he jumps across the stream to moor the boat. Previously it was, 'Watch *me* do this'!; now it is, 'I'll go to the village for the sausages! I've got a bike!' In all these activities it is no longer showing off which takes precedence, but the action performed for the good of the community.

If the phase of individuality is permitted full satisfaction and development, the child will naturally and without effort or stress pass into this phase of sociability.

It is at this period that *qualities of leadership* begin to emerge. Such qualities are partly constitutional, for there are people who are 'born leaders', people with strong personalities. But that is not all; leadership depends also on qualities of character which the child has developed, and the self-confidence he has gained, from the successful development of the earlier periods of his life.

Relation to other children: socialization. This is a phase of natural socialization in which children like playing together in groups and cooperating in their activities. It is in sharp contrast to the previous phase of individuality.

Laycock speaks of the phase, eight to twelve, as being the phase of the 'gang spirit'; but in my experience with children at the Leytonstone Homes, there were two distinct differences between the sociability at this age and the 'gang spirit' at puberty (twelve to fourteen). At this earlier age the children like to be in groups, but they are very loosely-formed groups. They join together for some common interest and then disband. Not so the gangs at puberty, which are very closely-knit and far more permanent, bound by loyalty to their leader and by a common interest. That is why I prefer to speak of this group as the 'primitive man' type and the later type the 'gang'. Thus it is that on the beach, on the street, or in the park, groups of children of eight to twelve will form together for a game of cricket, tennis, or rounders, and then break up after the morning's play. But while they are playing they are a cooperative group, not just each one waiting his turn, as in the phase of individuality.

There is this further important difference between this phase and puberty. At between eight and twelve, the group consists of both sexes, boys and girls playing together on equal terms with little distinction. Of course, it is the boys who are the 'Red Indians', and the girls the 'Squaws', but they all have their jobs to do. There is not the segregation and mutual disdain which takes place later at puberty. They respect one another for good work done, but there is no excessive show of chivalry. A boy is just as likely to smack the head of a girl who has burnt the bacon as of a boy who has tightened the guy ropes of a tent too much.

Romance is therefore at a discount. The six-year-old falling-in-love has long since passed; the children are too busy doing things that matter. At the cinema they are bored stiff with love scenes, which they regard as 'sloppy', and which simply confirm the view they have already come to, that adults are essentially silly.

The relationship between girls and boys is one of companionship rather than sex. After the break in this relationship at puberty, its revival at sixteen takes on a more definite interest in the other sex as such.

This, then, is a socially valuable pause, for it is a period when the partnership and cooperation between the sexes is well-developed before the sexual element protrudes to any extent in their relationships; and it is better therefore that boys and girls should not be completely segregated at this period.

The sexes learn to respect one another for the various functions they perform; a girl is not just a pretty thing out to attract, as she is at fifteen : she is a useful member of the group who can cook a meal or sew on a button if need be, and contribute other skills which she has learnt in the phase of individuality, for the common good. That and nothing else, from the boys' point of view, is what she is *for* !

The desire to conform. Because of this socialization, the child of eight to twelve is very concerned to *be* as the others are and *do* as others do. As in the phase of suggestibility, he takes over the moods and actions of others, but, unlike that phase, is fully conscious. How unhappy is the unfortunate boy who is sent to school wearing a sweater (however sensible) when the others are wearing only jackets; or the girl who is not allowed to ride a bicycle when, as she keeps on insisting, 'All the other girls do!' Parents who treat their child differently from the crowd, through a lack of understanding or because they themselves have other ideas, are storing up trouble for their offspring – and for themselves. It is true some parents cannot afford to do otherwise, but if so this should be fully explained to the child. A boy or girl, being reasonable, is quite ready to accept what is only due to force of circumstances and not to lack of understanding on the parents' part. They are at least grateful that the parents *understand* their predicament.

Relation to parents. As one might expect, the child of this age is so absorbed in his activities with other children that he is little concerned with adults, except in so far as the latter provide what he requires for his many activities. Otherwise he accepts adults as a necessary but not very important part of life. To the child, adults are the 'Olympians' of Kenneth Graham's book, always there in the background, but far removed from his ordinary interests. Their ways are incomprehensible and illogical to the intelligent child. They are tolerated and taken for granted. The children hurry over their meals which the mother has so laboriously prepared in order to get back to the game they are playing with other children.

The reaction of some parents, seeing the child's interests slipping away from them, is to try to keep a hold either by possessiveness (usually the mother's reaction) or authoritativeness (the father's prerogative). Nothing is more calculated to drive the child further away.

But the mother who provides him with the things necessary for his activities is a 'good sport'; the father who is interested in what he has been doing during the day is 'not a bad old chap!'

As regards affection, Laycock remarks, 'He dislikes public display of his parents' affection for him. He does not want to be called "Darling!" before the gang, or to have his mother kiss him in public.'

Relation to authority. The relation of children of this age to authority is characteristic; they will accept authority if it is *their* chosen authority; one sees that in the Cubs and Brownies. But they will resent all *arbitrary* authority and will rebel against it. This antagonism can take violent forms, as against a school teacher who is unfortunate enough to incur their dislike and against whom they hold a vendetta. Some teachers have had life made so intolerable for them that they have had to leave the school. The reasons for these dislikes are by no means always obvious. It does not seem to depend on teaching ability, or on athletic prowess. Some completely unathletic masters and mistresses are very popular. Perhaps it depends most on a sympathetic under-standing of the child's mind and an ability to enter into his interests. The boy does not demand that you play a game as long as you appreciate its subtleties as he describes it to you. It is still more unfortunate if this vendetta is against a parent. The more the parent punishes him the worse the child behaves, so that he may become 'beyond control'. Yet you often find that such children are very charming when they stay with relatives, well-behaved at school, obedient to their teachers, and devoted to some master or mistress who understands them.

Children of this age love to 'score' over adults even in fun, and every father has to learn to take it in good part if they play him some trick. A professional conjuror tells me that nothing makes an audience of children shriek with joy so much as when he makes an (intentional) mistake – when, for instance, the rabbit appears before it ought to. They feel they have scored off him!

Intellectual interests at this age are very strong, but not necessarily as regards lessons. The child wants to know, he has an innate desire to learn, and he asks numerous ques-tions, but instead of asking 'Why' and then passing on to something else like the five-year-old, he will persist till he knows all about a thing. He must know how people manage to swim the Channel or trap birds, because he is thinking of doing the same. But his curiosity is all for practical things; he will be eager to learn lessons only if he sees there is any purpose to be served in the learning.

Nowadays a good deal of education is given in this way, by means of practical work. In one school all the electrical fittings were installed by the boys, who, by doing so, learnt all about amps and ohms, which had become real things and not just words in books. In another school a piece of rough ground was levelled off in true surveyor's style to make a football field, and the use of mathematics was thus practically demonstrated. The parallelogram of forces may be learnt academically; but it makes more impression on the boy's mind when he discovers that it is the principle by which a sailing boat can sail against the wind.

Children of this age like fairy tales. Previously they exercised their imagination in a practical form. Now they enter into the realm of fantasy. Fantasy is the child's first introduction to abstract ideas. Children have subjective problems on their minds, but as they are extraverted and not introverted, they cannot solve these problems directly and must do so by working them out on an objective plane, by hearing stories about others. Fairy stories are symbolic of the child's own problems.

Bravery and courage are worked out in stories of brave and courageous men and women; the eternal conflict of good and evil is represented by witches and fairy godmothers; the overcoming of brute force by superior wit is portrayed in 'Jack the Giant Killer' and the story of David and Goliath. The boy and girl *live* in such stories, completely absorbed by them, because they represent their own problems. Biographies of great men and women, as long as they are men and women of action, are also of the greatest value, for children project themselves into the lives of these heroes with such conviction that they can have a permanent effect upon their lives.

Mental hygiene. As in all periods, the main task is to encourage all those activities and interests which are dominant at this age and to give every opportunity for their development. As usual, we must provide children with the materials and opportunities necessary to carry out the various 'primitive man' activities. They will need money – not a great deal, for they must learn how to lay it out to the best advantage – but they must have some to spend on themselves, rather than our buying what is necessary for them. We need to find them the materials for making a fishing rod or to help them make a canvas canoe – which they can do on winter evenings instead of watching television. By means of these various activities, they learn many skills – carpentry, mending their toys with solder, catching fish, riding a pony, replacing a washer or an electric fuse, blowing up a tyre. At this age they are quite prepared to have a try at anything. Let them have a shot; and be ready to teach them how to do it !

But when we have shown them the way, we must leave them to it. We must not expect formal thanks; the look of joy should be our sufficient reward. When a boy knows how to make the electric train work, he is too thrilled with the thing itself to express gratitude for advice. He has nevertheless registered in his mind that mother or father knows quite a lot, more than he expected of them – and also that they are useful, even if they do sometimes behave awkwardly !

Socialization of this period is directed towards those of his own age. Psychologically the boy (or girl) has finished with dependence on his parents; he must be given the opportunity to meet and play with other children if he is to develop his sociability and cooperativeness. Let him invite his friends in to meals, and don't try to choose his best friends for him. He has to learn to discriminate for himself : but how can he do so unless he tries out the good, the indifferent, and even the bad? And remember that class or colour mean little to children.

Of all the phases of childhood, this is the one I personally like most : boys and girls are so interested in life, so full of fun and vitality, so natural in their enthusiasms! If I were a schoolmaster it would certainly be boys of this age that I should choose to teach.

PLAY, HOBBIES, AND GAMES

Play is nature's method of giving a child practice in those activities which he will later require in earnest. By play he learns how to manipulate material, how to develop skills, how to avoid danger, and how to cooperate with others.

Play is different from work in that it is engaged in for the pleasure of the activity itself, without further purpose. When boys and girls play tennis, football, or hockey, it is for the enjoyment of playing these games, and for nothing else. Their elders may encourage games because they say it is good for their health or it 'develops the team spirit', but children are only out to enjoy the game itself.

In a broad sense 'play' includes games, hobbies, and sport, all of them activities indulged in for their own sake.

But we must analyse further. For us 'play' has a more restricted sense. Play is the *spontaneous expression of innate patterns of behaviour*. In *games*, on the contrary, there are rules to be observed. In *sport*, we keep not only to the rules but to the *spirit* of the game. *Hobbies* are a form of play directed towards a particular activity and interest. Hobbies may be pursued merely for the fun of the thing, like collecting bus tickets, or may have more serious intent, as in boat-building or fishing, in which case they border on work, since it is not merely the activity itself but an end, sailing the boat or catching the fish, which is the result.

Play. Play, as we have defined it, is a spontaneous expression of innate patterns of behaviour, like romping. These patterns of behaviour have been developed in the course of evolution in the animal species and are designed to maintain existence. The individual will need to stalk prey, and to hide from dangerous foes; there are patterns of behaviour laid down to enable him to do this. The first manifestation of this instinct in the child is in playing hide-and-seek.

Impulsive play. In its most primitive form, play is merely *exuberance of spirits*, 'letting off steam', the discharge of surplus energy. Boys kept in school all morning will, when let loose in the playground, begin to throw up their caps and push one another around. They fight with one another when they have nothing to fight about, and girls pull one another's hair.

Racial play. On less violent occasions, the excess of energy discharges itself in more definite patterns of behaviour characteristic of animal (racial) activity. Watch a kitten as you draw a bit of paper at the end of a string along the floor – the way it crouches, slowly moves towards it, and then pounces; indeed, it will itself push a ball of wool along and then jump for it. It is precisely the activity of stalking prey. A little child of one or two loves to play Peep-bo! and later hide-and-seek, which re-creates both lying in wait for a victim and escape from a prowling enemy. This game is a great favourite and never fails to meet with response. Gesell reports that Peep-bo! is played by over fifty per cent of children at nine months – a remarkable instance of innate behaviour.

Romping is a playful form of combat. It is the expression of the natural impulse to fight, but without serious intent. Dogs love to romp with you, with a child, and with one another. It is interesting to see that, in such romping, dogs may knock one another over and 'bite', but rarely hurt one another. If they do, the hurt puppy yelps and the romping is called off. It has ceased to be play. The same pattern can be seen in young children.

Even in a card game like Snap, the essence of the game depends on the expression of the innate need to spot and grab prey.

Imitative play. While a great deal of play is simply the expression of primitive patterns of behaviour, much of it comes from imitation of the activities of adult people, and this form of play often takes on adult forms. But imitation itself is of course an innate pattern of behaviour. Thus, the child plays at cooking, hospitals, or driving vans, which are not innate activities, like hide-and-seek, but are an expression of the urge to imitate. Children love to do these things to gratify their sense of achievement, although for the time being they serve no useful purpose.

Imaginative play is also very common, owing to identification. The child plays at being the grocer, the milkman, and the sweep. All this is a valuable preparation for life, for children are imagining the kind of situations they will meet with later, and this of course will help them to cope with these situations when they occur. Imaginative play widens the scope of their experience more than mere imitation.

Symbolic play. Imaginative play serves another interesting purpose, namely *the development of ideas*. Play is often symbolic : a child gets a bit of clay and calls it a bomb; he gets a bit of stick and calls it a ship. Two children playing on a veranda pointed to a pillar and said, 'And this is Daddy.' The father sitting by said, 'But I am Daddy, why not use me.' But they would not have it – their play had to be imaginative and symbolic, because these various objects represented ideas. Their own father would bring them down to reality too much. It had to be an imaginary father; the *image* of a ship, not the ship itself. An image is the raw material of an idea. A child can, of course, play ships with a toy ship, but he develops his imagination much more when he uses a stick to represent a ship. His imagination can make whatever kind of ship he likes of it. Children who are always given expensive and beautifully finished toys are apt to become stodgy.

Since such types of play are 'racial' in origin, they follow the various stages of maturation. A child of one or two likes to play Peep-bo! But try it on a boy of eight and see his reaction! A child of eight, however, will play hide-and-seek because he is still in the hunting stage, and this game is far more sophisticated than the infantile Peep-bo! A boy in the stage of individuality (four to seven) will play games expressive of his individuality, like King of the Castle. In the later 'primitive man' period (eight to twelve), he prefers to exercise his energies in more social activities like camping and doing things in groups. Later on, at sixteen, flirtation is a favourite innate form of play, again without serious intent. At this stage girls hunt in pairs in this new adventure. But this stage presently gives way to love-making, which is more serious in its intent, and more purposive. It is no longer 'play'.

In later adolescence play begins to take more intellectual forms, such as discussions, class debates, drama, orchestra, school magazines, athletics, practice in public speaking – all expressions of biological tendencies, for primitive men fought with words as well as weapons. A harangue before a battle is an abiding feature of warfare from the *Iliad* right through to generals during the Second World War. These adolescent activities, however, are all performed for practice and exercise, and are not to be taken too seriously. It therefore does not matter much what *views* a boy or girl holds in the debate; they are quite prepared to take the side opposite to their convictions for the sake of practising their skill.

Play is so natural a function and so needful to the soul of the child that even in the rigours of peasant life, where the child has to help with the work on the croft, he will still find time to play his own games after the day's work. Nor is elaborate equipment necessary. In Leicester Square, one of London's busiest thoroughfares, I saw a ragged boy of about nine pass water on the pavement, and then, with discarded matches which he picked up, began to dam up the main streams to form rivulets !

Play and mental health. The basic value of play is that it gives expression to those natural activities which are of value in the pursuit of life. 'All work and no play' *does* make Jack a dull boy, because work gives expression to only part of our personality; it leaves unexercised some of the qualities with which nature has endowed us. Indeed the character and mental health of a child are developed far more through pursuits outside the ordinary school curriculum than in school work, which most children do as a matter of necessity.

I have long advocated that schools should lay emphasis on the *natural* sports; and by natural sports I mean those sports like sailing, mountain climbing, swimming, cross country runs, and camping, in which we are competing against the forces of nature rather than with our fellow men. If you take a boy out sailing, and a squall springs up, there is no referee to whistle the wind 'off-side'; he has to cope with it as best he can. The same applies to swimming against a current, mountain climbing, tree felling, boating in a rough sea, and camping. The very fact that the boy is up against the forces of nature brings out his hardihood and makes a man of him. Facing a common danger also brings out cooperation, comradeship, leadership, and the team spirit far more than do conventional games.

Such activities *bring their own self-discipline*; they are the royal road to *self*-discipline, which is the only discipline worth cultivating. Emerson says of the education of boys,[*] 'Don't let them anticipate, ante-date, and be young men before they have finished their boyhood. Let them have the fields and woods and learn their secret ... then football and wrestling ... let them ride bareback and catch the horse in the pasture, let them hook and spear the fish and shin a tall tree before they begin to dress like collegeans and make polite talk.'

Games are different from play as we have used the term: they are organized and are determined by rules, to which the players have to conform.

Games are therefore of more value than play in teaching boys and girls *to keep to rules and to respect the rights of others*. They are a good training in citizenship, which may be why so much emphasis is laid upon them in British schools.

Games can develop qualities of character and social

[*] Quoted by Gesell, *Infancy and Human Growth*, p. 15.

consideration of others far better than school lessons, and should therefore be an *essential* part of school life. Boys and girls can learn in games what they can learn in no other way.

Games, like play, are often based on primitive activities. In primitive life one form of attack is to throw stones or spears at your enemy. He, on the other hand, evades the missile, stepping aside, using his shield, or running away. We do the same with strictly defined regulations, and call it cricket. Cricket is a sophisticated form of primitive combat by missiles.

Hobbies should have a place in every child's life and in every school curriculum. Games are *corporate*; the special function of hobbies is to give the child a chance to express his *individuality*. The 'gang spirit' is all very well; but it is a mistake to ram it down a boy's throat, as some schools do. Each boy wants a chance to develop his own individual interests to offset the communal activities. A hobby is of particular value to a boy who otherwise lacks prestige either in work or in play.

A hobby differs from games also in that there are no prescribed rules. It also differs somewhat from play, for although it is spontaneous and free, it usually has some aim, such as the building of a boat, upholstering a chair, keeping bees, or framing a picture. But while it has such a purpose, it is the activity itself which is pleasurable. Moreover, as in play, the child gives vent to natural innate tendencies. Stamp collecting reflects the collective impulse. Keeping pets is of great value; it is a reverberation of the time when man tamed animals for his domestic use, but it also develops a responsible parental impulse in boys and girls.

Play therapy. Spontaneous play serves one very important function, not recognized until recent years, namely the release of repressed emotional *complexes*. Play therapy is therefore largely used both as a means of diagnosing what is psychologically wrong with the child and for treatment.

The little girl scolded by her mother is resentful, but has

to suppress her feelings, so in her play she scolds her doll and thus lets off the aggressive feelings which she dare not express towards her mother. A boy who is made to feel that his excretions are 'filthy' is likely to be pre-occupied with the problem of the excretions of his teddy bear, which in play he always has to be cleaning up. Such play is therefore an immediate pointer to what complex the child is suffering from.

A great deal of a child's ordinary play *is* a working-out of its problems. As a case in point : a child of three was told she was going to get a baby sister and was duly prepared by her father for the arrival. But when she was taken to see the mother in hospital she took one look at her mother and the baby, and then got under the bed and started to play at 'lions', growling at the father's legs. It transpired in analysis that while she had expected the baby, she had not been prepared to see the mother looking so ill. She was naturally alarmed, and angry with the father for not having warned her. She could not express her anger openly and, therefore, got *under* the bed (indicative of hiding her emotions), and started to express her anger against him in symbolic form by growling like a lion. This is not an arbitrary interpretation imposed on her by the analyst, for she was a university student undergoing treatment when she revived this early experience, and in reviving it was also able to recall *why* she behaved in that way.

In play therapy the child is given play material consisting of all kinds of things and people in his world – trains, cars, policemen, farms, grown-up dolls, child dolls, boats, horses, and guns.

When a child is given such material to play with, he spontaneously and automatically sets about working out some problem which he cannot otherwise solve in his own mind, or even express. A Jewish boy had anxiety dreams. Given the play material he set out a farm with a house and fields. Into one field he put one cow, in another one sheep, in another one horse, and then stopped ! He was asked, 'Is that all?' He replied, 'Yes! we must be careful not to over-crowd them!' Why such a remark? Because he was himself too oppressed by an overcrowded life. At a day school he had not only had the usual excessive homework to do, but his parents made him do an hour's Hebrew every night. The poor boy had not time for himself! No wonder, when he created his new world, that his chief concern was that it should not be overcrowded!

An amusing incident mentioned to me by my friend Dr Emanuel Miller was of a child given a puppet show to play with. She set out a table with the father doll at one end, a little girl doll (herself) at the other end, and the mother doll standing in the corner, face to the wall! She also put a policeman looking through the window. An Electra complex indeed, including both the wish to oust her mother and have her father all to herself, and also the guilt of having that desire, symbolized by the policeman – her conscience.

Such play can be used not only for *diagnostic* purposes to discover what are the problems bothering the child, but for treatment, as play *therapy*. Thus a child might be led, in play, to act *cooperatively*, instead of jealously, and thus be brought to adjust himself to his problems without realizing he is doing so.

A case involving diagnosis, treatment, and cure was that of a small boy of three who could not be induced to pass his motions; coaxing and threats were equally unavailing. In play he re-enacted a scene which revealed the cause of his trouble. It transpired that after an operation in hospital, the nurse, trying to get him to pass a motion (which he could not do as he was still suffering from shock), threatened him that if he did not do so his mother would never come back to him. This morbid suggestion of fear in his mind made it impossible to do so thereafter, and caused both constipation as well as distrust of his mother. He had forgotten the actual incident but recalled it when he was questioned on the basis of the play material. No wonder coaxing and threats were unavailing, since those were the methods used by the nurse.

The revelation of the real cause and the removal of the false fear completely cured him.

Play and dreams. A child's play in fact serves precisely the same biological function as dreams, sorting out the unsolved problems of the day.* Many a scientific problem has been solved in dreams.

An example of the problem-solving nature of play can be seen in those children who were bombed out of hospital in Bristol. After a period of shock, they began to play at bombing, of all things. One would have expected it to be the last thing they wanted to be reminded of. But this was nature's way of getting them to acclimatize themselves to the problem, so that, if the bombing occurred again, they would be prepared by long experience of their own imaginary bombings, and so be less afraid. We find, too, that dreams of experiences at first terrifying gradually change, so that finally the child can cope with the situation.

That is why play and dreams are repetitive (p. 159). As long as the problem is not solved, it goes on repeating itself until it is solved. Nightmares are of this order.

A dream, therefore, is not, as Freud maintained, a mere wish fulfilment which allows the person to sleep, but has a much more important and valuable biological function. By repeating our problems, a dream works towards a solution of them.

We can, therefore, learn from a child's dreams, as we can from his play, what these problems are, and get help to solve them and so cure the neurosis.

But even if we do not interpret them and solve these problems, the play and the dreams are releasing pent-up energy and are constantly adjusting the child's mind towards a solution of his situation.

* See *Dreams and Nightmares* (Penguin Books), Chapter 4.

5

ADOLESCENCE

THE period of adolescence has fascinated people of all ages. Even Aristotle turned aside from his philosophical and ethical speculations to make a study of the adolescent. He realistically described a boy's voice as 'the bleating of a billy goat'. He also characterized the adolescent as being 'high-minded', but somewhat cynically put this down to lack of experience ! Plato devoted much time and thought to discover how best to bring up youth to true citizenship.

Growing-up. Adolescence means 'growing-up' and strictly speaking should apply to a child from birth to maturity. Why then do we use it for this teenage period alone? Because when we speak of the adolescent as 'growing-up', we mean that the youth is leaving behind the phase of protective childhood and is becoming independent, capable of going out to fend for himself.

Girls of this age used to be called 'flappers', a very descriptive term, for they are figuratively trying out their wings. Very often, like fledglings, both boys and girls require a gentle push off ! Sometimes they push off too soon and hurt themselves.

Venturesomeness. A characteristic of 'growing-up' is a desire to be *venturesome* – so unlike the dependence of the child and the set ways of the adult. He seeks for new experiences in life, and likes roughing it. In their camps and hiking, for example, boys and girls seek uncomfortable and difficult conditions – and then set about making themselves comfortable in them. They deliberately seek difficulties in order to overcome them.

Responsibility. The adolescent also loves responsibility. The boy likes to be given the job of packing the luggage in the car; the girl, the responsibility of getting the younger children ready for the trip. This is a natural urge and requires expression.

Unfortunately there are many youths who, because of insecurity in childhood, shrink from taking on responsibility; and many others who, because they were their mother's pampered darlings, remain childish, and later expect their wives to do everything for them. Many girls, instead of taking on the responsibilities of motherhood, still cling to their childish desire to attract attention to themselves. *Peter Pan*, the story of a boy who would not grow up, is full of happiness and adventure; its sequel, *Mary Rose*, is of that same (psychological) child who, because she never grew up, was incapable of facing the responsibilities of life and became a 'ghost', living in a world of unreality and escaping into ultimate neurosis.

Relation to life. The healthy adolescent boy or girl likes to do the *real* things in life, to do the things that matter. He would rather be a plumber's mate and do a real job that requires doing than learn about hydrostatics sitting at a desk, without understanding what practical use they are going to be. A girl would rather look after the baby than learn about child care.

Logically we should learn *about* things before *doing* them and that is presumably why the pundits enforce this in our educational system. But it is not the natural way – nor, I venture to think, the best way. The adolescent wants to do things first for only then does he appreciate the problems involved and want to learn more about them.

They do these things better in primitive life, for there at puberty the boy joins his father in making canoes, patching huts, going out fishing or hunting, and preparing weapons of war. He is serving his apprenticeship in the actual accomplishments of life. It is not surprising that anthropologists find that the adolescents of primitive communities do not suffer from the same neurotic 'difficulties' as those of civilized life. This is not, as some assume, because they are permitted more sexual freedom, but because they are given more natural outlets for their native interests and powers and are allowed to grow up freely into a full life of responsibility in the community.

In the last century this was recognized in the apprenticeship system, which allowed the boy to go out with the master carpenter, thatcher, or ploughman, to engage in the actual work of carpenty, roof-mending, or ploughing, and so to learn his trade. It was the same in medicine, in which a budding young doctor of sixteen learnt his job by going round with the general practitioner and helping with the bloodletting and physic. In our agricultural colleges at the present time young men have to do a year's work on a farm *before* their theoretical training at college. The great advantage of this system is that it lets the apprentice see the practical problems before he sets to work learning how to solve them, and he can therefore take a more intelligent interest in his theoretical work. That is also why a girl should be allowed to give expression to her *natural* desire to look after children, and then, when she comes up against difficulties, to learn the principles of child care.

If I may give a personal illustration. I have found that the students at Birkbeck College, most of whom have been teachers and have already had experience of children, and the higher degree students at the Institute of Education, take far more interest in lectures on mental health in childhood than my previous students at King's College, who came straight from school; for the former had already met with the problems and were therefore more interested to find some solution to them.

In civilized communities, it is true, the process is more complicated than in primitive life, for in order to fit himself for the functions of civilized life, the youth has to equip himself with a very great deal more knowledge. He has to learn hydrostatics if he is to become a master plumber; to learn the chemistry of the soils if he is to become a good farmer; medicine and surgery take the place of the simple concoctions of the Medicine Man. But he will do these more intelligently and therefore more effectively if he first tries his hand at them and realizes the practical problems involved. In the First World War medical students had full medical charge of destroyers as surgeon probationers, and in my opinion made better doctors later.

Since more knowledge of more things is now required in order to cope with the adult world, the period of growing up to independence takes much longer than it did in a more primitive community, and the responsibility for such education, which formerly was in the hands of the parents, is now necessarily undertaken by experts at school. But that should not make us lose sight of the basic principle, namely the need and the desire of the adolescent to engage responsibly in the 'real' pursuits of life and *then* to learn how – to learn *through* responsibility, not to learn before responsibility.

Relation to authority. Adolescents have the reputation of being rebellious and disobedient, but that is only because they are setting out to form their own views, and gain their own independence. They are no longer willing to submit without question to the authority even of their parents. They claim the right to their own judgement; they claim the right to make their own choices; to choose their own clothes; to choose their own friends, their own books to read, their own amusements; and they resent the adult dictating what friends, clothes, and amusements they should have.

The nature of the adolescent's relation to his parents is of fundamental importance. The adolescent is trying to grow up; the function of the parent is to *help* him to grow up, not to hold him back, as many parents try to do. This means that the child must largely be left to himself, to do things for himself, and only be given help at the appropriate times.

It is no use the parent trying to exert his or her strict authority over the adolescent. The adolescent won't have it! His natural impulses rebel. The parent replies, 'But the child must be disciplined!' All the training in discipline should have taken place long before this and self-discipline by this time well-established : it is no use for the parent to start now. *The influence which a parent has upon an adolescent child depends entirely on their previous relationship.* If things have gone wrong, far better to allow someone else to take him in hand – in extreme cases, even the child-psychiatrist. If you have lost the reins of a run-away horse, someone else must stop it.

Boys and girls should be given opportunities to be on their own, to meet their friends outside, and to have their own rooms, without constantly being asked, 'What do you do up there?' by a suspicious parent.

When an adolescent wants to leave home or make his own friends, it is not because he necessarily has anything against home, but simply because he feels this natural urge to be independent, as strong an urge as makes a swarm of bees fly off from a 'good home' into the discomforts of finding and establishing a new and perhaps far less comfortable home.

But all this is not to say that the youth is entirely capable of full independence. The mother who has always had the confidence of her daughter need not cease to help her over her adolescent problems. The sons whose father has been their companion will seek his advice on various matters – but it is only advice that they seek, not decisions or an authoritative laying down of the law. The parents must not be surprised if the youth refuses to take their advice. I should far rather have my son reject my advice and find out for himself that it was right than accept it against his judgement just because I said so. He must learn to think for himself.

However independent the youth is, he still likes his parents to take an interest in him and in his doings. He does not ask them to tell him how much better they did so-and-so when they were young; for he looks for encouragement in what *he* has done. Which of us indeed does not like others to appreciate our achievements? At school the boy is lost in a crowd and little notice is taken of him

by masters and others except in the case of outstanding
achievements. But to a boy it may mean a lot that, whereas
last term in a class of twenty he was third from the bottom,
this term he has risen to ninth from the bottom! After all,
the boy only has the intelligence of his parents, this being
an inherited quality, and a little encouragement goes a long
way, if not from the teacher, then from the parent, who
might point out that many great men did badly at school.
To have the assurance that someone believes in them is one
of the greatest incentives for children even in the midst of
failure.

Even a dull boy will thrive with encouragement, whereas
the boy whose parents laugh at or are uninterested in his
achievements will be discouraged and stop trying.

It is indeed extraordinary how many parents – and school
teachers who ought to know better – think they can spur on
a boy or girl to endeavour by scorn, disapproval, and blame!
The best that one can hope for is that such an attitude will
make the child rebellious, for this represents the child's determination to believe in himself, even if no one else believes
in him. It may at least drive him to make good in other
directions. Thus, a young boy, a friend of mine, whose
mother had little use for him, was so bad at work that he
was removed from his school and sent as a 'remittance man'
to Central Africa. Twenty years later he returned to see me,
flying his own plane, having built hundreds of miles of road
as a contractor. A relative of mine was so poor at school
that he was put on the 'commercial' side, which meant
addressing letters for the headmaster. He left at sixteen. At
the age of twenty-two he was a Professor of Chemical Agriculture. Adolescents are 'saved by faith', but it is the faith
of others in them, which in turn gives them faith in themselves.

So much for the general characteristics of adolescence.

The term 'adolescence' is usually taken to mean the age
from twelve to eighteen, the period of transition between

childhood and adult life. But this period itself consists of various phases differing fundamentally from one another.

We can subdivide it into : (a) *Puberty*, from twelve to fourteen years of age, characterized by the 'gang spirit' and rapid development of the physiological sex functions; (b) the *Transition Period*, about the age of fifteen, in which the youth is passing from the homosexual to the heterosexual phase; and finally (c) *Later Adolescence*, from sixteen to eighteen, characterized by heterosexuality and idealism.

PUBERTY

Puberty, which usually occurs about the age of twelve to fourteen, has always been recognized as of special significance; it is the turning point between childhood and adult life. In primitive tribes all over the world it is ushered in by puberty rites in which the boy and girl are 'initiated' into adulthood.

These puberty rites vary in significance. Amongst some primitive people they consist almost entirely of *sexual orgies*; amongst others puberty rites mean the *initiation into manliness*, the rites consisting of the infliction of pain which the boy has to endure with courage and stoicism. He will have his body scarred without flinching.

In Roman times this transition from childhood to manhood was signalled by the wearing of the toga. In this country, in medieval times, at the age of fourteen a boy became a 'squire'; his duties were to be in attendance on a knight, to accompany him into battle, and to bear his arms. All these rites and responsibilities emphasized the passing from the irresponsibility of childhood to the serious responsibilities of manhood.

Similarly there were secret rites when a girl began to menstruate, these naturally enough being more concerned with *fertility* than with toughness.

Physical development at puberty. We must consider the physical development of the boy and girl at puberty, because it has a bearing on mental health and development. Puberty is initiated by a period of rapid growth in height when the boy or girl 'shoots up'. That is because the long bones (the arms and the legs) grow more rapidly, giving the child a 'leggy' or 'lanky' appearance.

That is not, as might be thought, due to sexual development : on the contrary the sex glands, when they become active, work in the opposite direction and make for retardation of growth. That is why early maturing boys and girls often appear somewhat shorter, stockier, and heavier than the late maturing, who are more lanky. By contrast the lanky type of adolescent is usually less sexually developed than the stocky kind. There are exceptions in this, as in all else, but that is the general rule.

There is a difference between the sexes in the *times* of their growth. In early childhood boys tend to be taller than girls and remain so till about ten; but then girls forge ahead, and from eleven to fourteen girls are on the average taller than boys of the same age. But that is simply because their spurt begins earlier than the boys. After fourteen, the boys begin to take the lead from the girls, and they maintain this superiority in height from that time on.

This structural or anatomical growth is accompanied by corresponding physiological development and accounts for the fact that girls of eleven to fourteen are more precocious than boys and will begin to pester them before the boys are in any way interested.

At school the boy who is strong and good at athletics is admired by his fellows far more than the boy who is clever. But even amongst boys it is not mere brute force that counts, but the skill with which the boy uses his strength and also the purpose for which he uses it. The bully is not admired, although he may be feared, by his associates, for boys can differentiate between right and wrong uses of strength. On the other hand the boy who has no great strength but is 'daring' is admired by his fellows for this quality.

Since the opinion of the group is the all-determining

influence at this period, the boy who is elected captain of some sport has unrivalled opportunity for developing leadership and self-confidence. Thus the physical process at this stage often determines a boy's future relation to work and to his fellows.

Similarly whether a girl is beautiful or not (an accident of birth) may affect her whole outlook on life, whether she relies upon it and becomes vain, or whether she sublimates it as a model or actress, or whether she accepts it as a gift from the gods and becomes industrious.

Parents and relations pay too much attention to whether or not a child is pretty. It is unfair to the plain girl, who then feels unloved because of something for which she is not responsible. And it is also unfair on the pretty child, because it sends her out into the world thinking that there is no need for her to do anything since she gets all she wants simply by being pretty. I say 'pretty' and not 'beautiful' for beauty depends on qualities of character as well as on looks.

Many children in adolescence go through what is called the 'gawky' age; they are clumsy. It is said that a boy at this age will trip over the pattern on the carpet! The reason for this is that, with the development of the long bones, the arms and the legs lose some of their previous coordination. A boy handing you a tea cup has accommodated himself to move his hand *so far*; but if his arm has grown half an inch longer it reaches your hand too soon and knocks the cup over. Again, he makes to step over a hassock on the floor; but if his legs have grown an inch longer, he trips over it, is called 'clumsy' and 'stupid', and indeed himself feels stupid for his inability to do something he has always been able to do. It is the same with the girl; because of her hip development, in anticipation of child-bearing, she becomes knock-kneed and so waddles when she runs, instead of running straight-legged as she did before. She is laughed at by the boys and her self-consciousness is increased. She also feels self-conscious of her breast development and in order to hide it stoops her shoulders forward, which in fact only makes things worse, although she does not realize it.

The physical reasons for these awkwardnesses should be explained to the adolescent boy or girl; otherwise they are very apt to develop feelings of inferiority and excessive self-consciousness.

Reproductive functions. The name puberty comes from *pubis* (shame) and is obviously related to the genital organs. The word is retained in the adjacent 'pubic bone'.

It used to be thought that sexuality itself *started* at puberty. But those who held such a view must have been woefully lacking in observation or turned a blind eye to the very obvious earlier manifestations of sex even in infancy; or perhaps they saw them and regarded them as monstrosities.

Masturbation in the first year of life is very common. In a large baby show of infants in the first year of life, the two doctors judging the babies were interested in the subject and asked each mother, 'What do you do when your baby plays with itself?' Ninety per cent of the mothers replied, 'I do so and so!' implying that the babies did in fact play with themselves before they were a year old.* This 'play' is of course usually of a quite innocent type, similar to thumb-sucking, but it is undoubtedly of a sexual nature. The infant in fact is not only capable of sexual feelings, but also of getting an orgasm. This may be directly observed in some infants, and is also frequently confirmed in revival of childhood experiences in analysis.

Many boys and girls of five to seven 'examine' one another and indulge in sex play, just as you may see calves, even heifers, in a field 'mounting' one another in play long before they are capable of reproduction. It is an instance of the principle of anticipation (p. 61). Indeed, promiscuity and sexual intercourse are quite common in some primitive

---

* It is only right to say that Bühler and her co-workers found very few cases of masturbation in the first year, but perhaps their techniques of discovery was not as effective as that of the American doctors; or perhaps the cultural conditions were different.

tribes long before puberty; and at the present moment I have three adult patients under treatment whose neurotic disorders date back to sexual intercourse between boy and girl at the ages of six, eight, and twelve respectively.

Is there then nothing novel in sexuality at puberty? Why, if sexuality is found in earlier years, do we associate puberty with the emergence of sex? It is partly because of the considerable changes in the sex organs themselves, including menstruation in the girl and emission in the boy, in preparation for parenthood. Also, it is partly because sex feelings and emotions become far stronger.

But there is also a *qualitative* difference. In the prepuberty years, sexual feelings are aroused by *external* stimulation as in masturbation, by the irritation of tight nappies, the rubbing of towels after bath, and the climbing of ropes. Sexual feelings may also arise from a full bladder or rectum, and from a beating on the buttocks (which is a strong argument against this particular form of punishment). But these are all 'external' in the sense that they are external to the genital organs themselves.

But at puberty the sexual feelings are stimulated *internally,* as the result of the development of the sexual gland secretions, particularly of the pituitary gland at the base of the brain. This gland provides the gonadotrophic hormone, which originates both sex feelings and the sex cycle, and stimulates to action the gonads or testicles in the male and the ovaries in the female. Because of the pituitary gland being so close to the brain, sexual feelings can be stimulated just as much by imagination from within as by external stimulation and this applies all through adolescence and adult life, when sex fantasies play an important part.

There are other abnormal forms of sex stimulation. One, which I have not seen in books but which emerges over and over again in analytic memories, is that of suffocation, whether at birth, by a pillow, or at the mother's breast. This is understandable, for an erection is physically due to a congestion of blood in the sex organs. In suffocation there is also a congestion of blood : this congestion can produce an erection and with it sex feelings. The arousal of sex feelings is thus associated with the fear and horror due to this suffocation, and results in a consequent repression of sex. For instance, an infant was suffocated at the mother's breast where he choked with too much milk, and this gave him a fear of women. So he became homosexual, that being his only outlet.*

In analysis too, I have often found rage to be a cause of sex feelings, because rage also produces congestion. For instance, a patient as a child was 'baited' by his nurse and got into furious rages with her. The congestion of these rages gave him sex feelings; so he associated sex with hatred of women and suffered a sex perversion of sadism. Both these patients were cured by analytic treatment and are now happily married.

The exaggeration of sexuality may be physiological, due to the over-development of the sexual glands. A boy of eight, normal in other ways, may have the fully developed sex organs of a man. He is of the type known as the 'Infant Hercules'. This is to be distinguished from the type who develops *as a whole* more rapidly, like the girl of fourteen who always told people she was twenty-one because they would not believe she was fourteen. In these latter cases there is a *proportionate* development and they are only 'abnormal' in the sense that they are unusually early. A girl of eight in Peru has given birth to a child.

Deficiency in sexuality may be due to glandular deficiency. This can often be rectified by injection of pituitary gland extract which makes such a boy or girl grow up physically.

There are *basic emotional differences* between the sexes. In the main, male sexuality is aggressive (as witness the bull contrasted with the castrated bullock); female sexuality is receptive and seductive. The male wants to protect the female and the female wants to be protected while she pro-

* See my article 'The Cure of Homosexuality' in the *British Medical Journal*, 7 June 1958.

tects the offspring. Another factor which affects the relationship of the sexes is that the stronger male, if sexually aroused, can force the female to gratify his passions, whereas the female can do nothing about it if the male refuses to be attracted. I have seen a heifer tenderly licking the neck of a bull for a long period, but he remained impassive and couldn't have cared less! That is why the female adolescent is equipped with the will to seduce. Sexual play depending on this relationship is very common. You often see an adolescent boy bullying a girl and twisting her arm while she cries to him 'Stop!' But as soon as he stops she starts to provoke him again. He likes bullying to show his strength; she likes to be mastered. Both conform to their sexual natures.

The *physical changes at puberty* associated with reproduction are too well known to describe in detail. In the girl these changes include the widening of the pelvis (in preparation for child-bearing), and the growth of 'puppy fat' on the hips and elsewhere. This is a source of great annoyance and sometimes shame to the girl, until the slim mother tells her she was just as plump at that age. There is also the appearance of hair on the pubis and in the arm pits (which the girl often regards as an ugly blemish), and the enlargement of the breasts, a source of pride to some girls, of shame to others, but taken as a matter of course by the majority.

The age of menstruation. The data of the *menarche* in girls has been studied in all parts of the world. It is generally believed that girls in tropical and sub-tropical countries mature earlier than more northerly types. This view is wrong, as Robertson and others have found on closer study. It may have arisen because of the lower *resistance* to sex development in southern climes. Of 5,552 American girls the *menarche* started on the average at 14·2 years, whereas in Brazilian girls it was 14·47 and in Hindu girls in Calcutta it was 14·12.*

Admittedly, further north Mills found that in Edinburgh

* For a full study of this subject see Carmichael's *Manual of Child Psychology*, p. 270 ff.

it was 15·04, Finland 15·95, Russia 15·8, and amongst the
Eskimo of Greenland it was sixteen years. How far these
differences are due to climate, how far to nutrition (for
starved girls may not menstruate at all), and how far to
racial differences or just individual heredity, has not been
determined. What would happen if you took an Eskimo girl
from Greenland to Basutoland, or Maltese girls to Finland?
The tendency at the present day is to believe that nutrition
and general environmental conditions have a greater effect
on hastening menstruation than either climate or race.

In any case these are only averages, and even in our
climate and culture one girl will start menstruating at nine
or ten (the record, I believe, is seven and a half), and another
quite normal girl not until she is sixteen. It varies with individuals even more than with races or geographical dis-
tricts. It has been found that college women in America
start the *menarche* on the average of 13·5 years as against
14·2 of the general population.

It is often said that girls nowadays are much more developed than they used to be. The following was given in
the British Medical Journal in answer to the question :

There is a great deal of evidence that the age of puberty in
girls, and also in boys, is earlier than formerly. Unfortunately none
of the evidence comes from Britain, where up to about ten years
ago very little attention was paid to the growth of children; but
European and American statistics make it quite clear that the age
at which the first menstrual period occurs (*menarche*) has got less
by about a third of a year per decade continuously during the last
hundred years. The average age of *menarche* in England now is
approximately thirteen and a half years. So far as we know age
of puberty is not greatly affected by climate (contrary to what used
to be thought); poor nutrition retards the age of puberty, and poor
social environment does so as well. Various other factors influence
the age of puberty, the chief amongst them being the factor of
inheritance.

The age of nubility. But the appearance of menstruation
in girls or other signs of puberty in boys does not mean that

the boy or girl is then capable of *reproduction*. The age of nubility, as it is called, does not coincide with puberty and menstruation. There is a gap between them called the period of 'adolescent sterility'. This confirms what Aristotle long since observed, that a period of infertility follows puberty.

Evidence for this comes strikingly from a study of the Hindu girl. She marries before puberty, but does not go to live with her husband until the *menarche* starts. The marriage is sometimes then consummated immediately but sometimes deferred. But Robertson found that the time between the *menarche* and first conception was *two years and seven months*. Mondière (1880) found that in Chinese women the time between the *menarche* and first pregnancy was about three years, and Malinowski (in the Troubriand Islanders) found that although the girls were promiscuous, pregnancy was rare before *seven years* after the *menarche*. Obviously nature favours a delay between the preliminary preparation for reproduction on the one hand and actual reproduction on the other, and discourages early bearing of offspring.

This same gap appears on the psychological side of sex. Although sex feelings are greatly enhanced at puberty, they by no means immediately take the form of desire for sex intercourse. A number of preliminary phases are passed through, all of which prepare the individual for maturity.

To digress for one moment, the idea of many girls that evidences of maturation are shameful is partly derived from the fact that from an early age they have probably been taught and made to feel that their sex feelings are 'nasty' or 'disgusting'. This idea is accentuated by the fact that the sex organs are closely associated, especially in the girl, with the organs of excretion, which are regarded as 'dirty' or 'filthy'. There is probably a biological reason for the excretions being regarded with repulsion, for they are harmful in that they may contain certain putrid matter and dangerous microbes like typhoid. Nature therefore makes them evil smelling, so that we shall avoid them.

But there is no need for the mother to accentuate the horror. The mother who when changing an infant's nappy makes signs of disgust will not only transfer these feelings to the infant, who will then regard itself as disgusting, but will also give the child the feeling that it has done wrong to pass motions. In analysis this feeling proves to be one of the causes of constipation. The sensible mother who takes the child's excretions in a matter-of-fact way does her child a great service.

Masturbation. This habit, often called self-abuse, is very common in puberty and adolescence. It means 'manu-sturba-tion' rubbing by the hand, but includes any kind of stimula-tion of the sex organs. It bothers many parents – and youths. If it is not practised earlier in life (p. 81), it often starts in puberty, which is natural considering the extra strong feelings which emerge now.

Some people regard it as normal and harmless; others, and often the adolescent himself, regard it as a terrible and shameful sin. Indeed, even today some ill-conceived books make out that it is fraught with terrifying consequences, such as insanity and mental deficiency. I have even seen it stated that it produces tuberculosis !

It may be said at once that these dreaded physical con-sequences are simply old wives' tales, designed by well-meaning people, no doubt, to frighten the boy or girl out of the habit, and by others to make youths buy their quack medicines. They are not corroborated by the slightest med-ical evidence.

The idea that it gives rise to insanity probably arose from the fact that many insane or mentally deficient people in-dulge in sexual excess. It is a case of putting the cart before the horse. It is these people's lack of control which causes the masturbation – not the masturbation which causes the lack of control. You might as well, on seeing a ward full of maniacs all laughing, say, 'It is obvious what made them insane; it is over-laughing !' A good deal of what is ascribed in such books to masturbation is the result of venereal disease

– a very different matter, which may in fact produce insanity,
No! the harm of masturbation is psychological not physical.

We have already (p. 85 f.) discussed the possible harmful
affects of masturbation in early childhood. Where masturbation occurs in adolescence simply as a relief of tension,
little psychological harm is done, although there are those
who are strongly opposed to it on moral and religious
grounds.

It is therefore necessary, in investigating a case of *excessive*
masturbation, to discover what is the mental phantasy or
image by which the youth excites his or her sex feelings. In
early puberty (one finds in analysis) the image is of nothing
more than the feelings themselves – it is purely auto-erotic.
But usually there is a stimulating phantasy which it is important to discover; because it is obviously less psychologically perverted if the image is one of ordinary attraction to
one of the opposite sex, than if it is persistently homosexual,
or sadistic (such as beating), masochistic (of being beaten),
or fetichistic (attraction to objects like shoes or a waterproof
cape). In these cases we may have to deal with more serious
perversions derived from infantile complexes, which require
analytic treatment.

There are many boys who, having been told of the 'awful
consequences' of masturbation, think, when they have their
first emission from masturbation, that they have done themselves some grievous harm, and that increases their guilt in
doing what they know to be wrong. They are worried out of
their lives, yet dare not ask anyone because of their sense of
guilt and also because they dread to have their worst fears
confirmed. They sometimes spend years of their lives in
unnecessary misery. It is often the background of obsessional
acts and propitiations.

In cases where they are under the impression that masturbation leads to insanity or some such disorder, they
may be so terrified of it that they lose all confidence in
fighting against so overwhelming and tyrannical a foe, and
become helpless against it. The threats designed to frighten

them simply make them impotent against it. In such cases it helps a lot to disabuse them of these fears, which curiously enough does not encourage them to further masturbation but gives them greater confidence to avoid excessive indulgence.

Another harmful effect I have often met with in patients is that in infancy an orgasm produced by masturbation may be so overwhelming an experience (for the infant's cortical control has not yet been established) that it fills the infant with terror and dread of the sex feelings with which it is associated. This indeed is the origin of many nightmares of vampires and terrifying monsters which overwhelm one, suck one's blood, and rob one of vitality. The orgasm is thus objectified and personalized into these monsters.* The result is that not only do these night terrors make the child nervous and full of dread, but frequently the dread which accompanies the sexuality represses it, and this repression may result in impotence in the male, frigidity in the female, and sex perversions of various kinds. Thus sexuality which appears in excessive masturbation *becomes the means of its own repression.*†

It is also necessary to mention another unfortunate effect of masturbation which applies to the girl rather than the boy; it is sometimes the cause of frigidity in intercourse. The fact is that in female sexuality the focus of sexual excitement before puberty is external, in the clitoris, and after puberty passes internally into the vagina in anticipation of sex intercourse. If, therefore, a girl masturbates by external stimulation before puberty and continues to do so *after* puberty, the centre of excitement tends to remain external; which means that although the girl as wife enjoys external stimulation and may get an orgasm that way, she has no particular pleasure in sex intercourse *within* the vagina and has no orgasm. Marriage may therefore be a disappointment to both husband and wife.

* *Dreams and Nightmares*, Chapter 9.
† *Psychology and Mental Health*, p. 275.

Another serious objection to persistent masturbation is that it encourages self-love instead of object love for others – it is auto-erotic. Indeed, masturbation often originates in the feeling of deprivation of love, so the child says, 'Nobody else loves me; therefore I'll love myself!' A child whose feeling of being deprived of love has emerged in excessive masturbation may later in marriage seek only to gratify himself (or herself) and not the partner.

These problems suggest that persistent masturbation (on the psychological though not on the physical plane) is not as innocuous as some would have us believe and, whether in infancy or adolescence, is best discouraged, though never by threats.

What then are the causes of excessive masturbation, in the sense of excessive as beyond the child's control?

The cause may be some physiological condition, irritability from infection or need of circumcision, or sexual over-development. Amongst psychological causes is excessive sensuous or sexual stimulation so that the child cannot do without it. Most cases of persistent masturbation are found to be caused by the feeling of deprivation of love which makes the child resort to self-love as a solace, so that the whole of its love life is concentrated on physical satisfaction, the urge to which becomes therefore exaggerated and compulsive.

Further, the boy or girl who suffers from a feeling of inferiority will indulge in masturbation, for by this means he gives himself at least a temporary sense of well-being. But too commonly it is followed by an aftermath of disappointment and disillusion, which only increases the sense of inferiority.

It it quite obvious in such cases that to scold a child or to make him feel more guilty simply does more harm than good, for it throws him into greater depths of feeling unloved and inferior.

Sex perversions of sadism, masochism, fetchism, homosexuality, observationism, and exhibitionism often come to light in adolescence because of the upsurge of sexual life. But we should distinguish those cases in which sexual activities are more or less normal from those which are true perversions. The desire to see the bodies of the opposite sex, and to exhibit one's own, may be against social usage, but is quite natural. So is homosexuality in the homosexual phase we shall later describe, though it does not necessarily take an active form. These 'natural' activities will develop into normal adult sexuality, and must not be confused with true perversion. But if there have been sex complexes of that specific type in infancy which have been repressed, these link up with the activities in adolescence so that sexuality is fixated *to the exclusion of normal sexual development,* and thus form true perversion. *Sexual perversions are the persistence of infantile sexual activities which have been repressed.*

Masturbation may itself be a perversion of this sort, which never gives way to mature heterosexuality.

The repression of sex in these cases gives rise to a strange duality. We often find that it is boys and girls of high-minded principles, often of a religious nature, who are bothered with compulsive masturbation and sex perversions. Why is this? It is because in early childhood their sexuality has been repressed, usually by threats, and they then adopt the *opposite* character of being moral and religious, as approved by the parents. But in adolescence, their sexuality can be held in abeyance no longer and surges up in the form of compulsive masturbation or other sex perversion. This is a cause of acute distress to boys and girls of this character.

In these cases it is no use telling the children to exert their wills to stop it; they have tried and only wish they could. They cannot control it because the complex from which it comes is dissociated and beyond control of the will. Punishment is no use; they would be only too glad to suffer punishment, if it would cure them. Indeed they often punish themselves, physically or by obsession, but all to no purpose. Nor is it any use to tell them it does not matter and that there is no harm in continuing, for to them it matters over-whelmingly, since it is directly opposed to their moral principles.

Many adolescents, on the other hand, are cured of mas-turbation, even of the neurotic and compulsive type, by religious conversion, for that stirs up and re-orientates their whole emotional life, and transfers their self-love into love for God and for the service of others. But religious conver-sion cannot be ordered, and we must often resort to discover-ing and breaking up the morbid complex by the more mundane process of analysis.

LOVE IN ADOLESCENCE

'What is love?' That was a question which beat the Brains Trust.

We cannot understand or define the word love until we realize that love is not an 'instinct' like fear, anger, or sex, but is what psychologists call a 'sentiment'; that is, a *group of emotional tendencies centred round some object, person, or idea.*

The *objects* of love may be almost anything. We may feel love for our country (which we call patriotism), for home (a child being commiserated with for not having a home re-plied, 'We have got a home but we have not got a house to put it in'), for children, for our work, for golf, for art, for religion; love for our fellow men; or love for ourselves.

The *emotions ranged round* the object of love are tender-ness, sex, admiration, respect, pride, devotion, friendship, aggressiveness, submission, protectiveness, and loyalty. These are the main components of love. Love is a 'many-splen-doured thing'. Sex is only one of the components of love.

Each of these components of love has its function to fulfil in the development of a complete and fully developed per-sonality. Each can be recognized as a distinct entity in adolescence. For each serves a different purpose and we cannot fully understand this without understanding what each is *for*. As we have already remarked, just as you cannot really understand the *anatomy* of the lens of the eye or the valves of the heart without understanding their *functions*, what they are *for*, so you cannot understand love or other psychological processes without understanding their purpose. Maternal love and tenderness serve one biological purpose, sex another, and friendship another, and each has its own contribution to make to the development of the whole personality.

If therefore we regard these components of love *biologically*, that is to say in terms of the functions they serve, which is after all the most rational way of regarding them, we shall realize that they differ in their nature, in the functions they perform, and in the feelings associated with them. Indeed, as we shall see, one form of love may exclude another.

We then see why it is that many people have difficulty in defining love, for its meaning in any particular case varies according to which of these components is dominant. 'Love' means one thing to Hollywood, quite another thing to an archbishop, and still another to the poet. When 'love' is mentioned on the films it nearly always refers to sex; maternal love on the other hand it characterized by tenderness; while in religious language it means something spiritual, devotion to God. So 'love' can range from the most sensuous to the most sublime.

What we call 'falling in love' means that *all* these components of love are aroused towards the loved person – from strong physical desire to sublime idealism and self-sacrifice for the one we love.

What then is the difference between love and hate? They are both sentiments, a group of emotional tendencies centred round an object; but whereas in love the components consist of *attraction towards* the person or object, in hate the emotions are those of *repulsion from* the person and a desire to be rid of him.

All these forms of love emerge in adolescence, and to regard adolescence as characterized only by sex is to misunderstand the adolescent whose love is a mosaic composed of many parts.

Freud, for instance, regards those components of love such as friendship and admiration as sexual, but 'aim-restricted', that is to say bereft of their sexual aim of reproduction. He confuses love with sex; indeed he says in one place* that sex is all that we mean by the word love, and makes them synonymous. This is contrary to biological fact as well as contrary to experience of the *feeling* involved.

Let us then consider one or two of these components of love as experienced by the adolescent.

Friendship is an attraction based on common interest or common feeling. Friendship is particularly characteristic of the 'primitive man' period when boys and girls join together for their games and their hobbies, for a boating trip, for a visit to the Tower of London, or for other common interests. Boys and girls become *friends* because they play chess, collect stamps, enjoy the same kind of books, are keen on social problems, or travel; because they are devoted to religion or follow the same party in politics. Many people found a friendship in the Services which they had never found before, and were indeed disappointed when the war was over!

The distinction between friendship and sex is evident from the fact that we may have sex without friendship, as in prostitution, and we may have friendship without sex, as in ordinary neighbourliness.

Friendship may also be based on *common feeling*. Adolescents become friends because they have the same personal problems. This is typical of the phase we shall describe later in which the boy or girl has a bosom pal to whom everything is confided. These friendships may be associated with sexual interest and practices, but not necessarily so. Friendship as such is quite different from sex in motive, interest, feeling, and biological purpose.

* Freud, *Group Psychology*, p. 37. 'We call by that name [i.e. libido or sex hunger] the energy of those instincts which have to do with all that may be comprised under the word "love".'

Admiration. Admiration of others and a desire to be admired are very characteristic of adolescence. We admire a person because of some specific quality in him which we regard as of a high order and which perhaps we desire to emulate. We admire people for their goodness, their skill, their knowledge, their beauty, and the way they deal with the practical problems of life or organize their business. The adolescent is suddenly filled with wonder and admiration for the girl (or boy) with whom he finds himself in love. Hero-worship is mainly characterized by admiration.

Respect. We may respect a person without necessarily admiring him. We may respect a man for his teetotal convictions without necessarily subscribing to teetotalism ourselves. A boy may respect his schoolmaster, though he may not wish to be like him.

Far from being sexual, respect for a person may inhibit sex, as in the case of the youth, who, however strongly sexually attracted towards a girl he loves, will not force his attention on her because he respects her. Indeed, restraint from sex relations during the courting period encourages respect as well as other components of love, like friendship.

Romantic love is mainly sentimental. The word 'sentimental' implies *feeling without action*. We may be sentimental about the downtrodden people in Central Europe, yet do nothing about them. Some people like wallowing in sentiment; it is commonly a projection of self-pity.

The word 'romance' means 'unreal'. So the adolescent girl gets romantic about some cinema star whom she has never seen and is never likely to see. She weaves romantic stories about him; she worships and idealizes him and imagines him the most wonderful person in the world. The reason for all this is that she may enjoy the *feelings* associated with it. She even wallows in the pathos of parting from him, although she has never met him! – and all the time she has a *real* boy friend with whom she goes to the coffee-bar !

The mobbing of cinema stars by teenagers is not personal – that is why these 'fans' are not jealous of one another, but form clubs.

The attraction to a particular cinema star often arises because these stars symbolize, and therefore appeal to, something in the fans themselves.

James Dean, for instance (I am told by a teenage girl), was an unloved, adopted orphan, and he played the roles of unloved and lonely people. He appealed to the adolescent girl who herself feels unloved, and also whose maternal instinct makes her want someone who needs her and for whom she can care.

Maternal love is something very different and very real. It is characterized by *tenderness and protectiveness*. It is a component of love quite different from sex. In origin sex comes from the gonadotrophic hormone : maternal tendencies from the lactogenic hormone. Biologically sex is for the *procreation* of the species, tenderness for the *care* of the species. You may have the one without the other. Sex may be entirely devoid of tenderness; indeed it may be brutal and sadistic. Many women desire sex who have no maternal feeling, and no wish for children to care for; whereas other women would love to have children if they could only dispense with the husband !

What then do we mean by sex?

Sex is one of the most important components of love in adolescence, though not the only one. In evolution it takes precedence over other aspects of love like tenderness, for you must reproduce the species before you can be tender towards it. In ordinary language it is associated with reproduction and more generally with the stimulation, externally or internally, of the genital organs. We may then define sex as that group of functions and activities whose natural end is reproduction.*

As sex must be distinguished from love, of which it is only one component, so it differs from *sensuousness*. We have

* See *Psychology and Mental Health*, p. 342.

seen that sensuous pleasure accompanies many physiological functions like sucking, urination, defecation, and movement of the limbs. These are mainly self-preservative activities, the function of the sensuous pleasure being to enhance and encourage this biological function. Sexual functions also are sensuously pleasurable, but, unlike physiological functions like sucking and urination, serve reproductive rather than self-preservative ends.

Of course, one often merges into another. For the sensuous pleasure accompanying activities like an infant's sucking may be so intense as to spread and produce excited feelings in the sex organs. Thus an infant at the breast may be so voracious and sensuously aroused that it may get an erection, more obvious in the boy than the girl, and even an orgasm, though, of course, without an emission.

All these components of love are found in adolescence; but they appear, not at once, but in phases and ordered sequence, each making its contribution to the final fulfilment of love in marriage and parenthood.

Having glanced at the components of love, we must now consider the developmental phases of love through which the adolescent passes in ordered sequence.

We are too apt to think that when sex develops at puberty, it immediately takes the form of a desire for sex intercourse with the opposite sex. Far from it. It passes through many preliminary phases.

Tereschenko, in *Love and Friendship in Adolescence*, maintains, I think with considerable justification, that the adolescent in his or her love life passes through four distinct phases.

First, there is the attachment to a *group* of the *same* sex, such as boys in gangs. Then there is the attachment to a *single individual* of the *same* sex – the bosom friend. Thirdly, there is an attachment to a *group* of the *opposite* sex. Finally, an attachment to *one person* of the *opposite* sex, with whom the adolescent falls in love.

There have, of course, been love attachments prior to

these adolescent phases, each with its own characteristics. An attachment to the mother in early infancy is characterized by *dependence*. The 'primitive man' period, as we have seen, is marked by *friendship* between boys and girls. In the gang stage, love is characterized by *loyalty* to the group, and the phase of the one bosom friend is characterized by *personal affection* as well as friendship. The phase of attraction to the group of the opposite sex is first characterized by *sexual curiosity* and the *desire to attract*. The attraction to the one person of the opposite sex has two distinct phases : first, the *romantic* phase of *idyllic* love, followed by the *complete falling in love* with all the components of love, with the sexual component predominant. Later, the *parental emotions* emerge in which the family, children, and home are the dominant objects of love. But this phase is beyond our study.

All these phases are of importance for the development of a mature personality. Nature is never in a hurry. By leading the youth through these various phases, she is preparing him for the full responsibilities of adult love. Each of the phases of love contributes to the fullness of love, and therefore each requires its full opportunity for development, which it is the function of the parent to provide.

A phase in puberty, prior to those mentioned by Tereschenko but of considerable importance, is the *auto-erotic* phase, in which the sensations in the genital region call attention to these organs, and when the sex feelings themselves are the exclusive object of interest. This we may term *narcissism* or self-love. In some people it persists as such.

By a natural transition in most people this normally leads on to the homosexual phase, which is characterized by an attraction to a group of the same sex, the 'gang'.

THE GROUP HOMOSEXUAL PHASE : THE GANG

This 'gang' phase (twelve to fourteen) may be compared and contrasted with the group phase of the 'primitive man' period (eight to twelve).

In the 'primitive man' period, the groups consist of both boys and girls on equal terms, whereas at puberty these gangs are definitely homosexual, the sexes keeping to themselves, boys forming groups with boys only, and girls with girls.

There is this further distinction, that while in both phases the boys and girls form themselves into groups, in the 'primitive man' phase the groups are very loosely organized. As we have seen, on the beach or in the park they will pick up a few other boys and girls and play games, but the group will break up at the end of the morning. Not so the gang of puberty. Its members are very closely knit together with bonds of loyalty, usually under a leader whom they implicitly obey. An outsider is accepted into the gang only after considerable scrutiny.

The formation of gangs is a natural impulse, but boys and girls differ as regards the strength of the impulse. We found at the Leytonstone Homes that whereas boys *spontaneously* formed gangs of their own accord, girls needed to be encouraged to do so, but when they did, the gang persisted, as it does, for example, in the Girl Guides.

This, of course, is in keeping with biological functions in primitive life, for the men had to do the hunting and the fighting, in which combined action is called for and where loyalty was essential to success. The women, on the other hand, developed interests of a more domestic kind in which corporate action was not necessary, since they owed their allegiance to an individual 'lord and master', who provided them with food and protection. Girls are therefore more personal in their attachments, for their primal instinct is to get their man for procreation and for the care of their offspring. Other women are to them a secondary consideration – or even rivals.

Corporate activity seems to be an innate quality, for some species of animals like wolves have it, and others like tigers have not. It is variously called the 'herd instinct' or 'gregarious instinct'.

Gangs may be held together by a *common interest* such as football, photography, robbing orchards, or beating up rival gangs. Other gangs seem to hold together by nothing at all except the *impulse to congregate*. You see them wandering about on a Sunday afternoon with no common interest except a certain satisfaction in belonging to the gang. In other cases they are united by a *common need or distress*, as in the case of refugees.

Or they may join together because of a *common griev- ance*. I know of one of these gangs which consisted of boys and girls of thirteen and fourteen who were 'unwanted'. The member of the gang who came later for treatment was an illegitimate child in the middle of a large family who was scorned by the rest of the family. At fourteen she joined other unwanted boys and girls in the coffee bar. In adolescence she and the others formed a delinquent gang, and in adult life organized themselves into one of the most success- ful gangs of jewel thieves and robbers of large country houses. The gang held together for thirty years.

But in most cases gangs are held together by a common loyalty to a *leader*; for even if they meet for the reasons given above, they soon begin intuitively to follow one of their number as leader, to whom they give unquestioning obedience.

It is essential in a leader that he should be one of them- selves, that he should understand and represent the wishes and needs of his group.

That is the difference between a leader and a dictator : a dictator governs from without, he orders, he commands; a leader is one with the group and directs from within, giving expression to the desires and needs of the gang as a whole. Some teachers are regarded as dictators by their pupils, some as leaders.

The fact that the young adolescent will only willingly obey his chosen leader does not mean to say that he will not accept an adult as leader. There is no reason why an adult should not become the leader of a gang. Indeed, there are many Scoutmasters, club leaders, and school masters and mistresses who have constituted themselves leaders by the observance of this principle.

But what is required of such adult leaders, if they are to be accepted by the gang, is that they should be one of the gang in spirit and understanding, and that they should lead from within and not dictate from without. Hitler showed his intuition when he called himself the *Führer*, the Leader. He was in fact a dictator, but in giving himself out as 'the Leader' he was able to command the complete and loyal devotion of the youth of Germany. Stalin tried to do the same by perpetrating the myth of 'Uncle Joe', but with only moderate success, for he had to inspire fear in order to keep down the forces of revolt. He is now regarded as the *wicked* uncle !

It is not even necessary that the adult leader should be of the same sex. I recall in my adolescence the grown-up daughter at a country house being asked in an emergency to take a Sunday School class of young adolescent boys whose male teacher was ill, a task she had never undertaken before. She got on with the boys so well that they asked that she should remain as their teacher, which she did. They even insisted on remaining with her as the classes moved up.

Rebelliousness. It is sometimes stated that the adolescent is innately rebellious and disobedient. That is very true in his attitude towards *arbitrary* authority, especially the authority of those whom he refuses to recognize. But in point of fact the adolescent in puberty is extremely obedient and submissive, *but only to his accepted leader*, whether this be another boy or an adult. Obedience, not rebelliousness, is the law of the gang.

The devotion to the leader is often transformed into hero-worship. A boy *identifies* himself with a leader and in doing so takes on his characteristics, virtues, and even vices and peculiarities, and so forms or re-forms his own character. At this point he may completely abandon his identification with his father, whose authority he will no longer accept and whose character, previously adopted, he may now reject.

That is why it is of the greatest importance that the boy and girl should have the right leaders with whom they can identify themselves, for the influence of identification is much greater than that of teaching or command. The *characters* of schoolmasters are more important to a boy's mental health than his scholastic abilities. The schoolmaster who influenced me most at school was one without scholarship but who took an interest in supplying us with materials for hobbies.

Another of my schoolmasters was the famous 'Mr Chips' of Hilton's novel. W. H. Balgarnie was his name. I remember him over sixty-six years ago as an excellent Classics teacher, but very shy. He was never married as in the novel. But what is not generally known is that he was not only called back from retirement in the First World War (as in the novel) but also to the same school in the Second World War! I had a letter from him a little before he died in 1957 in which he recalled the names and characteristics of many boys all those years ago.

Parents would do wisely to consider this characteristic of adolescent psychology, and the necessity to lead from within rather than lay down the law from without, if they are to keep the affection and regard of their youngsters. There is all the difference between the mother who gets the evening meal ready a bit early so that the boy can be in time to meet his pals, and the one who is always saying, 'Why do you always want to be going out.' She ought to know.

Loyalty. The specific component of love characterizing this phase is *loyalty*. Boys are bound to all other members of a gang by a common tie of loyalty and affection.

This loyalty extends to each and every member of the gang, not for personal reasons, and quite irrespective of any personal qualities, but simply because they are members of the gang. The love of the leader is also tinged with *admiration* and with a desire to submit to his leadership and to obey his commands. Loyalty, submission, respect, and admiration are therefore the main characteristics of such groups.

These factors explain why telling tales bears a different significance at different ages, according to the phase of development. A child of three will tell you that his sister stole a plum. To rebuke him and tell him not to tell tales bewilders him. You tell him to tell the truth when he does things, why not when others do wrong? In the gang it is very different and a member's loyalty to his gang makes it imperative that he should not sneak – it is the cardinal sin. Later on, however, he passes out of the gang age and at sixteen to eighteen, as a prefect, he is *expected* to report to the master.

But the morality of the child at puberty is strictly practical, not idealistic. Charity, for instance, was defined by one boy as 'When you give poor people some money'. Loyalty is being loyal to the gang. Bad behaviour is judged not by the motive but by the act. Stealing is wrong only because you get punished for it.

Nevertheless in belonging to a gang, a boy does not altogether lose his *individuality*. On the contrary, having developed his individuality (at the earlier phase of four to seven), he now makes his individual contribution, however humble, to the good of the whole. He wants to shine; not to show off, for that also is a cardinal sin, but to get approval for what he can do for the gang.

The boy who at a camp goes off to collect sticks for a fire is not just obeying the collecting impulse; he is acting as a member of a community, adding to his prestige, and acquiring a proper pride in making his contribution. If someone in a boys' camp has to go on an errand there are half a dozen who are ready to say, 'I'll go!' The concentration is no longer on himself, though he is proud to be able to do it, but on his service to the gang. The gang does not abolish individuality; it directs and makes use of it for the good of the community.

Nor does the boy lose his *freedom*, for it is only in a

community that we have our greatest freedom; he finds his perfect freedom in that service. What he *does* lose and should lose by belonging to a gang is not individuality, but childish egotism and self-centredness.

Another feature of this phase, as indeed it is of the previous and following phases to some extent, is *conformity*. An adolescent at this phase hates to be different — whether in dress, habits, speech, pocket money, or the things he is allowed to do. Parents should remember this law of conformity and not try to break it. The dress of the 'Teddy boys' with their 'Edwardian' pipe-stem trousers was a clear indication on the part of the youths that they were going to dress according to the pattern of the group, not according to the tastes of adults who neglected them in their childhood during the war. These youths belonged to the 'forgotten generation', and were determined to make themselves noticed and recognized in some way — preferably by dress, but in some cases by crime, which was a means of getting their own back on a society which had previously neglected them.

For parents, therefore, to insist that their boy should be dressed differently or treated differently from others in the gang is bound to bring humiliation and unpopularity to the boy, who comes to hate parents whom he conceives to have so little understanding of his needs. Motherly care goes too far when it outruns motherly understanding.

This is true of the boy who has little pocket money compared with others. It is not that the others necessarily look down on him — as a rule they do not — but he himself feels humiliated in being different. In the same way the girl who has *more* pocket money than the others is lucky if she is not regarded as 'putting on airs'. She is wise if she hides her good fortune. The fact of being different in any way takes a lot of living down. All such breaches of the law of conformity may make a child's life at school with his fellows intolerable.

Hostility to other boys. As boys are loyal to their own gang they are *hostile to all other gangs*, whom they regard as natural enemies. They can indeed be very cruel not only to other gangs but to other individuals – the boy who is a 'weed' or 'lanky' and useless at sport, or the girl who is admitted to a private school for girls at reduced fees. Even the deformed child or the stammerer will sometimes be laughed at and persecuted. It is unjust, it is cruel, but it is a too frequent feature of the gang. Yet for the teacher to 'protect' such a child does the child no good, for it is humiliating to the child that he has to be protected. However, a word in the ear of the leader of the gang may divert the gang's energies. You can best influence a gang through its leader. It is useless to try to influence an individual except through the gang because it is to the gang that he owes his loyalty.

Many adult groups retain the same characteristics of hostility to other groups, so that a Catholic will not take communion with a Protestant, and a Freudian is hardly on speaking terms with a Jungian. Heresy hunting is by no means dead even in psychological and medical circles. Loyalty to his trade union will make a man vote contrary to his own principles.

Those who, for whatever reason, cannot take part at this age in gang life miss much enjoyment and a vital phase in development.

The boy who has been *rejected* by a gang resorts to various means to obtain esteem. He may try to buy popularity. If he is well off, he will try to buy the love of others with presents of sweets; if he is not well off, he steals to make himself popular by such gifts – a common trait. Another such boy will try to get recognition by breaking rules and defying the masters, and thus get approbation and popular applause. Unfortunately, all too often he is mortgaging his future, for he gains nothing.

Another withdraws from the crowd and takes to bird-watching, music, or complete absorption in some hobby, in order to gain some self-esteem, since he can't get the esteem of others. It is possible indeed that he may succeed so well in his endeavour, say in musical or artistic ability, that he will be admired to some extent by the other boys.

Natural segregation of the sexes. Loyalty to a gang, as we have seen, means hostility to all other gangs. The same hostility applies to those of the opposite sex. There is a natural antipathy between the sexes, and consequently segregation, more marked in boys' groups than in girls', because the gang spirit is stronger. While at the earlier 'primitive man' period (eight to twelve), boys and girls played together on equal terms, at puberty they scorn to do so. Boys at this period call girls 'silly'. They are vastly contemptuous of love-making in films, which is 'soppy'. Dancing is equally stupid. Similarly, girls in this phase consider boys rough, uncouth, and ill-mannered.

This natural antipathy between boys and girls at this period subserves a useful biological function, because in early adolescence boys and girls are beginning to be capable of reproducing their species, but it is as yet undesirable that they should reproduce immature offspring. Therefore those races are more likely to survive in which there is at this period a mutual and temporary revulsion. This antipathy is reflected in the customs found in primitive life. For instance, in my birthplace in the Loyalty Islands, on the outskirts of the village is a large thatched house which is called the *Hmelhom* (a kind of Y.M.C.A., but not Christian), where youths went to live as soon as they reached puberty and whence they did not emerge until they went forth to marry. There they learnt the arts of manhood, to make spears and canoes, to hunt, to fish, and to fight.

This segregation of the sexes is not unnatural nor confined to humans. Outside my window in the country are groups of chaffinches. The curious thing is that at this time of year (autumn) the brightly coloured cock birds congregate together and the dull-looking females form another group. Indeed at one time the chaffinch was called the 'bachelor' bird because of this propensity.

Compare this with a 'rock 'n' roll' mixed club in Battersea; there the boys of fifteen and sixteen are all grouped together, the girls in separate groups. Indeed even when a couple get engaged at nineteen or twenty and come to the club, they separate inside and each joins the group of his or her own sex. But by this age the indifference is only a pretence.

Development. This gang spirit, rightly exercised, is transformed into social and communal life. Our clubs, our schools of thought, our churches, our political parties, our social class distinctions are all developments of the gregarious impulse. The loyalty developed at this period is of immense value later in life. Loyalty to one's husband or wife is probably fundamental to a happy marriage and the gang loyalty can be transformed sometimes to an entirely metaphysical loyalty to ideals of conduct.

THE INDIVIDUAL HOMOSEXUAL PHASE

As the group homosexual phase proceeds, out of it develops the need for an intimate friend. The gang does not satisfy this need, for it is too impersonal, too concerned with objective aims and actions, and the leader is too impartial. The boy and girl want some one individual with whom they can exchange confidences, and with whom they can share their problems.

This attachment comes about in an interesting way. It is not that seeing some other boy or girl calls forth this kind of love and yearning; it is the other way round. The need and yearning is felt, and is then followed by the search for someone to satisfy it. This accords with the general principles of maturation (p. 162), that first a natural impulse or desire is awakened, and then comes the need to satisfy it in some object or person. Tereschenko's John, at the age of fourteen, writes : 'I wish to write in my diary of how terribly keen I am to have a sincere, faithful friend.' Then he suddenly thinks of Michael, then of Andrew whom he had previously disliked, and later of Nicholas – upon each of whom he seizes as the boy who shall be his friend and satisfy his yearning. Of Nicholas, he says, 'I became awfully fond of him. I used to go to church on purpose to see him. I saw him in my dreams during the night. I thought stories and dreams about our friendship. I thirsted for it!' All this at a distance. It is the same experience as the later *romantic* falling in love, but at this phase it is with one of the same sex. Recently a boy of fourteen took his own life because he could not live without his friend who was killed in an accident.

As a rule this romantic love for another boy (or girl) is non-sexual, although of course it may take a sexual form with mutual masturbation and the interchange of sexual talk.

Nor is it surprising that sex comes under discussion, since it is one of the adolescent's main problems, but the phase we are describing is not primarily sexual nor is the yearning, curiously enough, associated with the genital organs, but with the breast. 'What', says John, 'is that strange physiological sensation that is in my breast?'

What then is the meaning of this need for a friend? There are two main reasons. First, it is essentially the need for someone in whom the adolescent can confide. At this period he begins to find in himself so many strange impulses, mysterious feelings and sensations within his body, such strange ideas within his mind which he cannot understand, that he feels unsure of himself and needs someone in whom to confide, to discover whether the other has the same feelings or not.

Another reason for such friendships is the strength of the physical urges within himself. They are so strong and they produce such a state of tension within him, that he finds them almost unendurable, and he must find relief : he must give expression to them by telling someone about it, preferably someone of the same age who presumably has the same feelings. So he first has the need of a bosom friend, and then goes out to find one such as John found in Nicholas.

Diaries. This yearning also accounts for another phenomenon of adolescence, namely the keeping of diaries. For
if a boy or girl has no bosom friend, or maybe even if he has,
he pours out his most secret thoughts in these diaries, which
become his most treasured possessions. It is the same strong
urge that makes adolescents declare their love in carvings
on tree trunks : 'Frank loves Susie !' They must tell someone ! So strong is this urge that even many adults cannot
help jotting down all about their love affairs in their diaries,
often to their subsequent regret.

But though the adolescent has the urge to give expression
to his feelings in these ways, he is not, as a rule, prepared
to tell his parents, for parents live in another world and
obviously don't have these feelings. They even call these
deep emotions 'silly'. Said the parent to his son who was
looking scornfully at lovers in the park, 'That looks silly to
you now. Later it will not look silly. But later still it will
look silly again.' So much for maturation !

Bosom friends share everything as secrets. They whisper
in quiet places, in the dark, down alleyways if there is
nowhere at home; they will allow no one to share their
thoughts. This secretiveness does not necessarily mean that
they are up to any mischief – it is a normal development
of this phase.

Rituals. The tendency of adolescents to perform rites and
rituals – hand-washing, tidiness – probably originates from
the same source. In some cases these ceremonials are of an
obsessional nature and due to a sense of guilt and the need
to propitiate. These are definitely abnormal but fairly common in adolescence, for the simple reason that the arousal
of sex often brings with it a sense of guilt. But there is a
normal type of symbolism and ritual characteristic of adolescent secret societies. For there are some feelings and
emotions which are too deep for words; they are mysterious
and cannot be intellectually apprehended. The only way in
which they can be expressed is by symbols or by rituals of
some kind or another. Thus in their gangs they symbolize

the unity of the gang by making a wound in the arm and mixing the blood to signify that they are all of one blood. Music and dancing, whether barbarous or sublime, are symbolic of feelings which could never otherwise be expressed.

'Pashes.' Girls have the same craving as boys for a bosom pal, but their yearning for personal love is greater. It takes the form of 'pashes' or 'crushes' of various types.

The simplest type owes its existence to the fact that girls, at boarding schools especially, live in an Adamless Eden, and their craving for love must attach itself to somebody. At one time there was the French master, but he is unfortunately a thing of the past; so they have to be content with another girl or games mistress. This is an innocuous infatuation which soon passes.

The second type occurs in the girl who in her earlier years has felt unloved; so that, when the craving for love emerges particularly strongly at puberty, it calls up all the old repressed longings. These are therefore of a sentimental type, accompanied by a good deal of depression and hopeless longing – even suicidal feelings. It is love and affection she craves more than sex, and provided she forms a good relationship with an affectionate man, this type of attachment has no serious aftermaths.

A third type is more definitely homosexual; for if a child has had her auto-feelings strongly aroused earlier and indulged in masturbation, her yearnings at this period naturally take on a sexual form and are aimed at one of her own sex. This may be fixated and persist as Lesbianism into adult life, instead of developing into normal heterosexuality. This condition may need specific analytic treatment to uncover the underlying complex.

THE TRANSITION PERIOD

Between the homosexual phase and true heterosexuality, there is a transitional period, usually about the age of thirteen or fourteen in girls, and fifteen in boys. One sign of this transition is that adolescents become very moody. They go off bicycling or for long walks in the country by themselves. Even a bosom pal *cannot understand.*

They are not even interested in the gang which till now absorbed their interest. Observing this change of mind the mother says, 'Whatever has come over you? You used to be so fond of Fred!' Or, 'Why don't you go out and play with the others as you used to?' The reply would be, 'I am no longer interested! I prefer my own company because I must work things out for myself.'

This phase was well described by Meredith. Richard Feverel showed 'the blushes of youth, his long vigils, his clinging to solitude, his abstraction, and downcast but not melancholy air'. He also wrote poetry, much to his father's horror. 'No Feverel has ever written poetry!' he said, and called in a doctor!

This brooding or introspective phase marks the transition from the homosexual to the heterosexual phases.

Early manifestations of heterosexuality. We can hardly count as heterosexual the love of the infant for the mother, for though there is sensuous pleasure in the breast-feeding period, this applies to infant boys and girls alike, and it is only if the infant is stimulated sexually with a subsequent repression that the boy develops a sexual fixation to the mother or 'Oedipus complex'.

At the age of six or seven, however, the attachment of boy to girl already described (p. 158) does seem to be specifically directed towards one of the opposite sex, though in the form of companionship and not of sexual attraction.

In puberty, as we have seen, the opposite takes place, for there the attachment is towards those of the *same* sex, whether individually or in the gang. As regards the opposite sex there is antipathy, which keeps the sexes apart during the initial phases of sexual development and so serves biologically to prevent the procreation of immature species.

There is however one exception to this rule, which concerns the opposite parent. Boys at puberty will have nothing to do with girls and vice versa, but we very commonly find that the boy is devoted to his mother and the girl to her father, playing in each case the adult role.

So the boy likes to play the man to his mother; to prove that he is grown up, to look after her, to see her across the road, to pay the fare for the bus, to see that she comes to no harm. Correspondingly he hates to be bossed by his mother, or to be kissed by her in public.

This 'being in love' with the mother is of value because it keeps alive the boy's heterosexual feelings in a non-sexual form and thus encourages a form of chivalry which is later to be directed towards his wife. It is playing at marriage at a safe distance and like so much play is really anticipatory. It also develops in the boy confidence in his relationship with the opposite sex in the art of love.

In the same way the girl tends to fall in love with the father; she has his slippers warmed for him when he comes home in the evening; she likes to play the wife to him, to take his arm when they go for walks (preferably without mother), and she is distinctly jealous of the mother who, after all, has the prior claim.

This phase is as valuable in the girl as we have seen it to be in the boy, since it develops qualities of character, like tenderness and devotion, before the reproductive functions come to maturity.

One of the drawbacks of a boy or girl going away to a boarding school at this age is that, being deprived of the opposite sex, even their parents, they miss the opportunities of exercising this art of chivalrous love, with the result that when at seventeen or eighteen they meet girls and boys of their own age for the first time, they are awkward and may even be unperceptive and insensitive to a degree that affects their later relationship in marriage and parenthood.

This attachment to the parent of the opposite sex is not necessarily a mother or father 'complex', for that term implies something abnormal and repressed. On the other hand, a mother complex formed in early childhood is of course liable to emerge at this phase. Such a mother complex may be of two kinds; it may be of a sexual nature, or it may be based on over-dependence on the mother, a clinging to her for security. The protective form of mother complex generally comes from insecurity in early life. When the time comes in adolescence for the child to go out into life, he shrinks from doing so and clings all the more to his mother and home. The girl too in such a state clings to her mother (not her father) and may develop a phobia against leaving home.

The other type of mother complex is definitely sexual. Sophocles mentions in his Introduction to *Oedipus Rex* that boys *in puberty* not infrequently dream of having sex relations with their mothers. In analysis we find that this occurs when a boy has been sexually stimulated by his mother (intentionally or unintentionally) in early childhood, and so gets a sexual fixation to her. The fixation is more likely to occur if the sex feelings are aroused and then repressed. The result is that when sexuality is spontaneously aroused at puberty, it naturally reverts to its first love, namely the mother, just as in other instances it reverts back to other perversions, like sadism. That is a definite, morbid, mother complex. But clearly the Oedipus complex is artificially produced and is neither innate nor inevitable as the Greeks represented it. The same complex in girls towards the father is the Electra complex,* but should be called the Antigone complex, for it was Antigone who for love of her father Oedipus suffered misery and poverty. This occurs in girls who have been sexually stimulated early by the father, and in whom the upsurge of sexual feeling at adolescence is directed back to the father.

But such complexes must not be confused with the *normal* attachment of each sex to the parent of the opposite sex, which occurs in the course of development in boy or girl and is a very valuable phase in the process of growing up. For the essence of such an attachment is not that of a

* See *Psychology and Mental Health*, pp. 385-9.

dependent child clinging to a parent, but that of a 'grown up' person to one whom he or she wants to care for and protect.

Between the phase of being in love with the opposite parent and falling in love with someone of the same age, the youth often falls in love with a girl older than himself. This is a transition between the mother and the wife, and combines both. The boy of fifteen often falls for a girl of twenty. She may be flattered by his attraction and play up to it, or she may scorn the attentions of a 'mere kid', filling him with despair and humiliation. Similarly a young girl may 'fall' for a young married man; but the attachment, unless taken advantage of, is purely romantic, temporary, and harmless.

An amusing instance of such an attachment was one I witnessed at a Teddy boy club. A new billiards table was being presented to a rather noisy audience of youths, by an attractive young lady about twenty-three. When she started her speech some raucous youth in the audience called out, 'I wish you were my mum!'

THE HETEROSEXUAL PHASE

The heterosexual phase emerges in late adolescence, about the ages of sixteen to eighteen (earlier in girls), in which the attraction is to those of the opposite sex.

But this is not, as some imagine, a complete falling in love with a desire for intercourse and marriage, for the components of love as well as the objects of love change from time to time. At one time sex curiosity predominates, at another the desire to attract, at another romance, and only later the urge for sex intercourse. Ultimately all combine to form the climax of love which we call 'falling in love' and in which all the components of love are united in the desire for friendship, for companionship, for sex love, for children, and for family life. There is a gradual development both as regards the *object* of love and in the *nature* of that love.

We shall describe three main phases: the 'polygamous' phase; the 'romantic' phase; falling in love.

THE POLYGAMOUS PHASE

The 'polygamous' phase, at about sixteen years of age, is one in which both boy and girl are attached to a *number* of *the opposite sex*, but of the *same age*.

It differs from earlier phases not only in the objects of love but in the *components of love*. In the 'primitive man' period it was friendship; in this 'polygamous' phase the components of love which are dominant are sex curiosity and the desire to attract.

The onset of this polygamous phase has been well described by Maeterlinck in his play *The Betrothal*. In this play, Tyl-Tyl of his previous play *The Blue Bird* has now reached the age of sixteen years. He wakes on the morning of his birthday to find himself in love with every girl in the village – the Burgomaster's daughter, the Smith's daughter, the Beggar's daughter – every one of them. This polygamous phase is very familiar to those who have to deal with youths. The boy feels no inconsistency in being in love with a number of girls at the same time, to each of whom he writes love letters pledging life-long devotion ! So the girl has a number of boy friends; she may be in love with a favourite uncle, a friend of her brother's, and the latest crooner to whom she writes adoring letters. Indeed I know a young lady who was *engaged* to three men at once ! It speaks well for the ingenuity of youth that she was able to extract herself without hurt !

To quote from Tereschenko again, his John has 'a peculiar feeling on seeing some girls in uniform, and on talking to a strange girl who shows him the way and from whom he tries not to part'. He crosses over the street in order to pass two schoolgirls. He blames himself that previously he used to laugh at dancing, decides to learn, but says they will tease him. He is attracted to a number of girls at once – to girls in general. 'There are many schoolgirls, dear little ones in their little brown frocks.'

Teasing. This phase is often ushered in by teasing. For a boy or girl to be attracted to one of the opposite sex is a surrender – a shameful capitulation. Has not the boy till now regarded the girl as silly, the girl looked on the boy as rough and uncouth? To fall in love with such a person is a complete reversal of the former attitude, and most embarrassing! What can they do about it? They cannot bring themselves to admit it. What they do is to tease other boys and girls, to show that they themselves at least have not fallen to so fateful an attraction! We may be sure that when a boy begins to tease other boys about girls, it is because he is himself on the point of capitulation. The teasing is designed to hide his own feelings of which he is still half-ashamed, but which nonetheless obsess him.

Teasing by a parent of a youth's calf-love is a different matter and must be exercised with caution. A little teasing does no harm and prevents the adolescent taking his love affairs too seriously. But it may easily go too far, for teasing a child about a subject which he or she takes very seriously may wound. Worse still, it might check a perfectly normal phase of adolescent love and send it underground to take less desirable forms. On the whole it is best left alone for natural development to take its course. Regard it as perfectly natural that the boy should bring Mary home one week and Phyllis the next! – that Bessie is 'gone' on Sydney one week and says he is stupid or 'not nice' the next!

The polygamous phase is no doubt a throw-back to an earlier phase of evolution; for most animals and many primitive tribes are promiscuous. Multitudinous offspring were necessary, since only a few survived. In the higher stages of evolution, the development of a strong maternal instinct for the care of the young makes polygamy less necessary, while monogamy has the advantages of strengthening family life, which is the best atmosphere for a child to grow up in.

This flirtatious phase in adolescence, even if biologically a throwback, still has its value, for it enables a boy or girl to choose the right mate. A girl is attracted to a handsome youth but then finds he is vain and thinks more of himself than of her. Then she falls for a most attentive and flattering youth but discovers that he is equally attentive to other girls. Then she is attracted to a boy who is kindness itself, but finds he is too sapless : she wants a more robust mate. So too a boy falls for a pretty face, but finds its possessor is 'dumb', has no ideas, and can't discuss anything; another is capable, but unfortunately bossy; another is very sexually attractive, but vain and selfish. Parents should realize, therefore, the importance of allowing many boy and girl friends, for only through this experience can the right partner be chosen. The golden rule of allowing opportunity for the natural expression of each phase applies here also.

But it would be a mistake to regard this calf-love as a true 'falling in love' : nor does it take the form of an immediate desire for sex intercourse as opposed to sexual curiosity. Nature manages things in her own way, for she has other qualities to develop in both the boy and the girl before true love takes place.

Sex curiosity. A typical component of love at this polygamous phase is sex curiosity. This is probably accentuated in our culture because of what those who approve of it call 'modesty', and those who disapprove call 'prudery'.

This is the age when boys and girls like to sit on the beach and watch others dressing and undressing and to look through cracks in the bathroom door – the 'Peeping Tom' complex. They are curious about the physical make-up and anatomy of the opposite sex, even though at an earlier age boys and girls of the same family bathed together and are familiar with how members of the other sex are made. Indeed, sex curiosity is, as we have seen, very characteristic of the much younger child, say of six or seven. But the curiosity at that age is mainly *anatomical* – how the other sex is made. In adolescence the curiosity is obviously not merely anatomical. The adolescent is interested in the *physiology* of sex, that is to say the functions of sex, how it works. Girls in particular are interested in how babies come, and what part the man plays. In one investigation, in which a number of girls of fourteen were free to discuss any problem and ask any questions, it was found that forty per cent of their questions related to reproductive functions in one form or another. That is quite natural and desirable; there is nothing abnormal about such curiosity. Given full and natural explanations, this curiosity is satisfied.

But there seems little doubt that the main reason for sex curiosity in adolescence is on account of the *feelings and emotions* aroused, for such feelings are both strange and pleasurable. Indeed the interest in the anatomy and physiology of sex is largely due to the pleasurable emotions which such contemplation arouses. Many medical students, who know all about the anatomy and physiology of sex, are still interested in nude shows.

Sex instruction to satisfy the sex curiosity is, of course, desirable. But do not imagine that sex knowledge is going to solve all sex problems. It is true that ignorance of sex often leads to shocks and unhappiness, but the reverse does not hold true that to avoid difficulties all that we require is sex knowledge. Indeed sex instruction has in not a few cases started undesirable habits.

Knowledge of the anatomy and physiology of sex is not enough. It needs to be explained to youths *why* nature makes the sexual emotions so strong and so pleasurable – namely that she wants to take no risks as regards the continuation of the species – and how this necessarily gives rise to emotional problems in civilized life where the problem is over-population rather than under-population, but where, nevertheless, the urge remains.

It is also of the greatest importance that in sex instruction emphasis should be laid on *the purpose and biological function of sex*, namely the begetting of children. That sounds obvious, but it is curious how often this is forgotten, or omitted, by those who talk and write about sex. I am informed by a woman doctor who deals with girls that a number of girls with sexual difficulties are straightened out completely by being brought to realize that sex is not simply a passion, nor pleasant indulgence, nor indeed something shameful, but that its primary and biological purpose is to bear children.

But to return : in this polygamous phase then it is *curiosity* about all these things, whether anatomical, physiological, or emotional, which dominates, rather than a desire for sex intercourse as such. The object of excitement on the beach, for instance, is the *sight* of the other person, which is the stimulus of the sex feelings; and if the youth is excited to the point of masturbation at night, his fantasies are of seeing girls undressing and not usually at this stage of sexual union with them.

The desire to attract. Another characteristic of the polygamous phase, apart from sex curiosity but complementary to it, is the desire of every normal boy and girl to be attractive to the opposite sex. The boy wants to show off his strength and manliness; the girl wants to be beautiful and attract the male. Even the South Sea Island girl, who wears practically nothing at all, adorns her hair with flowers and her arms with shell bracelets. In my boyhood I often saw native girls placing the insect called the Praying Mantis on their eyebrows, in order to have the eyebrows clipped, so that they would grow again more strongly and enhance their beauty.

The desire to call attention to oneself is of course nothing new. We have met it in the infant who calls attention to itself by crying when in need of protection. At the age of four to seven, the child calls out, 'Watch me do this !' but in a purely egoistic way to demonstrate its individuality and achievements. In puberty the desire is to get the approval of the gang; but this must be for some service to the gang and not for self-aggrandizement. Even in later adolescence the boy is at first as much out to get the admiration of other boys for his prowess in football or climbing, as he is to get it from the girls. Similarly at first girls like to be admired by other girls for being pretty as much as by boys. Later on, women dress, we are told, not to attract men, but to compete with other women! The child who, however wanting in looks, gets love and affection from her parents, will grow up to be happy, and will be attractive in spite of her features. She can even make fun of her large mouth because her confidence lies elsewhere.

Every girl in love, like every bride, is beautiful, and that is because she is happy. We speak of her as 'radiant'.

At this phase in adolescence, then, the one object is to attract, to make conquests. We must not make the mistake here of reading our own interpretation into the youth's behaviour. We who study these phases realize full well that the biological significance of the need to attract is to ensure procreation. But for the adolescent, the desire to attract stands in its own right, as it were, irrespective of any desire for sex union. Presently we shall probably discover some hormone which stimulates it.

The power to attract as a prelude to procreation is found amongst plants and lower animals as well as in man. The colour and smell of flowers attract the insects which pollinate them; the colour, display, and song of birds attract the mate. Not that there is any *intention* on the part of the flower or bird to attract, and still less is there any awareness that it leads to procreation

In the boy or girl of this age, however, the desire to attract is conscious and deliberate but motiveless. A girl's first preoccupation at a dance at this age is, 'Do I look pretty?' She may be provocative and display her physical charms, but will be insulted at any suggestion of sexual relations, and will break off with a boy who becomes too amorous. Her rejection is not because of prudishness, but because she genuinely does not yet want intercourse. Her sole desire is at present to attract and to know that she can attract.

That is why some mothers feel it advisable to tell their daughters that their provocative desire to attract, which to the girl is an end in itself, may mean something very different to the older boy of eighteen or nineteen, who may thereby be sexually aroused towards her, and demand of her what she is not prepared to give. Murders have been committed as a result of such frustration.

In maintaining that there is a phase in which the desire to attract is the one main desire in the adolescent, we must make room for many exceptions. Some boys and girls have been so often snubbed earlier that they are markedly shy and the last thing they desire is to attract attention; but that does not mean that the desire is not latently there. On the other hand, in analysis we find that there are boys and girls who have been prematurely sexually stimulated in earlier childhood and are therefore naturally preoccupied with sex – even sex intercourse – all through adolescence. There are also a few who are constitutionally highly-sexed, their sexuality being physiologically over-developed. There are also those who have felt deprived of love and whose craving for love is concentrated upon sentimental longings. But these abnormal manifestations of love should not blind us to its natural and healthy development.

What is the purpose of all this? For in nature, the characteristics are not developed unless they serve some useful end. The biological value of this phase is obvious. The girl's attraction to a strong and handsome man is nature's way of enabling her to choose a strong mate to breed with, and a protector to care for her while she bears and protects her offspring. So the boy for his part sets out to display his strength to prove himself a worthy mate *capable* of giving her the protection.

But what about the girl who attracts by means of her beauty. Why this insistence on *beauty*? Why does nature make the male so attracted to the physical beauty of the female, and the female so anxious to be beautiful? What is it about beauty *biologically* that it should be given so high a place in courtship?

It is in the main that beauty goes with health. In essence the beautiful girl is the healthy girl and the healthy girl is a beautiful girl. In seeking out beauty in his mate the youth

is consciously or unconsciously seeking out the healthy
mate.

Consider for a moment what are the attractive features
of a beautiful girl. A good complexion is obviously a sign of
a good circulation, and all the cosmetics in the world would
not give a girl the lovely bloom which comes from good
health. A clear skin represents a healthy blood-stream free
from toxins; good teeth, red lips, bright eyes, luxurious but
fine and glossy hair all come from good health and a good
supply of natural vitamins. Indeed you may judge of your
health by the state of your skin and your hair : illness makes
your hair lank and your skin flabby. A good carriage and
graceful walk come from complete muscular poise especially
of the abdominal muscles. Some of the most beautiful and
graceful walkers are the women of the more primitive tribes
who work in the fields and so keep healthy. One of the most
beautiful artist's models I know is a market gardener. Such
girls do not need to diet to keep slim, or to 'cultivate' their
walk, or to do tummy exercises; their gracefulness comes to
them by their health. Exercise and fresh air would save a
large proportion of the many millions of pounds girls now
spend on cosmetics.

Again, there is a beauty of expression that comes from
happiness. Happiness and health go together. In general, the
healthy girl is the happy girl; and the happy girl is the
healthy girl. The unhappy girl soon becomes unhealthy, for
her appetite and her general metabolism suffer. Happiness
stimulates all the metabolic processes of our bodies (circulation, respiration, and digestion), and this in turn makes the
girl attractive.

Health and happiness make an attractive girl, and they
also make of her a desirable mate. There is a biological basis
for aesthetics.

We may point out, *en passant*, that one of the advantages
of the endless changes in women's fashions in clothes is that
they give every girl a chance.

The parents' attitude towards a child's looks is a matter of considerable importance. It is natural for a mother to be proud of her daughter's good looks (especially if she takes after the mother), but it is a mistake to make her too conscious of them. For a child constantly to hear it said, 'What a pretty child', is unfair both to herself and to the ugly child. It is not fair to the ugly child because she feels rejected for something for which she is not responsible, and develops the further handicap of an inferiority complex. It is also unfair to the pretty child to be constantly told she is pretty because she then feels that that is all that is necessary and fails to develop other characteristics without which she cannot in later life make a mature relationship.

THE MONOGAMOUS PHASE: ROMANCE

It is said that man is a polygamous animal. That is true. But, like many lower animals (the gorilla, for instance), he is also a monogamous animal. He passes through the polygamous phase before arriving at the monogamous phase.

But there are different stages even in the monogamous phase. It is at first purely *romantic*; then comes a *complete falling in love*, with devotion for the one person and a strong desire for sex relations. This is then followed by a desire for the permanent relationship of marriage, for a home of one's own independent of parents, and for the establishment of a family. That, biologically speaking, is the fulfilment of life.

From the attraction to the group of the opposite sex, the boy suddenly finds himself attracted to the one and only girl, and the girl to the one boy. They have no thoughts for the others who now appear quite ordinary compared with the object of their love.

Let me again take a quotation from Tereschenko by way of illustration. At this stage John was fifteen years of age, and Elizabeth was just over thirteen. He had previously disliked her, especially when she kissed him on one occasion (an example of the boy's repugnance already mentioned, but

also of the girl's earlier maturation). Then he fell completely
for her. 'It happened one day : I took a walk alone with a
strange girl ! That night I slept very badly : all the time I
was thinking of her, I felt fine !'

And again : 'I am living through a very strange period.
The fact is I see a collapse of all my principles and convictions (his antipathy to the opposite sex), and this collapse does
not cause me any unpleasant feelings !'

Sitting with Elizabeth : 'I felt that all the time I had a
silly look. I even made an attempt to make my face more
sensible, but at once it would be silly again. I had changed
entirely. A new thing that I have not even suspected has now
taken possession of me. Wonderful Betty. Wonderful !
Wonderful !'

Meredith's *The Ordeal of Richard Feverel* gives a vivid
description of these phases of boy life. Richard has a bosom
pal Ripton, and has a scorn of girls. When he is in trouble
with a farmer for poaching, he reports to Ripton : '. . . to
complete it he brought in a little girl and says to me she's
your best friend and told me to thank her. A little girl of
twelve ! What business had she to mix herself up in my
matters. Depend on it, Ripton, whenever there is mischief
there are girls, I think. She had the insolence to notice my
face, and ask me not to be unhappy. I was polite, of course,
but I would not look at her.'

Then comes the idyllic phase. Two or three years later,
rowing in the early morning, he comes across a girl on the
bank, her mouth stained with the blackberries she is picking
(the same girl he had scorned). 'What is your name ?' said his
mouth while his eyes added, 'Oh ! Wonderful creature ! How
came you to enrich the earth ?' 'And you have grown to
this,' he said. 'The little girl I saw there ! You are very
beautiful !' He writes screeds of poetry to her, most of which
he tears up : it could never express half his feelings ! It is
then that his father, Sir Austen, scornfully remarks : 'The
Feverels never write poety !' and has a doctor examine him !

The quotations from John's diary and from *Richard*

Feverel just given are a true expression of romantic love. It is idealistic; it idealizes its object. It has little relation to reality.

In modern life the distinction between the polygamous and the monogamous phases is expressed in the common language of adolescence. The 'polygamous' phase is called 'dating' – the more 'dates', and the greater number of boys and girls 'dated', the greater the prestige. The monogamous phase is called 'going steady'. The boy or girl is not necessarily 'in love' with his 'date'.

The chief component of love expressed at this age is *adoration*. The girl who yesterday appeared to the boy to be a stupid female, like any other girl, suddenly becomes adorable! He cannot understand how he was so blind to her charms before, and it is equally incomprehensible how all other boys are not equally affected with them. They actually call her 'Fatty'! Similarly the pimply youth becomes to the girl a perfect Adonis, the handsomest conceivable. In her imagination his muscles expand far beyond the pads of his shoulders, and his personality takes on the most god-like proportions!

This idealization may be part of the general idealism which is characteristic of this period, and which I refer to later. But it may also be largely a 'projection' of the adolescents' own feelings and sensations. These are felt by them to be the most wonderful things they have ever experienced; and they transfigure the whole world for them. It follows that the person who is able to arouse these feelings in them is also endowed with the same qualities and must also be wonderful.

This romantic love is often accompanied by loss of appetite and the love-sick swain may literally lose weight and 'pine away'. This is not because he 'feeds on love' as the poet would have us believe, but for a more mundane reason, namely, that any strong emotion such as fear, anger, or love, stops the gastric juices and therefore hinders digestion. He therefore has no appetite for food, and if he takes food he may be literally sick with love, or rather with unfulfilled love.

In this romantic phase the boy and girl become 'bosom pals' in the way each did with one of their own sex previously. Boy and girl like to talk things over, to express their views to one another, to discuss the problems of life and of their future, what they would like to be, and what they would like to do; they like to share their secrets with one another.

But very often the romance is too deep for words, and because they lack the capacity for expressing themselves in conversation, the romance takes the form of just sitting and holding hands and saying nothing. The cinema is a god-send for all love-sick youths.

It is necessary to stress that while there is, of course, a physical side to the relationship, in the purely romantic phase the desire is not normally for sexual intercourse. Far from being essentially sexual we often find that boys and girls may regard their romantic love as incompatible with sex. As soon as John is romantically in love with Elizabeth he says, 'I stopped looking at bathing women because it became repugnant to me to do it when I remembered about Betty.' This is the phase in which the boy, being in love with the girl, feels that she is 'too pure' for sex, too ethereal and idealised. 'I experienced a tenderness and a reverence', says John. Similarly, the girl adores the boy but feels that sex would 'spoil it all'.

I believe that this romanticism is a natural phase of maturation; it is playing at love-making (however serious it seems), an anticipation of the real thing. But that does not mean that we can expect to find it in every boy or girl, for, as in all the phases of maturation, the emerging characteristics may be affected by circumstances : the potentiality is there but in some cases is exaggerated, and in others it may never get a chance.

This phase is not confined to this country. The South Sea Island boy offers flowers to his girl friend. I have it on the word of a Burmese woman magistrate that the boys and girls there pass through this romantic stage although they have been promised in marriage and betrothed long before, to some other girl or boy.

In questioning the headmaster of a co-educational boarding school, I was told that he had sometimes found boys and girls sitting in the dark together in empty classrooms, holding hands and talking, but when he had asked if there was anything sexual going on, they were genuinely shocked at the suggestion.

It is of practical importance that we should recognize this romantic and idealistic period of love, for failure to understand its nature means that many parents and teachers regard it as dangerous to allow their boys and girls to go out with their girl or boy friend, thinking they might 'get into trouble'. No doubt it may be so in some cases, and it is right that parents should be cautious. But in the normal boy or girl in this idealistic phase there is no danger because their interests are set on romance rather than on sexual experience.

This phase of heterosexuality is of great value, for it enables boys and girls to know one another more intimately than in the polygamous phase, and therefore to be better able to choose their partners for life. It is the phase of 'going steady' with another boy or girl, but even 'going steady' does not mean marriage, or even engagement. Even in this 'monogamous' phase they may change from one girl or boy to another. It also helps the development of a companionship as in the 'primitive man' stage, but with one instead of many. Thus it develops chivalry between the sexes, with admiration for the qualities in each other.

It is also of value in developing *cultural* qualities. As there is admiration for the loved person, there is the desire to be pleasing to the person loved, and therefore to be as the other would have them to be. Both boys and girls learn to be considerate, good-natured, polite, and courteous; to be at their best before others. *The essence of politeness is consideration for others.* So the boy at this period begins to attend to his appearance, to clean his nails, and to be less uncouth, while the hoydenish girl who is always coming apart between her blouse and skirt begins to attend more to her dress, to develop her taste, to read books, to improve her mind. Teddy boys, contrary to the general impression, are often scrupulously clean and tidy and see their girl friends home.

John, in his diary, says, 'Yesterday at dinner, Mollie [his sister] said that it is surprising I always have clean nails now. I, fool, could not help blushing, and answered that I did not like such remarks. Mother said that surely Mollie knew that from the Fifth Form nails always became clean!' A most understanding mother!

Unfortunately, during the war we witnessed a perversion of the romantic phase. For the first time in many years in our country, girls as young as fourteen to sixteen had to a wide extent *experienced* sexual intrigues. It constitutes one of the gravest problems of our time, the full extent of which has, as far as I know, not been investigated. Having had their fling, did they settle down to be good wives and mothers? Or will their old habits of promiscuity persist or recur after marriage, making a broken or unstable home for their children?

I was informed by a woman doctor, who had to deal with many of these younger girls who got into trouble with our gallant allies, that while they enjoyed the romance, the sexual aspect meant very little to them. They were attracted by the flattery, the attention they received, the excitement of being taken out to meals and away for weekends. It was the novelty, the good time which appealed to them more than the sex. I was further informed by another woman doctor, who had a great deal to do with girls who had got into the hands of the police, that while with the older promiscuous type of girl, say of twenty, there is some chance of reforming her from her life, there is little chance of reforming these girls of fourteen to sixteen, because to them, immature as they are, sex does not mean the same, and they have not the same sense of responsibility about sex as the more mature girl.

On the hopeful side, because it means little to such younger girls, it may affect their future married lives less seriously, for as they get older sexual intercourse is a more mature and fully emotional experience bearing little relationship to the earlier affairs.

This social danger has been met with in some cases by the formation of mixed clubs where boys and girls of this age can meet, have dances, and engage in healthy romantic friendships with their own kind. In such clubs, indeed, you may observe the transition from the 'polygamous' phase in which there is an attraction to many different boys and girls to the 'monogamous' phase of romance. For while many boys and girls may be engaging in games or dancing, others tend to pair off and spend their evenings in the corner together. But both boys and girls have very strict conventions amongst themselves regarding sex, and this has nothing to do with conventional morality or religion. The one desire of the girls is to be married, and this means much more than sex. It is the fulfilment, biologically and otherwise, of their personality.

Boys and girls, as we have seen, develop differently, both physiologically and emotionally, although of course there are many individual differences. The girl develops more rapidly and matures earlier than the boy. This means that the girl in later adolescence has a greater sense of responsibility than the boy of the same age. This is a wise and natural provision of nature for sexual relations mean much more to a girl than to a boy. To a boy it may be a passing fancy, to the girl the responsibility of offspring. So the girl of eighteen may scorn the boy of her own age and prefer the young man of twenty, more capable of giving her the care and protection she needs. At co-educational boarding schools she is more likely to fall in love with a young master.

In Homer's *Odyssey*, there is a description of Nausicaa, the most charming picture of maidenly modesty that you could wish for. In a dream the goddess Athene, another name for her intuition, comes to her and tells her that it is time she gave up her tomboyish ways and made herself smart.

With her maidens (the gang of the same sex) she therefore goes for a washing picnic to the stream. There she finds Ulysses on the beach, thrown up by the storms, and with a simple frankness says, 'That is the kind of man I should like to marry!' She directs him to the palace of her father, the king, where he will receive hospitality, and accompanies him so far. But as they come near the village she suggests that he should go on ahead, otherwise the sailors on the quayside would make ribald remarks about them being together. This combination of intuition, charm, frankness, and modesty gives a most delightful picture of the healthy adolescent girl.

THE MONOGAMOUS PHASE: FALLING IN LOVE

'Falling in love' implies that *all* the components of love – friendship, devotion, tenderness, protection, sexual attraction, and adoration – attach to some particular boy or girl. When that occurs the boy and girl can think of nothing but the object of their attraction. The boy adores the girl, desires to protect her, to fight and even to die for her. Similarly the girl adores him, is tender towards him, admires his strength, and desires to bear him children. Such love may be completely self-forgetting, yet at the same time bring the supreme joy in life. It can be compared only with the religious ecstasy experienced by people at conversion, which is not uncommon at this period.

The degree of each of these components of love differs in every case. Where the boy marries 'the girl next door' the element of friendship plays an important part. Such marriages often wear well because each partner marries fully aware of the other's faults!

It is natural and biologically desirable that sexual passion plays a prominent part in adult love, for nature's concern is the procreation of the species. But procreation is not nature's only concern : *survival* of the offspring is equally important.

The care of the offspring is provided for by the maternal instinct. For the full development of the child, the establishment of the home and family life are also essential, for the home is the training ground which fits the child for the full responsibilities of life, social as well as material.

In many girls, the maternal and home-building instincts have a controlling influence upon the sexual. Many a girl will refuse to have intercourse with a man, much as she may desire it in herself, because she wants to be assured that the man really loves her. That is what she means when she says she wants to be 'loved for herself', that is to say, wants to be assured that the man's love and protectiveness are likely to be permanent.

There can be little doubt that pre-marital sexual relations make it much easier for either partner to fall back into outside sex relations *after* marriage. And there is no doubt that such external relations are a prime cause of the break-up of family relations which in turn produces insecurity and neurosis amongst the children of the marriage. That is why society upholds the principle of monogamy, however much it falls short in practice.

The need to be loved is much stronger in the girl than in the boy. This probably accounts for the curious way in which a girl who 'goes wrong' is more condemned than a man; to do so she has to overcome more natural resistance in herself. The dual standard in sexual morality probably arises from this circumstance.

Where sexuality has fulfilled its purpose in reproduction, it then becomes a symbol or expression of love between husband and wife, quite apart from the begetting of children. This bond of love, physical as well as spiritual, also makes for the more permanent establishment of the home and security of the family. Where there is dislike of sex on either side, it impairs this love. But recent researches suggest that the importance of the sexual relationship of marriage may have been exaggerated. The other components of love, such as friendship and companionship, are equally important in making a marriage successful.

THE PHASE OF IDEALISM

Idealism or 'high-mindedness' was described by Aristotle as a feature of adolescence, although he regarded it as due to lack of experience – as indeed many fathers still do. ('You'll come down to earth when you have to get a job.') This scorn, however, may with equal justice be ascribed to the disillusion c. the middle-aged parent, for there is a reason for this idealism of youth; it is necessary for the full development of a man as a human being.

This idealism is found even in primitive life, though not of course in the sophisticated form which it takes in civilized life. Some puberty rites are concerned with initiating youth into an idealized form of manliness, courage, and endurance under pain. The youth will have his body scarred without flinching to prove his fortitude.

In classical times there existed the same call to public service, to endurance, and to self-sacrifice. In Athens, at the age of eighteen, the youth was taken into the Grove of Agroulos, where he took his oath : 'I will never bring discredit in these arms, nor desert the man next to me in the ranks, but will fight for the sanctities of the common good, both alone and with others.'

Idealism held a high place also in the Middle Ages during the so-called Age of Chivalry, in which self-sacrifice and service to others were in high esteem. From seven to fourteen the boy was brought up to serve at the court, and to protect women; he was encouraged in games, music, and religion, and steeped in stories of knight errantry. When he came to the age of fourteen, he was made a squire, and as such he attended his lord in the tournament and kept near him in battle to help and protect him. In so doing, he was expected to show courage, obedience, helpfulness, and self-sacrifice both in devotion to his lord and in maintenance of his own standards of conduct.

When he came to the age of twenty-one he became a knight. After a night spent in prayer and confession, he took these vows : 'To be a brave, loyal, generous, just, and gentil knight, a champion of the Church, a redresser of the wrongs of widows and orphans, and a protector of women.'

Idealism in youth comes at a very significant time. During the earlier years, as we have seen, each of the potentialities of the child has been developed in ordered sequence. In later adolescence all the capacities and potentialities are co-ordinated and directed towards one aim. In this way, the personality is made complete and the individual both biologically and psychologically becomes a complete and adult person.

The emergence at the same time of strong sexual desires on the one hand, and idealism on the other, often gives rise to conflict in the adolescent's mind, particularly if he has previously been given a sense of guilt regarding sex. How often the adolescent years have been made unhappy by this constant struggle between sex impulses and religion !

Yet both heterosexuality and idealism appear to spring from the same common source, namely, *the need for some-one or something outside the adolescent to fulfil and complete himself.*

The youth finds this fulfilment, physically and emotion-ally, in the mate, without whom he feels incomplete; he finds it also in idealism, for aims and purposes are necessary both to the harmonization and to the fulfilment of the whole personality. Later adolescence is therefore characterized by two main features, heterosexuality and idealism.

It is interesting to find that, according to Starbuck,* most religious conversions take place at the age of sixteen, a phenomenon which appears to be due to a longing by adoles-cents for something outside and beyond themselves.

Because of the high-mindedness of idealism, late

* *The Psychology of Religion.*

adolescence is often accompanied by dissatisfaction, self-questioning, inadequacy, inferiority, and insecurity. This general dissatisfaction is due to discrepancy between what adolescents are and what their ideal is. The discrepancy may take the form of a 'consciousness of sin' which often leads to religious conversion.

Another form this idealism takes is a search for a perfect world and perfect people. 'If the world isn't what it ought to be, then it ought to be!' said one youth. This usually occurs in a youth whose ordinary life is unhappy or unsatisfactory. If the real world is unhappy, he must create an exaggeratedly happy world of phantasy or imagination.

Children whose lives have been contented develop idealisms which are more practical and attainable.

Adolescence, therefore, which may be a period of great joy and happiness, is to some a period of disillusion and moody self-doubt.

The adolescent judges both himself *and others* by his ideals. We should therefore regard with patience, if we cannot view with good humour, the adolescent's criticism and dissatisfaction of what Guedella has called 'the incurable frivolity of our elders'.

The adolescent is expressing his opinions, not his convictions, for convictions can only be based on experience. He may sound dogmatic in his expression of his opinions, but his very dogmatism comes from his sense of insecurity : it is because he is so unsure of himself that he blames others for their shortcomings. For his dissatisfaction with the world and others is only a projection of his own inner sense of unrest. This makes him seek in the outside ideal world that peace and order which he cannot find in his own soul.

To get a better grasp of their problem and to formulate their opinions the better, later adolescents often form themselves into groups. These are not like the 'gangs' of puberty, bound in loyalty to a leader and to one another, but rather groups bound together in loyalty to truth, sincerity, and justice.

Far from meekly accepting the opinions of others in the group, as in puberty, they differ very widely in their views and are prepared to defend their personal opinion against all comers.

These discussions, whether at home or in discussion groups, should be encouraged. The best way to clarify our views is to give expression to them; and the best way to mature is to submit our views to free discussion, bring them under the scrutiny of others, and examine their validity.

The *content* of these opinions should not concern us too much; it is more important that the adolescent should think for himself, formulate his views, and give expression to them. It is more important that he should be sincere than that he should be right.

In the same way, *the adolescent's views should not be taken too seriously.* Some parents really think their children intend to put their political and social ideas into immediate practice. Adolescents are only experimenting with ideas and trying to formulate their opinions. Adolescence is growing up, not being grown up.

Parents should, however, be on their guard against the *exploitation* of youth. Thus, in some schools the clever boy or girl is exploited for the sake of the credit which scholarships bring to the school. It is the full development of the child's personality which is our aim; the harm done to boys and girls over-stretched in the pursuit of scholarship prizes may be permanent. The exhaustion of scholarship children when they reach university level is one of the more disturbing features of our time.

6

ABNORMALITIES

DISORDERS IN ADOLESCENCE

ADOLESCENCE is generally considered a time when we look for disorders. Indeed the term 'adolescent instability' is commonly used, as though the adolescent is necessarily unstable. That is far from being the case. Children brought up sanely in earlier childhood pass through adolescence healthily and happily without any disorders or instability. Just as an infant's teething should not produce anything but teeth, so adolescence should produce nothing but 'growing up'. But the fact remains that adolescence is a time when disorders are more *liable* to happen than in earlier years. There are reasons for this, both physiological and psychological.

In the first place, there are rapid changes taking place in the physiological organism in adolescence, which may give rise to endocrine lack of balance and produce what we may justifiably call 'temperamental instability'. For temperament is the influence of the physiological organism upon the mental and emotional life. An extreme illustration of this is schizophrenia, which at one time was called 'adolescent insanity'. But there are numerous minor disorders of the same kind, where, for example, a youth's physical development outruns his intellect, or, on the other hand, where he is physiologically underdeveloped; either state can produce instability (pp. 44 f.).

Other reasons are psychological. We have touched on one of these, namely, the disillusion which comes from excessive idealism.

A further reason for adolescent instability is that the basic impulses, such as aggressiveness and sex, develop so fast that they get beyond the youth's control.

There are various factors which may cause lack of control. The first is the physiological instability already mentioned. The second and more obvious is that the youth has *never learnt self-discipline*. Sometimes this is because he is the spoilt child and has never been disciplined, or because the parents have shown him no example of self-control. People says, 'A little more discipline in childhood might have done him good' – and sometimes they are right.

But it must not be assumed that lack of discipline is the only cause of disorders in adolescence. It is sometimes the very reverse; for the same rebelliousness may occur because the child has been *too rigidly 'disciplined'* (in the wrong sense), so that when he attains more freedom he revolts and kicks over the traces.

Again, if the parents have always kept the child under their thumb and always made his decisions for him, or demanded strict obedience, he will not have developed the capacity to make his *own* decisions. When, therefore, he goes out into life – to work or to university – he will be completely at sea. He will be devoid of will and character, and when he has freedom he will not know how to use it, often with unfortunate results. Just as he has always had his parents to make decisions for him, so he will now be dominated by the will of others.

Another and most important reason for adolescent instability is that *complexes formed in early childhood and latent since then are apt to be revived at this time*. The reason for this is that in adolescence the impulses are more strongly developed, while at the same time the old fears and threats which repressed them are wearing thin. In adolescence, therefore, the impulses will no longer brook being kept under.

If the old fears are dispelled, the old repressions may emerge to the surface. It may be that a number of early obsessional traits are automatically cured in time. But if a child has had his aggressive or sex instincts repressed in early childhood, he may become a good and obedient boy out of fear; and nothing may happen for some years. But in adolescence the old conflict is re-activated, and the impulses may burst out like a suppressed volcano; the 'good' boy may turn overnight, as it were, into a moody uncontrollable adolescent, beyond the understanding and influence of his parents.

Or the conflict may take the form of neurotic anxiety, which represents the re-activation of the fear of his forbidden impulses. The youth has no idea why he is anxious, and so puts his anxiety on all kinds of other things, fear of leaving home, fear of knives, and other phobias – which are, however, fear of his aggressive impulses.

Similarly, the girl, becoming aware of her reawakened but forbidden sexual impulses, begins to feel guilty and to become over-conscientious or to do all kinds of propitiatory obsessional acts, like counting the windows in every room, hand-washing, tidying, or saying her prayers. If it is a childhood craving for love which has been repressed, it may emerge as a hysterical pain or illness. These disorders are very common in adolescence, and often pass as the child gets more confidence and the infantile fears are removed. But they sometimes persist and require expert treatment.

But a great deal of disturbance in adolescence comes from conditions which are preventable, such as *lack of outlets* for natural energy. If natural urges are frustrated, they take unnatural forms.

Other disorders are occasioned by the parents' attitude. The parents should realize that the youth is growing up to greater independence. He wants to go his own way, make his own decisions, and order his own life. If the parents try to keep a hold on him and interfere with his normal development by laying down the law, he will naturally resent it and kick over the traces. It is no use a parent starting to discipline his son or daughter at this stage; that should have been done long before. The whole of earlier childhood is designed to enable the child to learn *self*-discipline and to adapt himself to life and its responsibilities.

Some parents can't bear to see their children slipping away from their protective care (usually the mother), or from their authority (usually the father), forgetful of the fact that their function in life is *to prepare the child to grow up*, to be independent, and to take on the responsibilities of life for himself. Those parents who encourage the growth of independence usually retain the love and devotion of their children, and thereafter have an influence that no amount of coddling or laying down the law will achieve.

Further problems arise from lack of adequate advice. For adolescence is growing up, not being grown up, and needs guidance. One of the difficulties of the present time is that adolescents are completely bewildered on all kinds of problems, their work, their careers, their love affairs, their personal impulses and desires. Parents themselves find it difficult to advise them because of the confusing opinions, even of the experts. Most parents have, in fact, enough common sense to advise if adolescent sons and daughters ask their advice, but frequently parents are the last persons whom the adolescent is likely to approach.

All in all, if things go seriously wrong in adolescence, it is little use for the parents to try and deal with the problems; and it is better for them to hand over to someone in the confidence of the adolescent, or in very serious cases to an experienced child psychiatrist. But remember that the psychiatrist who is a genius at treating small children of six to twelve is not necessarily the most competent to treat the adolescent.

In my opinion there should be specific adolescent clinics staffed by those with a special aptitude for dealing with the problems of this phase.

DELINQUENCY AND ABNORMAL CHARACTER TRAITS

Delinquencies, abnormal characteristics, and 'naughtiness' – such as lying, stealing, truancy, cruelty, cowardice, conceit, arrogance, jealousy, and idleness – are common especially during adolescence, as the child wins greater independence.

What are their causes, and how do we treat them?

The *individual causes* are too many to mention; and many people have their pet theories – poverty, bad housing, too much coddling, too much strictness. But we very soon discover that there are not only many causes, but that these disorders can be grouped into several *types* of delinquency, which have different types of cause and require different types of treatment. This simplifies matters.

I have dealt very fully with the whole subject in my *Psychology and Mental Health* (Chapter 3), to which the reader whose work lies with children is referred. But a brief illustration of these different types may be given.

1. *Benign delinquencies.* A boy may take another boy's fountain pen just to tease him; another boy, camping in some wood, may cut down a sapling to act as a tent pole. They ought not to do these things, which are wrong from the sociological point of view, but such delinquencies do not show a *vicious* nature and are not necessarily wrong from the mental health point of view. I call them 'benign' delinquencies, because like benign tumours, such as warts, they ought not to be there but they do no particular harm. They ought also to be dealt with benignly! Boys playing football in the back streets are breaking the law; but they are not necessarily bad boys. Children often do 'wrong' things which they don't know to be wrong. To deal with them too seriously is to turn them into criminals!

2. *Physiological or temperamental abnormalities* are those which have a physiological not a psychological cause. Mental deficiency is a constitutional disorder due to a physiological development. A mental deficient may have no sense of right and wrong and will unashamedly come up to you and rifle your pockets. A girl at the time of her periods may be so unbalanced that she steals or runs away from home. An 'acidosis' child may become cantankerous, irritable, and 'imposible'. A man with low blood sugar or with a hidden epilepsy may suddenly become violent and commit a murder. Many delinquents are found to have abnormal

brain waves. Children who are tired, or lack sleep or proper food, will become bad-tempered from lack of control. But why labour the point : which of us, teachers or parents, have not found ourselves getting irritable and even unjust with our children when we feel tired or out of sorts?

Temperament is our *mental* make-up as determined by our *physiological* make-up. Minor or passing phases we call *moods*. So a child may be in an angry mood or pleasant mood. In a bad mood he may commit a delinquency. The treatment of all such disorders is obviously along physiological lines.

3. *Simple delinquencies*. But a boy may steal because he lacks moral standards. If he has never been disciplined or taught to tell the truth, or if he has a dishonest father or a bullying mother or a broken home, he will naturally lie, steal, bully, and assault. So he steals a watch or money because he wants it and doesn't see why he should not have it, so long as he is not found out. What they need is a change of *character*. These are not cases for the psychiatrist, for they are not 'ill', but for the teacher, the parson, the sociologist, and the magistrate – although it is a wise precaution for a child psychiatrist to examine them to make sure that they are not suffering from physiological disorder or from psychological complexes. Such children require to be given new moral standards. A new foster home, or a good club where they can get a new outlook on life, may be the best form of treatment. In extreme cases punishment may be called for when all else fails to turn them from their ways – as mentioned later (p. 276).

4. *Reaction delinquencies*. These are most important because they are least understood and therefore often wrongly treated, and wrong treatment often makes them worse. They are too often confused with the 'simple' types. Take a case of this kind : a child of three at the arrival of another baby feels left out and unloved. He pushes the baby aside and gets punished – sent into another room. What does he then do? He may come back and be a 'good boy'. But on the other

hand he may change his whole attitude and say, 'I don't want anybody's love : I can do without them ! They can go to hell !' – and so he becomes truculent, defiant, unco-operative, and anti-social, making as much of a nuisance of himself as he can and being thoroughly bloody-minded.

This is a reaction trait – he reacts to the craving for love by repulsing it and then goes to the opposite extreme. It is obvious that punishment, which is usually prescribed in such cases, does no good at all, but only makes things worse, for it gives him a greater sense of grievance. Many of our 'in-corrigible' youths on whom punishment has little or no deterrent effect are of this type : they are 'beyond control'. What we should of course do is to deal with the *underlying* condition, in this case the need for affection, and not simply the outward behaviour of defiance which resulted from it. So a child may be outwardly conceited or become the 'lime-light child' because deep down he feels inferior; to snub him only makes him worse.

5. *Psychoneurotic delinquencies*. But supposing in the last defiant case we do succeed in bringing the boy to heel by our punishment. He then represses his aggressiveness for fear of the consequences, and becomes a 'good boy'. In this case his repressed aggressiveness forms itself into an *unconscious complex*. Later on, especially in adolescence when he is more independent and less afraid, this complex may emerge in the form of stealing. Every school master and mistress is familiar with the high-minded, hard-working, conscientious type of boy who to everyone's surprise is found to be the boy who has been stealing from the other boys' lockers. They cannot understand it and he himself cannot understand why he did it. As often as not he does not want what he stole; and when he is discovered, far from being defiant like the reaction type, he is full of shame and remorse, and would do anything to put things right. Punishment does no good, although he would gladly have it if it would put things right. Punishment cannot cure a complex. Nor it is any good to preach to him or try to give him better moral

standards. His moral standards are as good as if not better than others!

These cases are easy to spot because the delinquent behaviour is *contrary to the boy's usual behaviour*, which is often exaggeratedly good. 'I never thought *you* would do a thing like that!' says the shocked mother or schoolmaster. 'I don't know *what* has come over you!' Nor does the boy!

These cases do very well with analytic treatment to unearth the basic cause of such a delinquency, which is usually some *buried* resentment of a former age; and they are easy to treat because such children are most willing to cooperate.

Analytic treatment is also called for in the reaction type; but it is not so easy, because this type is defiant. ('It's my mother who wants treatment, not me!') But such a boy is very unhappy, and if you get his confidence and let him give expression to his sense of grievance (which is often justified), he responds very well to analysis, and the results are most gratifying.

In early and in mild cases, the mother who recognizes the real cause of the child's condition will settle his sense of grievance by giving him that affection which is his basic need – and will persist even if the child at first rejects her advances.

It will be obvious from a consideration of these different types that those which advocate one form of treatment, whether it be more strict discipline or more affection or better housing, will be right in some cases but wrong in others, and even do harm.

To take a case of an entirely different sort : that of bed-wetting. This may be 'physiological', because of too acid urine. It may be 'simple', where the child has never been trained and is too lazy to get up. It may be a 'reaction', a deliberate attempt to annoy the mother or force her attention, because the child has a sense of grievance. Or it may be psychoneurotic, as in the case of the child who *unconsciously* wants to be a baby again – a very common type amongst evacuated children. Such a child, unlike the reaction type, can't help bed-wetting and is very ashamed of it. Each of these needs to be treated quite differently.

Minor cases of such disorders can be dealt with by the parent and teacher, provided they have sound understanding of the type of case they are dealing with. We can't be running off to a psychiatrist every time our children are naughty! But it is also necessary to know the differences in types to avoid making things worse, for then expert treatment *is* necessary.   .

WHAT IS NEUROSIS?

Since this book is largely concerned not only with the principles of the maintenance of mental health, but also with at least an outline of morbid disorders, we must very briefly consider what is a neurosis — what is its mechanism, and what its cause.

Mechanism. A neurosis is characterized by *dissociation* of consciousness, a part of the mind being split off from the rest.

This dissociation may be produced by shock (as Janet points out), but most commonly it is due to *repression*, as Freud has made us believe. We repress what is distasteful to us, and what is incompatible with the rest of our personality. The repressed and split off part then forms what we call a *complex.*

A complex is simply some experience of the past which because of its incompatibility with the rest of the personality is automatically repressed and dissociated.

But though repressed the complex is *still active* and may emerge in the form of a neurotic symptom. Being dissociated, these symptoms, like a hysterical paralysis, or a phobia like claustrophobia, or an obsessional compulsion to touch every lamp-post, are *beyond the control of the will.*

It is like a naughty boy thrown out of school; though dissociated from the class he can still throw stones, and we now have no control over him at all. Better to keep him in the class room – that is, in consciousness. Because such neurotic complexes are beyond the control of the will we regard them as 'illnesses' and not as moral faults. It is useless to tell a soldier with a hysterical paralysis to exert his will to walk. The will has no authority whatever over dissociate complexes. It is useless to tell a man who has a phobia for travelling in tube trains that it is silly – he knows that, but it makes no difference whatever – or to tell an obsessional patient to pull himself together. They are suffering from illnesses which require expert treatment.

So far we agree with Freud.

What then is the basic cause of neurotic disorders? *The basic cause of neurotic disorders is the sense of insecurity.* But since a child's security springs from the love which comes from the mother, the child feels insecurity in the specific form of *deprivation of love.** Protective love is the primal need of the child, occasioned by the child's helplessness and provided for in the maternal instinct in animals and men.

Given protective love the child has confidence to face life. Given protective love, the child is free to experiment and venture and explore in an atmosphere of security. So he gets adaptation to life. Given protective love, the child responds with love for others, grows up to be sociable, and is happy in his married life. Given protective love the child identifies himself with those he loves and so takes over stable standards and ideals which act as his guide through life.

Deprived of protective love, the child has no security and no confidence to face life; he is timid, anxious, and apprehensive. Deprived of protective love, he is afraid to venture and

* This theory, that the basic cause of the neuroses is insecurity experienced by the child as a deprivation of protective love, which is based on my experience in treating those suffering from neurotic disorders, has been put forward in my lectures in the university for the last thirty years, and is fully described in my *Psychology and Mental Health*, published in 1950. I am glad to find this insistence on the need for protective love put forward independently and convincingly by John Bowlby, the psychoanalyst, in his Pelican on *Child Care and the Growth of Love* published two years later.

to give expression to those activities which will enable him to cope with life. Deprived of love, he cannot *afford* to love others but is absorbed in self-love and is incapable of joining in that communal life by means of which alone he can get full scope for the development for his personality. Deprived of love he is deprived of the means of developing stable aims and ideals in life.

You can observe the formation of neurotic symptoms in any large nursery and specifically from the above cause.

An infant feeling left out and unloved gets into a state of *anxiety* or fear; or he may get into a state of *depression*. Another infant, feeling the lack of love, resorts to *masturbation* as a solace. A child a little older in the self-willed period, who feels left out perhaps because of the arrival of another baby, gets angry, *aggressive*, and jealous. A child of two and a half to three falls into *self-pity* and says, 'I have a sore back; I don't feel well' as a means of getting sympathy. He is a potential *hysteric* – for illness is the royal road to the sympathy of which he feels deprived. The hysteric does not want sympathy because he is ill; he is ill because he wants sympathy. A four-year-old child has greater independence and if he feels left out he becomes rebellious, anti-social, defiant, and may develop into a *delinquent*.

All these are neurotic reactions and all are due to the feeling of deprivation of love.

Whether neurotic reactions will lead to neurotic symptoms in the same or another form depends on how they are treated. Take the hysteric child who, feeling left out, says, 'I have a sore back.' If you say, 'Nonsense!', it makes him feel more unloved; if you fuss about him, he says to himself, 'This is fine!' and uses it another time to get attention. If you detect the underlying cause and begin to play with him and give him assurance, he will soon forget his fictitious pain.

Again, take the case of a child who feels left out and resorts to masturbation as a solace. If he is severely threatened or punished he feels a deep sense of guilt and may repress all sexual urges as being dangerous or wrong. But when sex inevitably emerges in adolescence, it may be turned either simply into an anxiety-state (fear of the threat), or a feeling of guilt and self-consciousness; or appear in the form of over-conscientiousness or propitiatory acts, like hand-washing, to compensate for his guilt, although he is quite unaware of why he is afraid, or why he feels guilty, or why he has to perform these acts, which he realizes perfectly well are stupid.

These neurotic symptoms need expert treatment if they persist. It is no use telling such sufferers to pull themselves together. But with right parenthood almost all of them could have been prevented. This can be affirmed dogmatically because if we look through the cases whose causes have been discovered and cured, we find that these causes lay in experiences which with more adequate parenthood could have been avoided.

Some are unavoidable, for there are some circumstances which are beyond the control of the parent. A difficult birth may be the predisposing cause of a claustrophobia; an operation in hospital the origin of a separation anxiety. But these early traumatic experiences do not develop into neuroses provided the child is later reassured. He realizes that life is not as bad as he thought. But if the child does not get adequate assurance, or if a later experience, like being buried in a trench, recalls the childhood pattern, the original fear may be revived as a neurosis.

Thus the early predisposing causes in infancy may never produce a psychoneurotic condition provided the child is given assurance later on. And later untoward experiences – such as an unfortunate love affair, or getting blown up, or a car crash – do not themselves produce a nervous breakdown unless there were predisposing causes making for insecurity in early childhood. That is why it is so important to prevent these conditions by right parenthood *in early childhood*.

7

THE PRINCIPLES OF PARENTHOOD

THE PRINCIPLE OF PROTECTIVE LOVE

In Chapter 1 we considered the parents' dilemma. This concerned discipline and freedom. We were told by the Victorians that to spare the rod was to spoil the child, and that a failure to discipline the child meant that he became a wastrel and a delinquent. We were told by the Neo-Georgians, on the other hand, that if we frustrated or repressed a child he would become a neurotic. What is the parent to do? Are we condemned to choose between our child being bad and healthy, or being good and neurotic? That was our problem. Are we now any nearer a solution? I think we are.

What are the principles of parenthood? There are three cardinal principles, not to speak of many subsidiary ones :

The Principle of Protective Love.

The Principle of Freedom.

The Principle of Discipline.

These three principles, far from being incompatible, as generally supposed, are necessary to one another and to the full development of the child's personality. Only in an atmosphere of security is a child free to act, to venture, and to be spontaneous. Only by discipline can these spontaneous tendencies be directed and coordinated, so that the personality is free. Discipline, therefore, is as necessary to true freedom as freedom is necessary to true self-discipline. And a sense of security, is a prerequisite to both.

It is a curious fact that the higher in evolution we go the more helpless the offspring. The lizard and the fly are much more capable at birth of fending for themselves than the human infant. That is because they have fixed reflexes which enable them to cope with the ordinary dangers of life, whereas the human infant has relatively few fixed reflexes. Of all creatures at birth the human infant is the most helpless. But this helplessness of the human infant has its corresponding advantages; for the human child, having fewer fixed reflexes, has a greater *variability of response*.

The insects' fixed reflexes enable them to cope with the *ordinary* contingencies of life; but if these vary, say by a marked change in the temperature, the insects cannot cope with them and 'die off like flies'. The human child on the other hand is far more capable of adapting itself to changing circumstances than the insect; his intelligence enables him to vary his responses to life.

Moreover, the helplessness of the infant is compensated for by the maternal love and care of its mother. So the higher you go in evolution, the more helpless the offspring; but the higher you go, the more developed is the maternal instinct, which gives to the child the care and protection necessary to its survival.

On the other hand, if the child is denied this protective love he is much more helpless and exposed to dangers than the lizard and the fly. That is why the human being is presumably so much more prone to develop neurotic disorders, for, as we have seen, the basic cause of neurotic disorders is the sense of insecurity expressed in the feeling of deprivation of love.

If, therefore, you want your child to grow up strong, independent, and well-adjusted to life, first of all give him a sense of security. This gives him confidence – confidence in his parents on whom he depends, and then confidence in himself to face life and its responsibilities.

This need of protective love is of course greatest in infancy. By the time the youth reaches adolescence, he feels capable of fending for himself; indeed, he now resents the intrusion of the parents into his activities, however patently he may require their help.

This need for protective love means, from the practical point of view, that in early childhood all forms of exaggerated fear should, as far as possible, be avoided, such as accidents, separation from the mother, severe punish-ment, and other assaults upon the child's sense of security.

There are, of course, some occasions of fear which are un-avoidable, as in the case of necessary operations in hospital; but when such occasions arise, it is of the greatest importance that the child should have reassurance. Such reassurance on the mother's part will help to counteract that fear.

Let us take two instances frequently found in the history of patients suffering from neurotic disorders : separation from the mother, and the coming of another child.

A young patient was left at the age of three at a nursery school, since both parents had to work. When she discovered her mother had gone she first felt miserable and desperate and then furious. This mood persisted, so that she was thoroughly antagonistic towards the teachers at the school and the other children. She therefore became unpopular and was teased, which did not improve matters. This made her isolated, so that she adopted an aloof attitude towards people in general. Later when any young man was attracted to her, and even when she was attracted to him, she could not help being stand-offish. At home she suffered from bad tempers and depression, which were the emergence of her repressed misery and anger in childhood. When in analysis the cause was revealed, she completely readjusted herself to the situation, was cured of her tempers, depression, and aloofness, and married her boss.

An explanation beforehand by the mother, and a more 'comforting' and understanding attitude on the part of the matron when she became 'difficult' and screamed for her mother in fear, might have prevented the whole trouble.

The following reactions of the child left in hospital are often revealed in analysis and are confirmed by direct ob-servation.*

The child first cries and even yells for his mother to come

* Edelston and Bowlby have independently made a study of the reactions of a child when left in hospital.

back. Then he falls into a state of shock and despair. He then recovers from the shock and begins to play with his toys and become acclimatized to the ward, and the nurse says, 'You see!' But when the mother returns to see the child, we often find that he does not respond; he goes on playing with his toys. His attitude is, 'You did not come when I wanted you; I am not going to respond when you want me!' This may continue at home, making a breach, sometimes permanent, between mother and child. She has 'let him down' and he has lost confidence in her. Finally, the child may develop a neurosis, it may be within days or weeks, or it may be some years later – such as fears at night, which are the revival of his repressed fears; or he may bed-wet in the *unconscious* desire to pay her out. At this stage if the mother approaches him with love he may reject her. But even in such cases, persistence on the mother's part in giving the child love and affection will usually overcome his resistance and he will be restored to her affection. Unfortunately the mother, being thus rebuffed, often adopts the attitude, 'Very well, then!' and leaves the child to himself, thus perpetuating the condition.

The mother, therefore, provided she is calm and reassuring, should be allowed to be with the child when he is being given the anaesthetic (instead of leaving him to feel he is being suffocated by queer people in witches' clothing), and also when the child comes out of the anaesthetic (when he is wondering what has happened to him and what this strange place is into which he is wafted, and where his mother is). Nurses can, and indeed often do, give the child this comfort, and that is all to the good, but it does not take the place of the familiar face of the mother, for she is known, whereas the nurse is a stranger.

But unexpected things may happen. I had a patient who as a child was having a circumcision operation at his home with the mother present. But her presence made things worse and gave him no reassurance, because in his distress he saw his mother standing by joking and flirting with the doctor, indifferent to his fear and suffering. To her and the doctor the operation was a trifling affair; not so to the child, who was filled with terror that his mother had let him down! The mother should have had more understanding of the child's feelings.

It is because of the recognition of the ill effects of such separation from the mother that the modern method has been increasingly adopted of getting the mother to stay in hospital to help with the nursing of her sick child, a method inaugurated by Dr Spence in the north of England. The reassurance that this gives to the child helps both in the physical recovery of the child (for the anxious child wears himself out), and also will no doubt save many children from later neurotic disorders.

Another very common situation which produces anxiety and later neurosis is *the coming of another baby*. In going back to the cases of neurotic disorders, I find this to be one of the most common and one of the most serious. Since the first need of the child is for security in his mother's love, if he sees that love passing to another, he is thrown into a state of panic and this gives rise to jealousy and anger : he has to fight for his life. Jealousy is simply self-preservation, and every mother should understand this. If the child is punished for this he is thrown into a still greater sense of insecurity. His fear may compel him to be a good boy, for by that means he recovers his mother's approval. But the repressed fear may later emerge as an anxiety neurosis or his repressed resentment may come out later in truculent behaviour, to get his own back.

Most mothers therefore now realize that it is not enough to tell the child of the coming of the baby, but that they must give the older child particular love and attention *after* the baby is born. The child will then feel reassured and very likely (if a girl) identify herself with the mother and start to 'look after' the baby, as many children do quite happily.

I have stated that all exaggerated forms of fear should as far as possible be avoided. Does this mean that a child should be protected from *all* fear and dangers? By no means! There are many lesser forms of danger in the everyday life of the child which cannot be avoided anyway, and *it is not desirable that they should be*. Falling off chairs, cutting themselves with a knife, bruising their knees in the playground – all these are more or less inevitable if children are to be allowed freedom to be venturesome. But such fears and hurts should immediately be accompanied by reassurance.

Indeed, provided these situations are followed by reassurance the child gains *greater* confidence to face life, for he learns that even dangerous situations are surmountable; and his mother's quiet confidence in dealing with the situation gives *him* confidence, enabling him to be adventurous but also cautious.

Pain and fear. As a child needs to be protected from fear, so he needs to be protected from unnecessary pain. Pain is closely linked up with fear – for *fear is the dominant element in pain*. In nature the function of pain is to call attention to the fact that something is wrong; that we are in danger. Pain is an alarm signal and is intended by nature to arouse fear.

Three-quarters of the distress of pain is the fear associated with it. If, therefore, the child is reassured, most of the pain goes. The small child who falls down some steps and hurts himself screams more in fear than in pain, and if the mother embraces the child and comforts it, the pain disappears because the fear goes, and the child runs off happily. That is why 'kissing it better' abolishes the pain. Similarly the expectant mother who is instructed to know just what is to be expected in labour does not mind the pain because she realizes that this is normal; she is reassured and if her fear is dispelled so is some of her pain! Many a child goes off to the dentist quite happily not in spite of, but because of, knowing what to expect. Pain which is robbed of fear loses its sting.

One of the most effective ways of making a small child

into a coward is to tell him, when he is frightened or hurt, not to make a fuss, for then he feels he has *no* security against danger.

Worst of all are the fears directly engendered by the mother herself, such as the fear of an ill-tempered mother. The mother's function is to protect the child. For the child to be told 'Mother won't love you if you do that' is devastating to a child who looks to her love for security. Punishment of a child may be necessary, but over-severity or a look of hate in the mother's eyes as she punishes the child puts a child into a state of abject terror, for he is left without security anywhere. You will sometimes see a child clinging to the mother who is beating him – pathetic sight! Little Red Riding Hood's experience of seeing a grandmother (or mother) turn into a wolf is no uncommon experience.

Even so, it is extraordinary how a child can acclimatize herself even to the cruelty of a parent. You may see a little girl (I saw one recently in a railway carriage) receive a vicious slap on the hand by her mother. She blanches, but does not cry : she is obviously used to it! But what influence will that mother have over her child when the latter reaches adolescence and can defy the mother?

The function of the parent is first of all, then, to give the child protection and security, for only in an atmosphere of security can a child be free. He wants to be assured that when he plays he will not be unduly hurt, that when he ventures he will be protected from harm; but that if he suffers hurts and gets into danger, his mother will be there to care for him. All this gives him confidence; it does not make him a molly-coddle, because he does play and venture – and even hurt himself – all the more because he has security behind him. It is fear that makes a child a molly-coddle who dare not leave his mother's side : it is the insecure child who dare not venture and whose timidity therefore robs him of freedom. The child is neither free nor happy who is always having to look over his shoulder to watch for danger.

Can a child, then, be *over*-protected? Yes, he can. By over-protection we mean being protected *when there is no call or need for protection.* If a child of two falls off a sofa, he naturally picks himself up, has a short cry, and climbs up on to the sofa again. It is natural for a child to repeat a situation so as to conquer it. If the situation is beyond him, say if frightened by a dog, let the mother reassure him *but only so far as is necessary for him to be reassured* – she must not get into a panic herself. As evidence of over-protection observe an anxious mother following her wretched three-year-old around the beach to protect him from dangers that don't exist! The child is wanting to explore the world *himself* and we should let him do so – watching him, but at a distance! To protect a child is not to coddle him!

Over-protection carries its own dangers. In the first place a child who is over-protected is made to feel that the dangers of life from which he is being so anxiously protected are worse than they really are. Secondly, an over-protected child, who has never learnt to recognize which situations are dangerous and which are not, takes stupid risks through ignorance and becomes the victim of those very dangers from which his mother all too carefully tried to protect him. She protected him, but never taught him to protect *himself.*

Finally, the child who is over-protected by being tied to his mother's apron-strings develops an inferiority complex before his play-fellows, and will behave with bravado to try to prove to himself and to others that he is not a 'sissy', and so does foolhardy things. The child, on the other hand, who is allowed to meet the ordinary risks of life with reassurance is bold and confident, yet cautious, for experience has made him so.

We may be told that many children become neurotic, not because they are deprived of love, but because they have too much love. That is because the so-called 'love' they are given is not a true love but a spurious love, one form of which is the over-protectiveness of the mother, just mentioned.

True love seeks first of all the well-being and happiness of the person loved.

Some mothers are *over-possessive*; they want to do everything for the child, for instance buttoning up his coat when he wants to do it himself. They must participate in every action of his life; they must make every decision for him. In medicine we have a term 'meddlesome surgery', by which we mean that the surgeon, instead of leaving well alone and allowing the forces of nature to do their healing work, is always interfering with the wound, fussing over it, and changing the treatment from day to day. There is such a thing as 'meddlesome motherhood', which cannot bear to stand aside and see the child developing naturally, but must always be interfering, scolding one moment and fondling the next, changing treatment from one day to the next.

The child does not flourish under that form of 'love', which gratifies the mother at the expense of the child. When the child manages to break away at adolescence, the mother charges him with ingratitude. His attitude is 'If only you would let me alone, I *should* be grateful.'

Another type is the *over-anxious* mother who is always worrying that the child may catch cold or run risks. This is sometimes because the mother herself has had an anxious childhood fraught with illnesses, and not necessarily, as some psychoanalysts would have us believe, because the mother unconsciously *wishes* the child to be ill or hurt.

The effect of this over-anxiety on children of a more sensitive temperament is to transfer the mother's anxiety to them and make them timid; the more robust types are more likely to go to the other extreme and become foolhardy, taking unnecessary risks.

Another spurious form of 'love' is *vanity*. A mother may be absorbed with her child, and people may say what love she has for the child, when really her adoration of the child is mainly for the reflected glory – that people will think what a wonderful mother she must be to have so clever, beautiful, or good and polite a child.

There is also the spurious love of the mother who satisfies her *sensuous pleasure*, especially with her little boy, with the result that he becomes sexually attached to her and develops a full-blown Oedipus complex.

But let us not be mistaken. There is nothing wrong with these qualities in themselves. It is quite natural that a mother should feel proud of her child's cleverness, prettiness, and achievements, but not natural for her pride to be simply for reflected glory, so that she gets angry with the child when he 'lets *her* down' before visitors. It is natural that a mother should protect a child and be careful lest the child gets into real danger, but not natural when it makes *her* frightened when he does, nor to the extent that the child is so protected that he is rendered unfit to face life. It is natural that a mother should feel possessive of her child, for after all she produced him – 'these are my jewels' – but not so as to restrict his development and hold on to him when he wants to spread his wings. After all what she has produced is not a jewel but a personality which must be free to develop. Furthermore, it is natural that a mother should find sensuous pleasure in feeding and fondling her child, for nature has provided it thus, so as to enhance the mother's love for the child. But the mother acts unnaturally if she so stimulates the child's sex feelings that he becomes sexually fixated to her, and makes as a result a deplorable marriage.

It is natural that a mother should provide a child with all he needs to fit him for life, but the kind of 'love' which says, 'He is such a darling I can't refuse him anything' is not true love, for it is doing him the worst possible service for his future life, when he will still feel 'I should have all I want.'

True love seeks the happiness and welfare of the child. All these spurious forms of love, instead of contributing to the child's health or happiness, only contribute to its inadequacy and ultimate unhappiness.

One of the greatest problems with which every child psychiatrist is confronted is the neurotic complexes of the mother or the father. The over-anxiety of the mother already mentioned, which will not allow the child to be free to explore and venture, is a case in point. So is the sex-starved mother – a widow perhaps who finds her sensuous gratification in her son. Jealousy in the family is an extremely common form. We often meet with a mother who is jealous of her own daughter because of the father's devotion to the child, although she may herself be quite unaware of that jealousy. We have not infrequently come across fathers who are severe with their sons, when all the time their severity is due to their jealousy of their sons. A mother's phobia for thunderstorms may develop the same fear in her child. The neuroses of parents are not hereditary, but they are transmissible and the neuroses of the parents are then visited upon their children.

On the more positive side, every child wants not only protection and security, but *personal* love – that is to say, to be assured that he is loved for himself alone by the mother.

It is of course difficult for a mother who has a large family and the housework to do, but even so she should try each day to give a short time to each child alone, even if it is only having him on her knee as she chats to them all, or next to her at the table, or reading a story which *he* chooses. 'It's my turn to sit next to Mummy!' may seem unimportant to the parent but it means a lot to the child. To the child it means the assurance of her personal love and that means security. It is the deprivation of this which makes a child jealous, and to punish him for jealousy does nothing to remedy this.

It is this personal note which is inevitably missing in institutions where too many children are cared for by too few house mothers. The child has the necessary care, but lacks the personal affection.

Working with the children in a poor law home at Leytonstone, my impression was that institutional children can, with the care they receive, grow up into efficient and mentally healthy members of the community – but that they lack something of the joy of life, and that this appears to apply also when they are adults. They have the necessary care, but they lack that personal love which brings the greatest happiness and confidence to a child.

This is confirmed by an experiment by Bühler in which two groups of two-year-old children living in the same institution were segregated from each other and subjected to two divergent types of treatment. One group was given very little tenderness, although adequately cared for in every other respect. In the other group, a nurse was assigned to each child and there was no lack of tenderness and affection. At the end of half a year the first group was mentally and physically retarded in comparison with the second. Individual care and devotion are indispensable in the upbringing of small children.

Thirdly, the child requires a love which is *constant,* that is to say that the mother will love him *whatever happens* – even if he is naughty. Indeed patients have often told me that they were deliberately naughty to test their mother's love.

Finally, the mother's love should be an *understanding* love. Many mothers have a natural flair for understanding and sensing the child's need; they intuitively understand why the child acts in often bizarre ways, and by their love and understanding know just what the child is feeling. Such mothers do not need to go by rules, and they do just as well without books on psychology. But most of us can do with a little more understanding of what is going on in a child's mind, and in such a case, books and the experience of others can give us considerable help.

THE PRINCIPLE OF FREEDOM

Throughout this book stress has been laid on the need for freedom if the child is to enjoy full mental health and to avoid neurotic disorders.

It is the function of the parent to provide the child with opportunities for that freedom.

In the first place the child needs *freedom for activities of all kinds*, because only by experimentation and exploration can he develop conditioned reflexes which enable him to adapt himself to the conditions of life.

He also needs *freedom for his native impulses* and emotions, such as assertiveness, love, fear, and curiosity; for these primary instincts and emotions are the source of strength which nature has designed to overcome the obstacles and difficulties of life.

All these potentialities are distinct entities, each with its own function to perform.*

But although they all have distinct functions they do not exist for themselves; *they exist to serve the personality as a whole* and should be directed to that end.

It is like the body, which consists of a number of organs – the lungs for breathing, the stomach for digesting, the heart for circulating the blood – each of which has its distinctive function to serve, but each existing not for itself but to serve the function of the body as a whole. So with the personality: the instincts and other potentialities are distinct entities, each having its own special function to perform – fear to escape danger, aggressiveness to overcome a foe, curiosity to search out whether the strange object is friend or foe, desirable or undesirable, the maternal instinct to care for the young. But each of these potentialities exists only to serve the purpose of the personality as a whole. They cannot exist apart from the

---

* Some scholars would deny that we have any right to consider the instincts as separate entities, regarding them only as ways in which the personality works. We are justified in distinguishing them, as McDougall does, because some of them at least are motivated by distinct hormones of the body. There is one hormone (the gonadotrophic) of the pituitary gland in the head which is the primary stimulus of sex feelings and sex functions. The instinct of fight and flight are associated with secretions from the adrenal glands, and the maternal 'instinct' is probably stimulated from the lactogenic hormone which also produces milk. We may some day find hormones which give rise to such potentialities as curiosity, self-display, and social propensities.

personality; and the personality cannot exist without them. In this mutual service both the potentialities and the personality find their freedom and fulfilment.

There is, therefore, as we have seen (p. 114), no incompatibility between the freedom of the instincts and freedom of the personality provided that these basic impulses are used and directed to the service of the personality as a whole.

Moreover, nature herself has provided the child with the means of coordinating all these potentialities to a common end by implanting in the child by identification a stable standard or Ego ideal to which they may all be directed and by which they may be controlled.

By this means the *whole personality* is free to pursue its ends.

Nature also has given the child the means whereby his potentialities can be used to the best advantage, by giving him *intelligence*, *imagination*, and *reason*.

The parents should see to it, therefore, that the child has freedom to exercise these higher functions which nature has provided for man's use. By this provision the child need not be driven by the blind forces of his instincts, but is able to direct these forces to his ends and aims. Instead of having everything done for him, the child should be allowed to try to do things for himself; instead of having all his decisions made for him, he should be given an opportunity to make his own decisions and encouraged to think for himself. The child naturally wants to learn; he should be given opportunity to do so.

But as we have seen, nature helps the child still further by giving him *certain patterns of behaviour ready-made* – specific activities which the child will require in the later pursuits of life.

Nature has provided an outlet for these patterns of behaviour in *play*; and has also provided further exercise and practice in these activities through repetitiveness which makes a child perform an action over and over again till he is well practised.

Furthermore, nature provides that these various patterns of response should not be exercised all at once, but that each should be given a specific period in childhood in which it is given time for its development – one period to develop its aggressiveness, another for the development of individuality, another for sociability.

In this way each has time for full development and can make its contribution to the full development of the whole personality. It is for the parent to see that the child has the opportunity for exercise at each phase.

Here we meet with a principle of great practical importance – *spontaneity before discipline*. Nature carries out this principle by giving the child the aptitude to play. The child gives spontaneous expression to its activities before it directs them in its adult experience of life.

How we can follow this principle in practice may best be illustrated by an example, that of a child learning to swim. One school of thought says, 'Teach him to swim correctly from the start, so that he will not have to unlearn mistakes in his technique. That indeed is a principle I believed in before I had real experience of children. But it is rather boring to the child who may lose interest. The opinion I have formed as a result of further experience is that it is far better to let the child splash about and enjoy himself, so that he feels thoroughly at home in the water. Then at a certain point he sees others swimming, tries a few strokes himself and, finding he cannot do it satisfactorily, asks you to teach him. He now *wants* to learn and so puts his whole heart into it and learns far more rapidly; it is to my mind the better method. The principle is : *first allow spontaneous expression to the natural impulse, and then discipline and direct it*.

If a little girl wants to bake a loaf as her mother is doing, give her the flour and water and let her muck about with it herself first and *then* she will want to learn how.

The two schools of thought exist in the world of art. The conventional school sets the child from the beginning the task of drawing correctly and symmetrically. Only a few survive such treatment. The other method, now increasingly adopted, is to let a child splash around with his paints, trying to draw a man or horse in this way or that (it is extraordinary how full of life his picture of a bucking horse can be!) and *then* teach him the technique. In this case his final product is full of life as well as being well disciplined. Augustus John remarked how many potential artists are ruined by schools of art. This is because technique may stifle spontaneity.

Adrian Hill, the artist, tells me of a child who was drawing a country scene with a boat in it. The art teacher said, 'That is not the way to draw a boat! I'll show you the way', and did it. The child replied : 'Yes, but it isn't my boat!'

This principle of spontaneity before discipline means that we must not be surprised if our small children at first fight and grab, get into a mess, and behave like little savages; for that is what they are. They cannot all at once spring from being children of nature to being 'polite members of society'. It is not only impossible, it is not desirable, for there must be spontaneous expression of the native impulses and patterns of response before these can be disciplined and directed to higher purposes. Children will learn to be polite by your politeness.

This task of becoming civilized while retaining all the power and drive that the native impulses have to give us is not an altogether easy task, and requires patience on both sides. It is made all the more difficult because of a problem brought about by civilization. Owing to the greater security of civilized life, we do not require our primitive instincts in their original strength. We do not need to fight one another like animals at the water hole in the primeval forest; nor do we need to produce innumerable offspring only for them to be killed off. The result is that there is a *surplus of instinctual energy* in us all which is apt to get out of control and lead to trouble.

In point of fact it is this very surplus of instinctual energy which rightly directed has gone to the making of civilized life. McDougall has shown us in his *Social Psychology*, that these instinctual energies, when they have performed their necessary tasks, can be transformed and re-directed to the higher uses of man. Aggressiveness is transformed into will power; curiosity into scientific research; maternal instinct into care for the sick; fear into devising means of protection and security; rivalry into personal achievement.

The same principle was later enunciated by Freud who called it *sublimation*, but he confined the process to the sex instinct only.

This principle is the *raising of the primitive instincts and impulses to a higher standard.*

It comes about spontaneously and naturally in the process of civilization, or, as Freud would put it, it is an unconscious process. But it is no easy task because of the surplus of emotion. So like all of nature's efforts it needs encouragement from the parent bringing up the child, but that takes the form of directing the child's energies in more serviceable ways and to more serviceable ends. That is the function of discipline.

THE PRINCIPLE OF DISCIPLINE

The old concept of discipline, based on the idea that the 'animal instincts' in man were essentially evil, was that they should be crushed or even thrashed out of the child when necessary – which was often.

The more enlightened view of discipline, based on the idea that native capacities were given by nature for man's use, is that discipline's function is to *direct and control* these natural forces.

Natural discipline. One would think from the way some psychologists talk, and some teenagers behave, that discipline, inhibition, restraint, and self-control were the inventions of mid-Victorian moralists.

In point of fact restraint and inhibition are a law of life, physiological as well as psychological and moral. In the brain we not only have the mid-brain, which is concerned with the primitive emotions, but the cortex of the brain, whose definite function is inhibition and control. The sympathetic nervous system stimulates the heart beats, but the parasympathetic system controls the beating of the heart so that it is regular and more efficient. Throughout the body we have these opposites – one function to stimulate, one to control.

Inhibition and efficiency. Take the simple illustration of the arm. In your arm you have both flexor muscles, which contract and bend your arm, and extensor muscles at the back of your arm, which extend or straighten it. But the curious fact is that when you flex your arm, say to carry a cup of tea to your lips, the opposing extensor muscles also come into play and contract, though to a lesser degree. These extensor muscles, by contracting, exercise a restraining or controlling influence on the flexors and *so steady the movements of the arm.* If you simply bent your arm without any opposing check, it would produce a jerk and the cup of tea would be spilt. Indeed, we may observe just that happening in a child whose nervous system is not yet fully developed. In drinking from a cup, pouring milk out of a jug, putting coal on the fire, threading a needle, he at first almost invariably overdoes it, and shoots past the mark. Only gradually, by the restraint of the opposing muscles, does he learn to control all his actions.

This illustration suggests that *restraint and inhibition are necessary to effective action.*

Discipline is a law of life, provided by nature and necessary to efficiency and the fulfilment of life. Those who advocate free expression of all the instincts are therefore not acting according to nature, but contrary to nature.

Discipline in this sense is not incompatible with freedom of the personality; it is necessary to it. You cannot have true freedom unless you have discipline.

Self-control means the use of our natural capacities and potentialities in the service of the personality. Self-control is very different from repression. *Repression* means the attempted obliteration of some natural instinctive urge, like aggressiveness, so that it is no longer at our disposal and may later emerge as a neurosis. Repression is thus not only different from self-control; it is incompatible with it. We cannot use and direct any impulse which is repressed, since it is dissociated.

Restraint. Whereas repression is incompatible with self-control, restrain is necessary for self-control. *Restraint is the temporary checking of some natural impulse so as to direct it to more useful channels.*

If a child is hitting another child, or throwing a newspaper on the fire, he needs to be restrained, but quietly and firmly in the manner already described (p. 106), and his aggressiveness diverted, perhaps by getting him to play a game, by romping with him, or by getting him to help with what you are doing. These are methods every mother employs. Restraint of the adolescent delinquent, who goes out to break things or to pull up the plants in the public park, is necessary. But it is also necessary for the community to provide other and more desirable outlets for the adolescent.

The difference between these functions can be made clear by the analogy of the mill stream. The miller wants to make use of the power of the stream to drive his mill. The way he does this is to dam up the stream, for by so doing he develops a head of water which, being directed, is far more powerful than the open stream itself.

Thus the function of restraint is to *canalize* all the forces in our nature; this increases their strength and also directs them. Repression, on the other hand, would mean damming up the stream so that it later broke its banks and flooded the countryside. So the repression of our impulses means that they overwhelm the personality and burst forth as a nervous breakdown with its floods of fear, sex, and rage.

Thus, while repression is harmful, restraint is necessary to the healthy pursuit of life. Restraint may be external or internal.

External restraint is necessary in the earliest years of life, before a child's self-control is established, to prevent him from harm and danger, such as rushing into traffic, tampering with a boiling kettle, or fiddling with the electric fitments. That is what a parent is for.

External restraint is also necessary in the earliest years to help to build up a child's will. As we have seen (p. 109), in those years the parent's will has to stand in the place of the child's, which he has not yet developed. By being dealt with quietly and firmly the child learns to be quiet and controlled himself. Once his Ego ideal is established he has *self*-discipline and *self*-control. This has been considered under 'The Child's Morality' (pp. 141 ff.).

When a child in the phase of individuality begins to pursue his own interests, building bricks, making shelves, mending chairs, or riding a bicycle, *the exercise of these activities brings its own self-discipline*. Very little external discipline is necessary. The function of the parents is then to supply plenty of material for such activities, to show the child how to do them, and to encourage him.

In adolescence, discipline comes naturally to members of a gang. In gangs strict discipline and obedience to the leader are insisted on, and arduous tasks are imposed and willingly undertaken.

But there are times, even in later childhood, when every parent finds that the child wants to pursue undesirable activities, in which some kind of external restraint is still necessary. A big bonfire in a small back yard may be dangerous, and robbing orchards, however natural and delightful, cannot be allowed, because of the rights of others. In such cases reason may be appealed to, but where this fails more stringent methods may be called for. Most of these take the form of an appeal to fear in one form or another. This is not surprising, for after all fear is nature's method of deterring us from harmful acts by the infliction of pain, as when we touch a thorn or hot stove, and should not be disregarded.

Disapproval. The simplest form of discouragement is that

of the mother's disapproval, for the small child depends for its safety and security on the mother's goodwill. For a mother to say, 'I don't like you doing that!' is often quite sufficient. But this can go to extremes, and for a mother to be 'grieved' and not speak to the child for a whole morning is devastating and may completely undermine a child's sense of security. He would much rather have a good smacking and have done with it! So we find in analysis.

Praise and blame are of the same order as approval and disapproval.

Warnings. Warnings are also necessary. No one would deny that it is not only legitimate but necessary to warn a child of the danger of eating poisonous berries, to point out to him that if he rushes into the road he will be badly hurt, or to warn an adolescent girl of the dangers of illicit pregnancy, and the consequent misery. All these are essential forms of discipline conducive to healthy living.

Threats. But warnings are very different from *threats*. In warning you *point out* what the consequences will be; in threatening you *impose* the threatened consequences. Threats are more personal and therefore the more resented.

But even threats have their place when all else fails. The threat 'If you can't play nicely with the other children you will have to go into the other room' at least gives the child warning and so gives him a choice. If he continues to be a nuisance and is removed, he only gets what he asked for and there is little harm done. He usually recognizes this. But it might be better to find out *why* the child is behaving so: it may be that he is not getting his just rights. On the other hand to say, 'If you don't stop crying, I'll put you in the cupboard!' when the child can't help crying is devastating.

Punishment. Is there any place for punishment? Yes, but not often. Punishment should always be applied as *one of the consequences of a child's action*. It should not be retributive; it should not be vindictive. A child naturally wants to do something because he finds some pleasure and advantage in doing so. If, however, one of the consequences is punishment, he may decide that it is not worth while : the advantage is outweighed by the disadvantages. If I overrun the traffic lights in a car, the magistrate does not get angry with me, he just fines me ! Indeed, one magistrate recently said to an aggrieved motorist, 'We are not blaming you; we are only fining you !' The punishment was simply one of the consequences of his act !

Punishments should not be given without due warning. All too often a small child has no idea why he is being smacked. A warning has the advantage that it gives the child the opportunity to make his own decisions, which is the essence of morality. He can choose either to stop pulling a valuable toy to pieces or he can have it taken from him. So with a boy who breaks the rules : he knows what the punishment will be, takes a chance on it and, if found out, is usually prepared to take punishment with no ill effects.

Rewards and punishments should be immediate. If there is too great a distance between the act and the reward or the punishment, the child no longer associates the two. Punishment should not only fit the crime, but should immediately follow the crime. That is why, if a boy steals apples, a kick on the backside by the policeman is more effective than appearance in the children's court a week later when there is no longer an association between the crime and the punishment.

Punishment should be inevitable, for the child (or the delinquent or the criminal) who gets away with it, either because of the weakness of the discipline or because he is not found out, is encouraged to do the same again. The best deterrent to crime is the certainty of detection. Few people would commit burglaries if they knew they were bound to be discovered and would be well and truly punished. So with the child.

Punishment should be neither too lenient nor too severe. If the punishment is *too lenient*, then it is worthwhile to defy the rules. To fine a prostitute two pounds is no deterrent when she can earn twenty pounds a night. There are some who maintain, therefore, that to deal leniently with a first offender in the courts is *not* the best way to handle the situation, and that a 'short, sharp smack' at the very beginning would be a better deterrent to crime and delinquency. For a parent to make a threat and not carry it out is disastrous : it encourages the disobedience.

If the punishment is *too severe*, it leaves behind a sense of injustice : it is *not* accepted. I recently had a boy of nineteen to treat for embezzling and forging cheques. It started by his father, a wealthy man, giving him 'everything of the best'. Even if he chose a second-rate bicycle, his father would give him a better one. (This was the father's vanity, not his love.) So he got the idea that he could have everything he wanted; and when at school, aged fourteen, he was short of money, he stole some. His headmaster rightly punished him for this 'simple' delinquency and he accepted the beating as just. But when he got home his mother sent him to bed without supper and further when his father came home he got a beating. These added punishments he felt to be an injustice as he had already paid for his crime; and this latent sense of injustice came out later at nineteen when he forged the cheque. If the incident had stopped with the headmaster's punishment, the boy would probably have learnt his lesson. But what the boy felt most deeply was that his father turned away from him as 'a disgrace to the family', lost his faith in him, and gave his affection to the sister.

Punishment should not make a breach in the love relationship between parent and child – whether that means being afraid of the parent or hating the parent. The father who says to a boy, 'You mustn't cheek your mother like that', and sends him out of the room, and later lets him come back to a friendly relationship and to join in the family life is not doing that boy any grievous harm. It might be better, however, to discover why he cheeks his mother; perhaps she is too domineering.

No punishment should be inflicted without finding out why the boy or girl committed the act. It is not always the child whom you see hitting another child who is the culprit. If an adolescent steals or lies, there is always a reason. Find it out. If a hooligan goes about hitting old ladies over the head, it might be because his mother constantly hit him over the head and he is getting his own back. He must be stopped doing it, of course, but don't put *all* the blame on him.

In general, the *positive* methods of dealing with a child are far better than the negative. Punishment, blame, disapproval are *deterrents to bad actions*; praise, rewards, approval, and encouragements are *incentives to good actions* – and are far more effective. They are better because the resultant action is then *voluntary*, whereas disapproval or punishment acts only through fear – and fear is not only a deterrent but often paralyses a child's actions, since he is afraid to do anything.

Those who train animals have found that positive incentives such as rewards are better than beating. Not all parents and teachers have discovered it yet.

Personally, I have a very poor opinion of blame, much as it is used by teachers, moralists, and churchmen as a spur to action. Encouragement is far more effective.

To take a simple example : obviously it is far better to say to a child, 'Will you do the washing up with me and I'll give you a swing afterwards', than to say, 'Do the washing up or I'll give you a smacking!' It makes all the difference to a child whether the attitude of the parent is 'Don't do that or else –' or 'I wouldn't do that if I were you because –' The one is the threat of fear; the other is the incentive of approval and reason. (You do, however, run the risk of an answer such as I got from a seven-year-old when I asked her if she would like to help me with the washing up; she replied, 'No, thank you !')

*

Throughout the book I have been writing for the ordinary, intelligent parent, about the ordinary, intelligent child, not primarily about delinquents. I am, however, glad to find these principles confirmed by a magistrate of great experience, John Watson, Chairman of the Metropolitan Juvenile Court in London (writing in the *Sunday Times*), who has had more than twenty-five years' experience in dealing with delinquent children, and has brought to his work a most humane attitude.

He writes : 'Without prejudice to modern researches into the subconscious motives, let us thankfully admit that there is still such a thing as a healthy-minded child.' (This corresponds to the group I have called 'benign delinquencies', namely, those which may be against the law but are not against the principles of mental health.

Further : 'Most of the more serious misbehaviour is due to lack of discipline – an old-fashioned word denoting something of what today is seldom preached, and much less seldom practised.' (I have stressed the need of discipline, with a new orientation.)

'Poverty is no longer a major cause of crime.' (This confirms what Cyril Burt in *The Young Delinquent* discovered a generation ago when in fact there *was* a great deal of poverty.) 'I believe', says Watson, 'that today a major cause is the availability of *too many* material benefits in return for too little effort.' Again, 'Parents neglect their children. . . . It is no compensation for that kind of neglect to load the children with pocket money and expensive gifts : the result is merely to create in the child an insatiable appetite for material possessions and in an attempt to satisfy it he steals. "We just can't understand it," his parents protest in court. "Ever since he was small he has always had everything he asked for. . . ." '

Watson further writes : 'But the most grievous problems in the juvenile court are neither the spoiled children nor the ill-disciplined, *they are the children who from their earliest days have lacked those essentials to their well-being, the loss of which nothing else in the world can compensate for. They are love and security. These are the gravely delinquent children. . . .'*

*

May I close with a definition of the principle of parenthood by Kahlil Gibran, a Lebanese poet who died about 1930.

You may give them your love but not your thoughts,
For they have their own thoughts;
You may house their bodies but not their souls,
For their souls dwell in the house of tomorrow, which you cannot visit, not even in your dreams.
You may strive to be like them, but seek not to make them like you.
For life goes not backward, nor tarries with yesterday.

INDEX

MORE ABOUT PENGUINS
AND PELICANS

If you have enjoyed reading this book you may wish to know that *Penguin Book News* appears every month. It is an attractively illustrated magazine containing complete details of the month's new books. A specimen copy will be sent free on request.

Penguin Book News is obtainable from most bookshops; but you may prefer to become a regular subscriber at 3s. for twelve issues. Just write to Dept EP, Penguin Books Ltd, Harmondsworth, Middlesex, enclosing a cheque or postal order, and you will be put on the mailing list.

Another Pelican by J. A. Hadfield is described overleaf.

Note: *Penguin Book News* is not
available in the U.S.A., Canada or Australia

Also by J. A. Hadfield

DREAMS AND NIGHTMARES

Dreams have a fascination for everyone, partly because of their bizarre nature, partly because these strange imaginings come from within ourselves, and partly because of the effect they have upon our daily lives. It is not surprising that efforts at dream interpretation have been made throughout all ages, by the most primitive tribes, who regard them as premonitions, no less than in the attempts at establishing a scientific method made by Freud with his sexual wish-fulfilment theory, Jung with his archetypes from the racial subconscious, and Adler with his urge to power. In this book, Dr Hadfield attempts to show that dreams have a biological role, and may be useful in the solution of the practical everyday, as well as of the deep-rooted problems, of our life. Many mathematical problems have been solved in dreams, and many scientific discoveries made by their means. We cannot, therefore, afford to ignore the significance of our dreaming, just as we cannot afford to ignore that of our intuition. This book, then, is a brief sketch of the mechanism, nature, and importance of our dream life.